PRAISE FOR

Positive Discipline for Working Parents

"Positive Discipline for Working Parents will make life easier for any parent juggling the needs of work and home, empowering them to guide and love their children from a state of overflow. The authors give working parents a rich, practical source of hope and help!"

—Judy Ryan, owner, Expanding Human Potential, LLC

"As a full-time human resources consultant and a mother of two teenagers, I often feel that I've cornered the market on the term 'busy'. Nelsen and Larson's book is like having your best friend coach you through the labyrinth of parenting. The best news of all is that the advice offered can be applied at home and at work with equally positive results! *Positive Discipline for Working Parents* should be on every working parent's nightstand."

—Liz Butler, human resources consultant for Fortune 50 Insurance Company

"*Positive Discipline for Working Parents* is a welcome addition to the POSITIVE DISCIPLINE series, focusing on how sound parenting principles can be used in the busy, often chaotic lives of dual-career families. As always, the authors provide easy-to-implement, highly effective solutions to the day-to-day problems faced by families trying to juggle jobs and kids. Thank you Jane and Lisa for your on-target ideas!"

—Anne Bain, CEO, The Armrel-Byrnes Company

"This book is a must-have for all parents and managers. Besides the great parenting tips, I received practical knowledge about how to have more successful meetings, effective brainstorming, and group consensus with my staff. This book will help any parent or manager succeed in all aspects of life."

—Dana Nelsen, manager for Fortune 500 company

"Managing a career and family can be quite a challenge. *Positive Discipline for Working Parents* allowed me to refocus and recommit. Nelsen and Larson's strategies are easy to implement and redefined my balance and view of success at home and work. This book is perfect for parents and teachers."

—Michele Mills, coowner, Phoenix Schools, California

ALSO IN THE
POSITIVE DISCIPLINE SERIES

Jane Nelsen, Ed.D, and Lisa Larson, M.A.

Positive Discipline

FOR WORKING PARENTS

Raising Responsible, Respectful,
and Resourceful Children When
You Work Outside the Home

THREE RIVERS PRESS • NEW YORK

Published by Three Rivers Press, New York, New York.
Member of the Crown Publishing Group, a division of Random House, Inc.
www.randomhouse.com

THREE RIVERS PRESS and the Tugboat design are registered trademarks of Random House, Inc.

Printed in the United States of America

Illustrations by Paula Gray

Library of Congress Cataloging-in-Publication Data
Nelsen, Jane.
 Positive discipline for working parents : raising responsible, respectful, and resourceful children when you work outside the home / Jane Nelsen and Lisa Larson
 p. cm.
 Includes index.
 1. Discipline of children. 2. Child rearing. I. Larson, Lisa. II. Title. III. Series.
HQ770.4 .N4354 2003
649'.64—dc21   2003002116
ISBN 0-7615-2510-6

10 9 8 7 6 5 4 3 2 1

First Edition

To Jamie Miller, the publishing world's
best acquisition editor.
—Jane

To Jason, my firstborn and
my greatest teacher.
—Lisa

CONTENTS

ACKNOWLEDGMENTS

Jane's Acknowledgments

I HAVE MANY mixed feelings as I write these acknowledgments. I just learned that the Prima Lifestyle's Roseville, California office is being closed. I have worked closely with Prima for over 15 years and have become very fond of and friends with many of the people who have worked with me and pampered me. I feel so much sadness about losing this Prima home. I will especially miss Jamie Miller who always calls me back and helps me through both professional and personal challenges. Jamie has given me book ideas (both *Positive Discipline for Preschoolers* and *Positive Discipline for Childcare Providers* were her idea) and has gone to bat for me with my ideas. I can't imagine having a better relationship with an acquisition editor and can't imagine what publishing will be like without her.

Shawn Vreeland has been the project editor on many of the Positive Discipline books and is extremely responsive and helpful. He found an excellent copy editor, Janelle Rohr, who went the extra mile to make this book much better. She is a very industrious editor who took the time to move things around, and even add a sentence or two, to make things flow better.

Because I have been so "spoiled" by these people (I have never had to write a proposal or send printed manuscripts), I don't know how or if I'll adjust to the "normal" publishing world. My deepest thanks to all of you.

We also learned that *Parents Who Love Too Much*, coauthored by Jane Nelsen and Cheryl Erwin, was being discontinued. Cheryl graciously gave her permission to use some of that material in this book because it is too good to be lost. Cheryl also brainstormed a lot of the material that is included in this book. She also did some editing and gave us very valuable suggestions for improvement. We feel so fortunate that a talented journalist like Cheryl is so generous with her contributions and is a coauthor of several of the Positive

Discipline books, including *Positive Discipline for Preschoolers, Positive Discipline the First Three Years,* and *Positive Discipline for Single Parents.*

Thanks to Deb Cashen for her many contributions. And, as usual, we are delighted with the illustrations of Paula Gray.

Of course, I also thank my husband, Barry, who supports and cheers me all the way.

Lisa's Acknowledgments

I WOULD LIKE to acknowledge the tremendous work of Jane Nelsen and thank her for bringing me the Positive Discipline tools and principles at a time when I desperately needed them. Her work changed the course of my relationship with my teenage son, Jason. Years of conflict and power struggles were avoided, and today we enjoy a loving, supportive relationship. I am grateful to the Positive Discipline principles for teaching me how to be an encouraging parent as well as an encouraging wife.

Most of all I want to thank my three children, Jason, Kelly, and Annie for their tolerance and love while I made numerous parenting mistakes. Jason, thank you for giving me the chance to show you that I love you no matter what. Kelly, thank you for making me laugh, and Annie, thanks for letting me know when I am out of line! You keep me honest. I'd like to thank my husband, Pete, for his unwavering support of my children, this book, and me. You are a special gift in my life.

Working Parent Dilemmas: "Will My Children Suffer?"

The Question That Plagues Working Parents

DO YOU FEEL as if there just aren't enough hours in the day to complete everything at work? When you get home from work, do you have enough energy left to meet the demands of your children, your home, and a social life? Are you laughing (or crying) and asking, "What social life?" Are you feeling torn between pressures at work and at home? Last, but certainly not least, are you *enjoying* either your work or your family?

> *Lord, help me to sort out what I should do first, second, and third today and to not try to do everything at once and nothing well. Give me the wisdom to delegate what I can and to order the things I can't delegate, to say no when I need to, and the sense to know when to go home.*
>
> —MARIAN WRIGHT EDELMAN

Most working parents feel both an obligation to their workplace and a strong sense of responsibility to their family. They are frustrated by their inability to balance the two. This conflict has a deeper impact on the workplace and the home than most people admit. Research has shown that stressed parents create stressed employees, managers, and CEOs. When parents find answers, the workplace will improve. Most important of all, children will benefit.

Has It Always Been This Way?

LIFE HAS NOT always been this complex. We live in a fast-paced world, one that seems to accelerate every year. Thirty years ago, few mothers worked outside the home. Today, there are few mothers who *don't* work outside the home. As a consequence, new opportunities and problems are surfacing. *Work-family conflict,* a relatively new phrase, is the conflict that occurs when people are required to fulfill multiple tasks at home and at work. This demands more time and energy than is available to most working parents, few of whom have been trained in time management, home management, and effective parenting. The toll on parents, children, and employers is monumental.

It is well known that the number one cause of employee absenteeism is family-related issues. These work-family conflicts create stressors that result in physical and psychological damage to the health of parents and children, which contributes to more absenteeism. Even though issues such as equal pay, childcare, and feeling overwhelmed from juggling home, family, and work arose as women entered the workforce, these issues aren't affecting just women. Fathers also struggle with work-family stress. In two-parent homes, when Mom puts in more time at work, Dad is expected to become more involved with the children. Many men have stepped off the "fast track" at work because of the overwhelming stress inherent in trying to meet the unending demands at home and at the office. Chronic stress takes a huge toll on families. With divorce holding steady at about 50 percent for the last two decades, single parents and stepparents juggle multiple-family issues. More and more single dads are working and raising their children. No matter what your family situation is, it may seem to you that there is never enough time to get everything done.

> The number one cause of employee absenteeism is family-related issues.

And then, of course, there is the biggest concern of all—the question that creates the greatest stress—do children suffer when parents work outside the home?

"Will My Children Suffer?"

MOST WORKING MOTHERS wonder, "Will my working hurt my children?" (Fathers don't ask this question nearly as often; we'll explore the reasons why in chapter 2.)

Being a working mother can be beneficial to your children—and it can be harmful. It all depends on how you handle the following nine harmful and nine beneficial factors of working parents:

Harmful Factors	Beneficial Factors
Feeling guilty	Feeling confident
Poor childcare	Quality childcare
Not understanding why children misbehave	Understanding why children misbehave
Pampering	Respectfully involving children
Lack of effective parenting skills	Effective parenting skills
Lack of social and life skill training	Social and life skill training for good character
Lack of organization	Organization with your children
Neglecting children	Planning for special time with children
Workaholism	Balancing family and work

Since these nine factors are so important in determining whether your children suffer or benefit from your working, an entire chapter (and sometimes more than one chapter) is dedicated to each. These chapters will help dispel the myths about working parents and applying the ideas will increase your efficiency and joy as a working parent.

What You Believe Affects How You Feel and What You Do

WORKING IS SUCH a fact of life for so many parents that they may not understand the significance of what they *believe* about working. But what you think, feel, and believe about your decision to work has everything to do with how working affects your children. Parents who believe their children will suffer spend a lot of time and energy feeling guilty. They feel stretched to the limit as they try to compensate for being gone. Children sense the guilt and usually learn to use it to their advantage. Parents may overdo, give too much, pamper, rescue, and render their children incapable by robbing them of opportunities to contribute and solve some of their own problems. Pampered children create a whole new set of issues and stress. It can become a vicious cycle. (We will discuss this in greater detail in chapter 5.)

Where Did the Myths About Working Parents Originate?

MANY PEOPLE HAVE deep convictions about parents—and mothers in particular—who work outside the home. But where did these beliefs come from? Who said mothers should stay home? Who said mothers who work should feel guilty? Who said fathers should not be the ones to stay at home with the children? We often hear, "They say . . ." Who are "they"? Where do they hold their meetings? Wherever they are, they need to be told about the thousands of children who do very well when their parents work.

During a simpler time it probably made sense that fathers hunted while mothers cooked the food and took care of the children. Breastfeeding was an

important factor—infant formula wasn't around, a family may not have had cows or goats to milk, and so the mother's need to breastfeed likely led to her being primary caretaker for children. Also, without birth control, women were pregnant much more of their lives than a typical woman is nowadays. Both roles were very important jobs, however. In food-gathering clans, mothers strapped their children on their backs and gathered berries and tilled the soil side by side with fathers. As soon as children were old enough they helped—and it wasn't called *child labor*. Times are different now. Why is it that customs that made sense at one time become dogma at a later time?

There is a wonderful story about a family who had a custom of eating ham on Easter Sunday. They would buy a large ham and cut about one-fourth off the end before putting the ham in the oven. When the third-generation daughter started cooking the ham, she asked her mother, "Why do you cut off so much of the ham?" Her mother replied, "I don't know. It is a tradition. That is how my mother always did it." The curious daughter decided to ask her grandmother who replied, "Because my only pan wasn't big enough for the whole ham."

Some "traditions"—and many of our beliefs about men, women, families, and choices—were simply a necessity at one time and don't make sense today. They are stifling and create conflict. They are continued because people don't think about what makes sense for the benefit of all concerned. On the other hand, many traditions are wonderful and create a feeling of family or community. Conscious people will use their thinking abilities to understand the difference.

Blasting the Myths About Working Mothers

RECENT STUDIES HAVE shown that children thrive when mothers give 100 percent of their energy to their jobs while they are at work and 100 percent to their families when they are at home.[1] Galinsky was brilliant enough to go to the source. She asked *children* how they felt about having a working mother. She discovered that children actually feel proud of their working mothers—so long as mothers don't neglect their children when they are home. It is reasonable

---

1. Ellen Galinsky, *Ask the Children* (William Morrow, New York, NY, 1999).

> Children thrive when mothers give 100 percent of their energy to their jobs while they are at work and 100 percent to their families when they are at home.

to assume that children would feel the same about their working fathers.

Common sense tells us that when parents feel good about what they are doing with their children, they will feel less anxiety and will be capable of contributing more to their employer. As a consequence, more corporations are offering work-life programs to help families find a balance between work and home. Family and work can be a beneficial partnership rather than a conflict.

Because society has focused most of its attention on working mothers, the first myth that needs to be challenged is the one that states, "It is always best for mothers to stay home with their children." We are not advocating that all mothers should work. We believe it is best for some mothers to work and for some mothers to stay home—and that it should be a personal choice. Some mothers (and some fathers) stay home and love it. Some stay home and hate it—and their children feel and mirror the stress this causes. Unhappy parents create unhappy children. Children absorb the stress and unhappiness of their parents and express it in many kinds of "misbehavior" including fussiness, defiance, temper tantrums, or outright rebellion. Too many parents do not accept accountability for their part in the misbehavior. We don't say this to place blame, but rather to increase understanding about the dynamics between parents and children. A mother who isn't happy staying home would create less turmoil for her children by working outside the home, if she then can be an effective and loving parent with her children when she is home.

The decision to work or to stay home is not as black and white as some people might think. There are many variables to consider. Advocates of stay-at-home moms make it sound like staying at home is the only variable that accounts for success or failure in a child's development. We know of stay-at-home moms who are depressed, who watch television or talk on the phone much of the day, or who run from one social event to the next—none of which are beneficial for their children.

Simply staying at home does not guarantee that a parent will have effective parenting skills. Some mothers pride themselves on being supermoms who, in the process, overprotect their children, do too much for them, and give them too much materially. These children do not develop into capable people. We also know stay-at-home moms who are happy, efficient homemakers and who use excellent parenting skills.

The same is true for working parents: Some are depressed, stressed, tired, and do not have any energy left for their children. Other working parents know how to balance work and family and are delighted to be with their children after a long day at work. They get their children involved in creating routines and problem-solving sessions. They establish healthy priorities, find ways to attend important functions most of the time, and help their children deal with disappointment when everything doesn't work out perfectly.

> Perfection isn't necessary, as long as wise priorities and effective parenting skills are in place.

The truth is that most parents are not perfect in either situation, staying at home or working. The good news is that perfection isn't necessary, as long as wise priorities and effective parenting skills are in place.

Who Said It Would Be Easy?

WE AREN'T SAYING it is easy to be a working parent. Parenting isn't easy whether you work or don't work outside the home. Working requires juggling numerous competing balls at work and at home. School and childcare problems contribute to the stress working parents experience. They wonder how to find good childcare, and then worry about how to handle illnesses. Should they miss work to take care of their sick children? And, if they find someone who is willing to take care of their sick children, how do they deal with the heart-wrenching decision to work when they want to be home comforting their children? Even when good childcare is found and the problem of sick children is dealt with, what happens when parents must miss their children's special events? You'll find lots of help in chapter 3 about childcare.

So now you know. Neither working parents nor stay-at-home parents experience total joy and bliss all the time. All children, from either situation, do not turn out "all good" or "all bad." There are assets and liabilities that go along with any decision and any situation. In all cases, helping children thrive will be both a continuing challenge and a continuing joy. So follow your heart, do your best, and see all situations (including mistakes made by you and your children) as opportunities for learning.

Follow Your Heart

DO YOU WANT to work or do you want to stay home? If you have the choice and you want to stay home, follow your heart and do everything possible to make this dream a reality. Tighten your belt, trim your budget, and focus on your children. If you need money to survive, find a way to work at home. If you are the type who goes *stir crazy* when you stay at home full time, it is just as valid to follow your heart and join the workforce. If you can't follow your heart because you simply must work outside the home, give up your guilt, find quality childcare (discussed in chapter 3), and use the suggestions in this book to help you find peace while you prioritize what is most important to you at home and at work.

You Can Do Both—With Less Stress

THIS IS A BOOK for working parents because we believe work is an honorable option. For decades women have been taught that it was more honorable

to stay home rather than to work outside the home. Was it really more honorable, or simply the only option? Considering the fact that millions of mothers do work, does it really matter? Working mothers are here to stay, so how to make the best of it—for parents, children, and employers—is the only helpful question.

As Galinsky's research demonstrated, children can thrive when parents have a healthy attitude about working, have effective parenting skills, and learn how to create a healthy balance between work and family. The suggestions offered in this book are designed to help parents feel confident about working and caring for their children.

Raising children is a complicated task, whether one parent stays home or not, and we see no evidence that it's going to get simpler any time soon. Regardless of whether you are a full time parent or are working in or out of the home, balancing work and family is one of the greatest challenges you will face as a parent. Take it seriously, think it through, and make the best decisions you can. When you feel good about what you are doing with your children, you will be a better employee and a happier person.

Give Up the Guilt and Proudly Say, "I Am My Child's Working Parent"

Feeling Guilty vs. Feeling Confident

SOME PARENTS WORK because they have to. Others work because they want to. In either case, many parents still buy into the old myths and feel guilty if they don't have one parent who stays home. Media "experts" such as Dr. Laura have exacerbated the problem by asserting that "good" parents always stay at home with their children ("Hi! I'm my kid's mom!"). There is nothing wrong with being proud to be your kid's mom or dad, but Dr. Laura goes on to advocate that being your kid's mom means staying home with them instead of working.

Parents who believe their children will suffer when they work spend a lot of time feeling guilty. Children sense the guilt and learn to use it to their advantage. If we had a radio program, we would start by saying, "Hi! We are our kids' working moms. We hope you'll join us by being proud of what you do."

Guilt, a Useless Emotion

HAVE YOU EVER known guilt to solve anything? Oh, it might—if the guilt leads to change. However, many people feel guilty because on some level they believe that their guilt proves they are a good person with a conscience. "Well, at least I feel guilty for doing what I'm doing. What kind of person would I be if I didn't at least feel guilty?" In other words, some people use guilt to help them *look* good while they are doing things they intuitively believe are *bad*.

If you truly are going against your internal values and doing "bad," it would make more sense to change your behavior, instead of feeling guilty, so you can live peacefully with yourself. But if you aren't violating your inner truths, it doesn't make sense to feel guilty. Many parents haven't developed their inner truth because they have focused too much on what "others" say. Our guess is that the question that haunts you is, "Is it bad to work outside the home when I have children?" As we said in the last chapter, it depends. And the critical factor is whether you feel guilty or confident about the choice you have made.

The Consequences of Feeling Guilty

IF YOU THINK that your children will suffer when you work outside the home, you may spend a lot of time feeling guilty, and your guilt will cause problems for both you and your children. Again, children absorb your attitude and use it, one way or another. They may develop a sense of unease and insecurity that they don't understand, a free-floating sense that all is not well in their world. This could cause crankiness, depression, defiance, or a hundred other confusing emotions and behaviors. Or your children may use your guilt to manipulate you into pampering them. Neither is good for your children or for you.

> Stop feeling guilty and start feeling confident in your role as a parent and a provider.

It is important to realize that none of these behaviors occur at a *conscious* level. Children don't consciously think, "My parent feels guilty and this makes me uncomfortable, therefore I will misbehave." Guilt creates feelings of insecurity that unconsciously translate into many different kinds of compensating behaviors. Stress creates additional emotions and behaviors. Human beings, old or young, simply don't do well when they feel insecure and stressed.

So, if you are going to work and you don't want to harm your children, one of the first steps is to stop feeling guilty and start feeling confident in your role as a parent and a provider. Fathers offer a good example. Have you ever noticed that most working fathers don't feel guilty and thus don't create at atmosphere of insecurity? Why don't fathers feel guilty for working?

Why Most Fathers Don't Feel Guilty (and Why Some Do)

FOR CENTURIES, CULTURES have dictated that fathers should work; in fact, they may be considered lazy bums if they don't. In other words, we have learned that fathers "should" work whereas mothers in the workplace are a relatively new phenomenon. In more recent times, since fathers started bonding with their children at birth (by being allowed to be present during the births of their children), many feel guilty for not being able to spend more time with their children. Is this really guilt, or is it frustration over the difficulty in being a successful parent and a successful career person? Of course, some fathers feel guilty because they work too many hours—something that can be difficult to change.

Guilt is one of those traditions that could benefit from some rethinking. Guilt makes sense only as a motivator for change. If change is not possible, guilt makes no sense at all. The following story illustrates what can happen before you give up your guilt, and the great possibilities for parents and children when guilt is no longer part of the picture.

"Tell Me Another Story": The Guilt-Anger-Remorse Cycle

"TELL ME ANOTHER story," whined four-year-old Angela. Mom was getting angry. She had already given in to the plea for three stories. But she felt guilty for leaving Angela at the day-care center while she worked all day. Mom felt she had to make it up to Angela, even though she felt angry because she also wanted some time to herself. So she gave in and told Angela a fourth story.

When Angela whined for one more story, Mom was at the end of her rope. She scolded, "Angela, you are never satisfied. I'm never going to tell you another story because you just want more, more, more. You can just do without until you learn to appreciate what you get!"

Angela burst into sobs. Mom ran to the bathroom, locked the door, and burst into tears herself. Then she remorsefully scolded herself. "She is only a child who wants to spend some time with me. If I'm going to leave her alone all day, the least I can do is read her as many stories as she wants." Then the guilt started again. "It isn't her fault that I'm tired. I don't want my poor daughter to suffer because she has a working mom. How will I ever manage?"

What is truth and what is fiction regarding this scene? It is true that Angela needs time with her mom. It is fiction that she needs to hear four stories. When Mom allows Angela to push her guilt button, she is teaching Angela the skill of manipulation.

When Mom learns to allot a reasonable amount of time, she can avoid the anger stage. After one or two stories (in the amount of time Mom can give with enjoyment) Mom can say, kindly and firmly, "Story time is over. Time for my hug and kiss." (The importance of kindness and firmness at the same time will be addressed in chapter 3.)

Angela will know if Mom means what she says, just as she will know if Mom's guilt button can be pushed. However, when Mom is just learning to give up her guilt, it would be only natural for Angela to up the ante in an attempt to keep the old game going. She may scream, "I want another story!"

Again, kindly and firmly, Mom can say, "Do you want to go to sleep without a hug and kiss or with a hug and kiss?" This may be enough to distract Angela from the power struggle by giving her an opportunity to use her power to make a choice. If Angela keeps whining or screaming, however, Mom can say, "I'll just sit here for five minutes to see if that is enough time for you to get ready for a hug and kiss." (After all, Mom helped Angela perfect her manipulation skills. It may take patience for her to learn mutual respect.) If Angela continues the manipulation pattern, Mom can say, "I can see you are not ready for a hug and kiss now. We'll try again tomorrow night," and then leave.

There are several parenting skills that can eliminate the guilt-anger-remorse cycle.

1. Give up your guilt buttons. Children know when you have guilt buttons that can be pushed, and they know when you don't. Guilt buttons send out a certain kind of energy that speaks louder than words.

2. Avoid pampering in the name of guilt—or for any other reason. When parents feel guilty about working, they often try to assuage their guilt through pampering. (The ill effects of pampering are so profound that we have devoted an entire chapter 5 to this issue.) Pampering is not healthy for children for a number of reasons. First, children see through what you are doing (even if at a subconscious level). They know that you think they are being deprived. If *you* believe this, why shouldn't they? Second, pampering invites children to form unhealthy beliefs such as, "I feel loved only if I'm pampered" or "I'm entitled

to special service." Third, children are likely to learn unhealthy manipulation skills instead of respectful life skills. All of the parenting suggestions in this book are designed to help children develop respectful life skills such as self-discipline, responsibility, cooperation, and problem solving.

3. Decide what you are willing to do and state it specifically. "I will read two stories." Again, confidence, kindness, and firmness are the keys. Deciding what you are willing to do is a demonstration of self-respect. The willingness to spend reasonable time and perform reasonable tasks for and with your children demonstrates respect for them. However, if you state your intentions in a threatening way instead of a respectful way, the effectiveness is diminished.

4. When you say it, mean it, and when you mean it, follow through with dignity and respect. It is far more effective to *act* than to use words. Children respond to actions but become "hearing impaired" with too many words. Let your kind and firm actions speak loud and clear. If you say you will read two stories, stick to your decision. At the end of the stories, give a hug and a kiss and leave the room with confidence.

5. Avoid lectures and scolding. When you don't feel guilty, there is no need to make your child feel guilty. Lectures and scolding are usually designed to manipulate through guilt. Even if they work, the price of lowered self-confidence in your children is a price that is too high to pay. Limit discipline words to ten or fewer. One is often best. For example, the meaning is perfectly clear in the following words: Towels. Dishes. Bath. It is disrespectful of yourself and of your children to think they don't know what you mean, if you have discussed routines and procedures respectfully together, in advance, as described in the next skill. When your child pleads for another story, you might smile and say, "Bedtime," before leaving the room.

> It is usually more effective to act than to use words.

6. Plan ahead. Another way to avoid the "tell me another story" scene is to talk about it in advance. Engage your child in planning for the future. When you decide to make a change, it is respectful to let your child know and to work on a plan together. Mom decided to try this with Angela.

While driving home from day care, Mom shared her feelings with Angela. "Sweetie, I love you so much. I want our time together to be happy time. I'll bet you and I can figure out a plan to make bedtime a happy time. Okay?"

Angela caught the spirit of Mom's new attitude and said, "Okay."

Mom continued, "I'm willing to read two stories. I know it upsets you when I yell at you, and it upsets me when you whine for another story. What could we do instead after I read the two stories?"

Angela said, "I know. You could give me a hug and kiss?" This was already part of their routine, but it seemed very different to Angela when it was her idea.

Mom said, "I like that idea. And why don't we figure out a signal we can give each other to help us remember to stop if we start getting upset? How about tugging on our ears or a wink, or do you have another idea?"

Angela said, "We could tap our knees."

Mom said, "Great. Let's try that."

That night their plan worked like a charm because it was a plan that they worked on together. This is why routines can be so effective. When parents and children plan routines together (bedtime routines, morning routines, mealtime routines), the routine becomes the boss. Parents can ask their children, "What is next on our bedtime routine?" Children feel empowered because they can check it out instead of being ordered by their parents and because they helped plan the routine in the first place. (Creating routine charts is discussed in more detail in chapter 5.)

7. Allow time for your child to adjust to your new behavior. You have helped create the troubling patterns that are now established. Change may take time—for both of you. It may take a while for your child to believe your guilt button is gone for good, that you mean what you say, and that you will behave respectfully, kindly, and firmly.

Attitude Matters

WE REPEAT: *Children can thrive with working parents.* Your attitude is the key. If you feel guilty and believe your children may suffer, they are likely to adopt your attitude and to develop manipulation skills. If you feel confidence in your abilities and the abilities of your children to create a happy, successful home, they are more likely to adopt that attitude and to develop cooperation skills.

Do what is right for you. If you truly have made a poor decision, wouldn't it make more sense to change instead of continuing to do it while feeling guilty? Focus on the attitudes, behaviors, and skills that will make your working beneficial to your children. You will feel the atmosphere in your home change when you adopt an attitude of confidence. Learning effective parenting skills and involving your children in problem solving and family meetings will help your family become a place where children learn to be capable, competent people. Have faith in your children to deal with your working as comfortably as you do. Of course they will experience some frustrations. Knowing they can deal with frustrations is essential to their healthy development. Remember, they take their cues from you and absorb your attitudes.

Confidence about your decision to work is one thing; confidence in your parenting skills is another matter. In the following chapters we will offer suggestions that will help you continue to gain confidence in your parenting skills by following these positive discipline concepts.

3

The Agony and Ecstasy of Childcare

Poor Childcare vs. Quality Childcare

SELENA AND ROSIE became friends when they both started working for a large corporation in their hometown. Both had found excellent childcare for their three-year-old children. Selena lived next door to a widowed grandmother who was delighted to take care of Selena's child. Rosie found a licensed preschool with an excellent reputation. At the end of the day, both children would cling to their childcare providers. They did not want to leave them. This

caused Selena to feel agony. Rosie felt ecstasy. Because they both had excellent childcare, why did one feel pain and the other joy?

Selena was jealous. She was afraid her child would love someone else more than she loved her. Rosie was thrilled that her child felt so loved and so happy in her day-care situation that she didn't want to leave. Her child adjusted quickly after they left childcare, and was happy and cuddly with her mom and dad for the rest of the evening. Rosie was able to give up her guilt about working when she knew her child was receiving so much care and nurturing from her childcare providers.

It helped Selena to talk to Rosie about their different feelings. She realized she was not being very practical to feel bad about the fact that her child was happy and felt so loved by her next-door neighbor. Rosie changed her attitude of jealousy and focused on her gratitude for finding such excellent childcare.

Home (with Parents) Care or Quality Childcare

AS WE HAVE seen, the debate goes on and on as to whether children do better when at least one parent stays home or whether they do just fine—if not better—in a quality day-care situation. The results of a recent study suggested that children can thrive in quality day care.[1] (It's important to note that the study stated *quality* childcare. There is a wealth of information stating that much of the available childcare is mediocre and is indeed harmful to children.) This caused uproar among "moms-should-stay-home" advocates.

Some stay-at-home advocates claim that many of the problems youth experience today, such as drugs, vandalism, and teenage pregnancy, could be prevented if mothers were home to supervise and nurture their children. But many of the problems are caused by other factors such as too much television; overindulged, pampered children; a culture that promotes constant busyness

1. NICHD (National Institute of Child Health and Human Development) Early Child Care Research Network, "Characteristics of Infant Child Care: Factors Contributing to Positive Caregiving," *Early Childhood Research Quarterly* 11 (1996): 267–306.

as a virtue; poor parenting skills; and woefully inadequate communication skills in marriage. These factors can be seen in families where mothers stay home as well as in families where mothers work.

We don't know which is best for you and your children—to work or to stay home. We will point out, over and over, that what works for you depends on your attitude, your needs, your hopes and dreams, your situation, and your parenting skills. The following story, about a woman who felt her deepest needs could be met if she worked at home, tells of the problems she faced and how she solved them through effective parenting skills. Whether you work at home or outside the home, this story illustrates many typical parenting problems as well as the parenting skills that solve them.

> What works for you depends on your attitude, your needs, your hopes and dreams, your situation, and your parenting skills.

The Best of Both Worlds

SANDY IS A single parent who wanted to have the best of both worlds—to work at home so she could earn money while being with her two children, four-year-old Kyle and six-year-old Joey. To accomplish this, she decided to create a day-care program in her home. However, her fantasy of having the best of both worlds was failing miserably.

Sandy told her parenting group that she needed help. Near tears, she reported that Joey was driving her crazy while she tried to manage the day-care program. "He taunts the younger children, hits them, takes their toys, uses nasty language, and fights with the older boys over the use of the equipment. Joey doesn't get into trouble at school or at his friends' homes. He misbehaves only with me. I think the day care is too hard for him to handle because I'm a single mom and he doesn't want to share me with so many other kids. He's constantly saying I'm unfair. It is so bad that I think I should stop having the children come to my day care right now so I can give him the attention he needs."

Sandy continued to share: She told Joey she would stop running the day care in June. She couldn't stop sooner because of her obligations to the families who counted on her and because she needed the money to support her family. She hadn't figured out how she would earn money when she gave up the day care, but Joey was her primary concern.

The parenting group facilitator asked, "Do you want to give up your day-care business?"

Sandy responded with passion, "No, I love it; but Joey is more important. I want peace and harmony between us and I worry about his self-esteem."

The facilitator asked, "Would you like to keep your day-care business if you could also help Joey be happy about it?"

Sandy didn't hesitate. "Of course I would!"

"Okay, then," said the facilitator. "Let's look at some basics first, then we'll work on some suggestions. Can you give up your day-care business without some hidden resentment?"

Sandy thought a moment, "No, probably not. After all, I'm doing this so I can stay home while earning money. I'm doing it for my children, and Joey doesn't understand or appreciate that."

"Who is in control if you do give up your day care even though you don't want to?" the facilitator asked.

"Well, obviously Joey is," Sandy shrugged. "I know that isn't healthy, but I can't think of what else to do. He obviously needs my attention."

The facilitator continued, "What message are you sending to Joey by allowing him to manipulate you with his emotions?"

Sandy smiled wearily. "That he can be a total tyrant—and that's what it feels like to me. I'm so confused. I love him and want to be a good mother, but

I will feel resentful if I give in to him and give up a job I love and can do at home. Having a day-care program in my home seemed like the perfect way to earn money without having to leave my kids. But the dream has turned into a nightmare."

The facilitator said, "As a group, we can show you many ways to get beyond control and power struggles and use ideas that involve cooperation. Are you interested?"

Sandy agreed, "Of course."

The facilitator turned to the group. "It's time for some brainstorming. Let's see how many ideas we can come up with that could help Sandy and Joey."

The group came up with a long list of ideas Sandy could try. She was invited to choose the one she felt most comfortable with. Sandy heard so many good ideas, however, that she chose a combination of several of them:

1. Meet with Joey at a calm time and use the four steps for winning cooperation. (We'll explain these shortly.)

2. Let Joey have some things that he doesn't have to share with anyone.

3. Spend scheduled, special time with Joey (and with Kyle).

4. Give Joey some jobs so that he can feel he's making an important contribution and can also earn some extra money.

5. Get Joey involved in finding solutions to problems so that he will feel he belongs and is significant.

6. Reach out for support by talking to someone in a similar situation who can share his or her experience.

Sandy started with the last suggestion. She called Betty, from the day-care association, and shared her problem. Betty laughed and said, "Am I ever glad I'm over that one! I had the same problem when my kids were younger. I think it's very normal. It's hard for kids to share their moms, even when they aren't single moms. Two things helped me. I wouldn't play the 'no fair' game, so my kids didn't hook me with that one. Children know what your buttons are, and they will push them, so I gave up my 'no fair' buttons. But I did allow them to have toys that were their own and didn't have to be shared by anyone. The other thing was letting them know how much I enjoyed making a good living while still being with them. It helped them to see the benefits as well as the problems."

Sandy was encouraged and relieved to hear that her problem was normal and wasn't happening just because she was a single mom. All kids need attention, but Sandy was giving Joey attention in a way that invited unhealthy manipulation. She realized that she had fallen into the trap of trying to "make it up to her kids" because they didn't have a father just as many parents try to "make it up to their kids" because they work outside the home. It was a relief to give up that belief and all the guilt that went with it.

> Many parents try to "make it up to their kids" because they work outside the home.

After talking to Betty, Sandy felt validated in her desire to make a living while being with her kids the majority of the time. Betty had made enough money to stay home with her children and even enough to help put them through college. Betty said, "Of course there were some problems and some hassles, but what job *doesn't* include some problems. The benefits for me far outweighed them, just as the benefits of parents working outside the home work for some families."

By reaching out for support, Sandy learned the importance of filling her own cup—getting strength and encouragement—before she could fill Joey's cup and resolve the problem. She was able to work with Joey on positive solutions because she was able to drop her misplaced guilt. Now that she was ready, Sandy decided to start with the four steps for winning cooperation.

Sandy was glad to see that Joey was still awake when she finished talking with Betty. Kyle had gone to sleep. It was a perfect, calm time to try the four steps for winning cooperation. Sandy started by asking Joey, "Honey, could we have a special talk just between me and you while I'm tucking you into bed?"

"Yeah, okay," Joey replied.

Sandy continued. "I was wondering if you feel like you aren't important to me when I'm running the day care."

Sandy had struck a nerve. Joey replied angrily, "It's not fair that I have to share all my stuff."

Sandy reflected and validated his feelings. She offered her understanding and a story of her own. "I can see how you would feel that way. I can remember when I was a little girl and my mom made me share all my clothes with my

FOUR STEPS FOR WINNING COOPERATION

1. Get into the child's world and make a guess about what he or she might be feeling. (If you're wrong, guess again.)

2. Show understanding and validate feelings. (Sometimes it helps to describe a time when you felt the same.)

3. Ask your child if he or she is willing to listen to his or her feelings. (Children listen better when they have agreed and when they feel listened to first.)

4. Work on a solution together. (The first two steps create a feeling of closeness and trust so children will be more willing to listen and to work on solutions in a cooperative manner.)

younger sister—even my favorites. I hated it. I can see now that by trying to be fair to all the other kids, I was very unfair to you. I made you share your dinnertime chair even when you tried to tell me you didn't think it was fair. I'm so sorry I didn't consider your feelings. I'll try to do better from now on."

Joey felt understood. He was touched by his mother's admission and apology and started to cry. "I'm sorry for being so bad." (Children often cry from relief when they feel understood. They have a tendency to drop their defensiveness. And, when parents take responsibility for disrespectful behavior, children often follow their example.)

Sandy reassured Joey. "Honey, you aren't bad. We both made some mistakes. I'll bet we can work on some solutions together. First, would you be willing to hear some of my feelings?"

Joey sniffled. "Okay," he said.

Sandy drew Joey close to her. "You're more important to me than any job. And I'd really like to keep the day care so I don't have to go to work outside our home. I like being able to work and be with you at the same time. I know you have some great ideas that I haven't listened to before. I'd really like to hear them now. And maybe you'd like to hear some of mine. I can't do it without your help. Would you be willing to help find ideas that work for both of us?"

Joey grinned. "Okay!"

Children feel empowered when they know they can be helpful and when they are respectfully involved in figuring out how to be helpful. Together, Sandy and Joey came up with the following plans: Joey and Sandy would spend fifteen minutes of special time together every day with no phones, no little brother, and no other children. Joey agreed that Kyle should have the same amount of time and that they would all work together, during a family meeting, on a specific time schedule and what each could do while the other was spending special time with Mom. Joey was enthusiastic about the possibility of helping out and earning some extra money. They agreed that he would earn one dollar every day by helping Mom make the lunches for the day-care children the night before. He volunteered to take on other jobs, such as picking up toys. They also decided that no one else could sit in his dinner chair un-

> Children feel empowered when they know they can be helpful and when they are respectfully involved in figuring out how to be helpful.

less he gave permission. They ended their talk by agreeing that in the future, if something was bothering them, they would talk about it and work together on solutions that felt respectful to all.

Sandy was ecstatic at her next parenting group. "I can't believe how well this stuff works! Joey is now helping and seems to feel great about himself instead of misbehaving because he feels left out. At our family meeting he told Kyle how lucky they are to have a mom who can work at home. When I got Joey involved in problem solving, he had so many good ideas. I'm so glad that I got to tell him how much I love him and that he could really hear me. Thank you all so much!"

Sandy was able to turn a "nightmare" back into a dream. She found a way to use her problems as great opportunities to learn and grow. Sandy and Joey learned listening, problem-solving, and cooperation skills. All of this learning could not have happened if Sandy had not honored her dream while finding a way to honor Joey at the same time. She received help in getting out of the win/lose struggle. It would not have been healthy for Joey to "win" at Sandy's expense, nor for Sandy to "win" at Joey's expense. Control and manipulation stopped being an issue when she learned to "win" cooperation *with* Joey, rather than winning *over* Joey. Remember, there are opportunities for learning in any situation—staying at home or working.

Sandy resolved her work-family conflict by combining work and childcare. That may not be a viable option for you. Whether you currently have satisfactory childcare or you are just beginning to search for an appropriate placement, there are many factors to consider.

Searching for Childcare

CHILDCARE OPTIONS FALL under two main categories: in your home or outside your home. If you choose childcare outside your home, you may prefer the structure and child centeredness of a quality childcare facility or the family atmosphere of a private home. In either situation, there is a huge difference between quality childcare and poor childcare.

The book *Positive Discipline for Preschoolers* contains an excellent chapter on finding childcare.[2] You can also get information on quality childcare from the National Association for the Education of Young Children (NAEYC). In any case, we can't emphasize enough that poor childcare can be very harmful to your children, while quality childcare can benefit your children. In addition to the above sources, here are some things to consider.

Childcare Inside Your Home

You may choose the services of a live-in nanny or someone who can come to your home on a daily basis. The media is filled with horror stories of nannies who have been physically and/or emotionally abusive to the children in their care. However, many people have found qualified people who provided such quality childcare that they were almost like a family member.

Finding well-qualified people is a challenge for any kind of employer whether you are hiring for your business or for your childcare. However, much more is at stake when employing a childcare provider—your children. It is essential to check references and to be very clear (in writing) about your expectations and your discipline philosophy. Once you have found someone you like, we suggest having the nanny start during a vacation period or a weekend, so

---

2. Jane Nelsen, Cheryl Erwin, and Roslyn Duffy, Chapter 23 "Identifying Quality Child Care," in *Positive Discipline for Preschoolers* (Roseville, CA: Prima Publishing, 1998), 319–329.

you can be in the home with your new childcare provider for several days before leaving that person alone with your children. You can learn a lot in a few days about a nanny's attitude, skills, and relationship with your children.

Be in the home with your new childcare provider for several days before leaving that person alone with your children.

Linda, a single mother of three young children, found in her church a part-time student with excellent references to come to her home forty hours a week. Linda had the added benefit of knowing this person and her family. She found it was more cost-effective and less stressful to have someone in her home. As she put it, "I needed someone wonderful to watch my kids, and I also needed a helper to do some of the things stay-at-home moms have time to do! After long days selling print advertising I was able to come home to a tidy house, with the laundry done and dinner on the table (expectations that had been agreed to in advance). My kids loved her, and they loved having someone in their home because they could have their little friends over. My nanny would also do errands like grocery shopping, buying birthday presents, or picking up the dry cleaning. That way I was able to relax and really enjoy my kids when I came home at night. I can't imagine how stressful it would have been to pick up my kids from day care and go home to a messy house and an empty refrigerator. This arrangement worked beautifully for me for seven years. My kids never had to miss out on anything because I worked, and I was able to attend most of their events because I didn't have to take time to do all the other chores and errands."

Another mother shared, "I learned the importance of regular communication with my husband and our nanny after discovering poor Julianne got peas and spaghetti for lunch *and* dinner two days in a row—I guess I should be thankful she didn't get it for breakfast, too! The nanny gave her the same lunch twice in a row, and my husband fed her the same dinner twice in a row." That led to the creation of daily journals and regular family meetings that included the nanny. The parents completed the daily journal while they were with Julianne to convey key information to the nanny, and the nanny completed the other parts of the journal while she watched Julianne so the parents were informed. Part of the family meeting included menu planning that involved everyone. (See page 133 in the chapter on family meetings.)

JULIANNE'S DAILY JOURNAL

DATE: _____   **BATH?** ❏ Yes   ❏ No

SLEEP: Woke up _____   Napped _____   Went to bed _____

MEALS & SNACKS: **Beverage**   **Time**

Breakfast _____   _____   _____

Morning Snack _____   _____   _____

Lunch _____   _____   _____

Afternoon Snack _____   _____   _____

Dinner _____   _____   _____

Comments on mealtimes?

ACTIVITIES, NEW ACCOMPLISHMENTS, ETC.:

HEALTH & GENERAL DISPOSITION:

MEDICINES:

Jane Nelsen had a live-in nanny, Joanne, for eleven years. Joanne was willing to read several *Positive Discipline* books and to implement the discipline theories. She understood the importance of not becoming a slave to the children, but instead supervising their involvement in chores and following the other routines they helped create. Joanne is still a close family friend.

Many working parents feel it is an invasion of their privacy to have someone in their home and prefer childcare outside their homes.

Childcare Outside Your Home

If you are one of the many parents who have decided that childcare outside of your home meets the needs of your family, there are several additional factors you should consider.

Childcare Facilities

A childcare facility is a center that is dedicated solely to the care of young children (as contrasted to a childcare provider's home). The advantage is that childcare is the sole occupation of the staff and a quality facility will be filled with age-appropriate equipment and toys. However, not all childcare facilities can claim the "quality" label. Personal research regarding the following questions is imperative.

- Is the staff well trained? What kind of training do they get and how often? Does the staff receive training to detect learning disabilities or

physical and cognitive problems? Does the center do a background check on their employees? How is this background check performed? *No matter what form of childcare you select, be sure you take the time to do background checks.* Personal references are nice, but a background check of the individual or facility may turn up information that will help you decide whether or not this is the provider for you.

> *No matter what form of childcare you select, be sure you take the time to do background checks.*

- Does the facility meet or exceed the minimum standards outlined for your state? You can do an online investigation to determine what the minimum standards are where you live. The National Resource Center for Health and Safety in Child Care (http://nrc.uchsc.edu/states.html) is a Web site that will give you licensing information in your state. In addition, some organizations provide special accreditation. The best known is the National Association for the Education of Young Children (NAEYC). Programs that receive this type of accreditation truly have earned it.

- What is the turnover rate for the staff at the facility? Very young children need consistency, not only with curriculum or daily routines, but also with those who care for them. Will your child consistently interact with the same provider?

- Is there a discipline policy? How are problems handled? Observe how teachers interact with the children. The best childcare is void of any kind of punishment (shaming and blaming) and uses discipline based on kindness and firmness at the same time. Many parents aren't sure how this looks in practical application. You will be familiar with many nonpunitive discipline methods by the time you finish this book.

- Does the provider prepare meals and/or snacks? If so, what do the meals and snacks consist of? When and how are meals and snacks prepared and served? Childcare facilities that appreciate the importance of involving children to enhance their sense of belonging and capability will allow children to take turns with meal preparations and will allow children to serve themselves as much as possible.

- How does the center handle toilet training? What is your responsibility regarding extra clothing, providing diapers, and so on? What are the sanitary conditions in the toileting area? Many childcare facilities are willing to toilet train young children. This works very well because the childcare staff are not emotionally invested in your child's toileting. It is especially effective when the facility has small toilets and a regular schedule for toileting. Your child will see other children using the toilet and usually want to follow their example. "Accidents" are handled with a minimum of fuss—simply allowing a child to change into clean, dry clothes, helping only as much as necessary—without any sense of blame or shame.

- Does the center have an open-door policy? Can you drop by unexpectedly to visit with your child during your lunch hour? Can you volunteer in the classroom for special events? This is a very important point to consider. Some centers may tell you it is disturbing to the child to have you visit, and this could be true. However, don't even consider leaving your child anywhere that doesn't have an open-door policy. If your visits disturb your child, consider finding a way to peek around corners once in awhile to observe without being seen.

The first thing you should do is spend several hours in the center with your child, quietly sitting on the sidelines where you can observe what goes on. You could use the observation checklist and give a rating of 1 to 10 (with 10 being the best) on each item.

> Don't even consider leaving your child anywhere that doesn't have an open-door policy.

A Private Home

Some parents prefer childcare in a private home because of the family atmosphere. Some are lucky enough to find a close friend or relative to take care of their children.

If you choose childcare in a home, we strongly suggest that you spend a full day with your child in the private home. Spend this time whether you know the provider well or not. If that is not allowed, do not consider this home. You cannot make a better investment of time to be certain your child is

OBSERVATION CHECKLIST

1. Staff seems to love and enjoy children.

2. Staff does not expect things of children that are not age appropriate, such as expecting a two-year-old to sit quietly during story time. (See chapter 6 for more information on age appropriateness.)

3. Staff uses kind and firm discipline and avoids all punishment. (See chapters 6–8 for what to expect.)

4. There are no televisions in sight.

5. Rate for cleanliness and safety.

6. There are routines without rigidity. For example, do they have a "reading time" but allow children to wander and play with other toys if they are not interested? Do they serve nutritious food, but allow children to eat only as much or as little as they want? Do they have nap time, but allow children who aren't sleepy to quietly read a book?

7. Are there plenty of developmentally appropriate educational, as well as just plain fun, toys?

8. Do they avoid pushing academics for children who are under six and learn best from play and socialization?

9. Do they treat parents as partners rather than as intruders?

receiving quality vs. poor childcare. The observation checklist can be used for observing childcare in a private home as well as a childcare facility. The exception is that you may see a television set in the home, but make very certain that it is turned off most of the time. Perhaps older children may watch an educational program while small children are napping.

Just as you hear horror stories about nannies and day-care facilities, there are horror stories about childcare in homes. Some are literally parking places for children who spend their day sitting in front of a television, are subjected to physical punishment, and are lacking in the kind of equipment that enhances child development.

On the other hand, many day-care providers have a solid background in child development and/or other training for quality childcare. They create an environment filled with developmentally appropriate equipment, flexible routines, and positive discipline. *Positive Discipline for Childcare Providers*[3] is an excellent resource for more information on quality childcare and positive discipline in a quality day-care setting.

After-School Care

Once your children enter elementary school, other childcare options become available. Many schools offer after-school care. Some schools have on-site care so your children never have to leave the school's grounds. Other schools will bus your children to a childcare center. The same licensing, safety, discipline, and parent-involvement guidelines listed above apply to those caring for your elementary-school-age child.

The Importance of Communication and Research

FINDING QUALITY CHILDCARE is a critical component in your success as a working parent. Regardless of what option you choose, it is important to stay connected to your child and his childcare provider. Take the time to keep your childcare provider updated about your child's development and anything happening at home; the birth of a new baby or illness in the family can have an effect on your child's behavior, and your childcare provider will deal with it best when the situation is understood. In addition, ask your provider to keep you updated. It is not always possible to chat for any length of time when dropping your child off or picking your child up.

---

3. Jane Nelsen and Cheryl Erwin, *Positive Discipline for Childcare Providers* (Roseville, CA: Prima Publishing, 2002).

As you can see, finding appropriate childcare is no easy matter. Take the time to research and investigate the options that would work best for your needs. Your child depends on you to select the best possible environment for his or her early learning.

Quick and Quality Parenting Tips

Separation Anxiety

It breaks my heart when my child cries and clings when I drop her off at the child-care center. It is enough to make me want to stop working.

Working Parents' Common Mistakes

1. Being riddled with guilt or uncertainty. Children absorb this energy. They also absorb an energy of confidence.

2. Not knowing that quality childcare can provide an extended community that reinforces the lessons of trust, connection, and respect.

Discouraging Words and Actions

It is never a good idea to tell a child to stop crying—or even worse to tell a child, "Big girls/boys don't cry." We know adults mean well when they say, "Don't cry," which is the same as saying, "Don't communicate. It makes me uncomfortable."

Respectful and Encouraging Actions

1. Use your intuition (and/or the Mistaken Goals Chart on pages 42–43) to give you clues about why the child is crying. He may be using "water power" as a misguided way to seek belonging.

2. For nonverbal children, separation anxiety is very real—and, when you follow all the precautions for finding quality childcare, your child will be fine. (Children raised in extended families seldom experience separation anxiety because they get used to many people who love them. Of course, their anxiety may kick in when they meet a stranger.)

3. Be sure your childcare provider is willing to rock and comfort your child if needed. Then, if your child is still having difficulty separating, leave as soon as possible so your child doesn't have to deal with the energy of your guilt and anxiety as well as making his own adjustments.

4. Have faith in children to survive separation so long as they are provided with love and support, both at home and in the childcare environment—and that some will adjust sooner than others.

Respectful and Encouraging Words

1. Sometimes it is okay to simply allow the child to have his feelings. You might say, "It is okay to cry. I hope you feel better soon."

2. Take time to teach skills that many help your child learn other ways to behave and communicate as soon as they are old enough, such as "Use your words."

3. Spray some of your perfume or aftershave lotion on your child's shirt. Tell her, "You can smell this when you miss me and remember that I'll be back to pick you up at the end of the day."

Encouraging Attitudes

1. Understand that the process of coping with separation is part of every child's normal developmental challenges.

2. You may feel differently about crying when you understand it is a language. You will be more effective when you learn to understand (not speak) the language. Crying doesn't always mean anxiety. Sometimes it is an expression of genuine need, and sometimes an expression of a preference. (Needs should be granted, but it is not always healthy to have every preference granted.) Sometimes crying represents frustration, lack of communication skills, or simply a transition method.

3. Encouraging dependence is counter-productive to the development of self-trust and leads to excessive dependence on others. Yes, babies must depend on others, but the goal of parents and caregivers is to help them develop a sense of trust in themselves—including the experience that they can handle disappointment and anxiety.

4. Remember the research that has shown that babies can thrive when they receive love at home and love in a quality childcare situation.

4

Why Childen Misbehave and What to Do About It

Not Understanding Why Children Misbehave vs. Understanding Why Children Misbehave

REMEMBER YOUR FANTASIES about what it would be like to have a child—before you had one. This child would never have a snotty nose, would always be well groomed, would be well liked, would always behave well, and, certainly, would never be allowed to "talk back." By now you have had your rude awakening, because the truth is that children don't always behave the way we expect them to or wish they would.

You may have fallen into the trap of thinking, "It must be because I work outside the home. Surely my children would behave better if I stayed home with them." Not so. In this chapter you will learn it is normal for children to misbehave whether or not their parents work outside the home. In fact, we recommend immediate therapy for parents who have perfectly behaved children—therapy for *them,* not for their children. Perfectly behaved children (if you can find any) are likely experiencing too much control or fear in their homes. Misbehavior is a normal part of a child's individuation process.

The Individuation Process

IT IS NORMAL for children to "test the waters" (misbehave) as they try to figure out how they fit into this world. How do they find belonging, connection, and capability (especially when they have to compete with those intruders—other children)? How do they find out who they are separate from their parents? How do they deal with their perceptions of being less capable than others? How do they deal with the frustration from lacking the skills to accomplish their desires? Often, the way they deal with their perceptions and frustrations is to feel discouraged and then to misbehave. As Rudolf Dreikurs (a Viennese psychiatrist who came to America and perpetuated the work of psychiatrist Alfred Adler, upon whose philosophy the POSITIVE DISCIPLINE books are based) said, "A misbehaving child is a discouraged child."

When parents don't understand why children misbehave and what to do about it, they often use ineffective, punishing parenting methods. Children become more discouraged and as a result, misbehave even more. Misbehavior, ineffective parenting skills, more discouragement, misbehavior, ineffective parenting skills—it becomes a vicious cycle. We'd like to add that parents also become discouraged and misbehave. Surely you, like most parents, have used an ineffective parenting method you later regretted, but had to admit you just didn't know what else to do. That is an example of discouragement and misbehavior. Just like you, your children feel discouraged and just don't know what else to do.

Why Children Misbehave

THE PRIMARY GOAL of children (and of all people) is to feel a sense of belonging (connection) and capability. When they "perceive" that they don't belong, they feel discouraged and misbehave. It is as simple as that. We repeat, as Dreikurs often did, "A misbehaving child is a discouraged child." Most misbehavior is based on a child's *mistaken* idea of how to find that sense of belonging, connection, and capability.

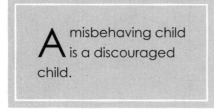
A misbehaving child is a discouraged child.

Often it is difficult to understand why children believe they don't belong. For example, why does a child "believe" she doesn't belong when her parents love her so much? Why does she decide she doesn't belong when her parents have another baby? Doesn't she know they can love more than one child? Why

does a small child believe she is not capable just because she can't do something as well as an older child? Doesn't she know she'll be able to do it as well once she grows older and develops the same skills? No, she doesn't know these things. Her mind has not developed enough to comprehend logic. This is why Dreikurs taught, "Children are good perceivers, but poor interpreters." In other words, children observe (perceive) a situation, interpret what it means (based on their illogical, undeveloped thinking skills), feel something, decide something, and then act (behave) based on their interpretation, feelings, and decisions about the situation.[1]

See the Discouragement Beneath the Behavior

ADULTS USUALLY LOOK at the behavior without understanding the discouragement that motivates the behavior. Instead of seeing a misbehaving child as a discouraged child, these adults give the behavior all kinds of labels such as naughty, hardheaded, stubborn, disobedient, bad, strong-willed, liar, lazy, irresponsible, spoiled.

---

1. Rudolf Dreikurs and Vicki Soltz, *Children: the Challenge* (E. P. Dutton, New York, NY, 1987).

These words create a very negative mind-set. They label the child without seeing that what the child is trying to say through the misbehavior is, "I'm a child, and I just want to belong."

Dreikurs was able to see past the behavior and identify four mistaken goals that explain the beliefs (the discouragement) behind the misbehaviors. They are called *mistaken* goals because the *real* goal is to achieve belonging, connection, and capability. The mistake is that children choose an ineffective way to achieve their real goal. As Alfred Adler taught, all behavior has a purpose. Understanding mistaken goal behavior helps adults understand that the real purpose (to belong) is hidden (like a code) in behavior that doesn't make sense to achieve that goal.

When you understand mistaken goal behavior, you will know that children are really speaking in code. When you understand the code, you can respond to what the child is really saying with her misbehavior and respond in ways that will give your children encouraging experiences that may lead to different decisions. When children no longer feel discouraged and find belonging, connection, and capability, they respond by behaving in positive, appropriate ways.

Clues for Understanding the Mistaken Goal

TAKE A LOOK at the Mistaken Goals Chart on pages 42–43. As you can see (look at the second column), the first clue that helps you understand the

FOUR MISTAKEN GOALS OF BEHAVIOR

1. Undue attention ("I'll belong if you pay constant attention to me.")

2. Misguided power ("I'll belong if I boss you around—or, at least, if I don't let you boss me.")

3. Revenge ("I don't belong, and that hurts. At least I can hurt back.")

4. Assumed inadequacy ("I don't belong and there is no hope that I can. I give up.")

child's *mistaken* goal is your feelings. The second clue (look at the fourth column) is how the child reacts to ineffective interventions (third column).

Are you now totally confused? Let's take each mistaken goal, one at a time, and look at typical "misbehaviors," the coded message, and some parenting skills that are likely to help the child feel encouraged, and thus eliminate the misbehavior.

Undue Attention

When you feel annoyed, irritated, worried, or guilty, your child is involved in the mistaken goal of undue attention and has the mistaken idea that she will belong only if you give her almost constant attention.

The reason this goal is called "undue" attention is because everyone has a healthy, appropriate need for attention. Children are very resourceful. If they believe they don't belong and choose the mistaken goal of undue attention, they may try:

- Interrupting
- Crying
- Acting helpless
- Manipulating through tantrums
- Acting silly
- Pretending to forget
- Clinging
- Whining
- Pestering
- Clowning

Children mistakenly believe that these irritating behaviors will be effective to help them find belonging, connection, and capability by getting your attention. Instead parents feel annoyed, irritated, worried, or guilty. When you understand mistaken goal behavior, you can ignore the irritating behavior and focus on what the child is really saying—the coded message.

The coded message for children seeking undue attention is, "Involve me usefully." When parents respond to the coded message, their response can

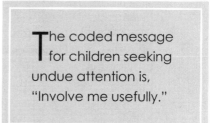

The coded message for children seeking undue attention is, "Involve me usefully."

help children achieve their goal to belong and feel significant. Their mistaken goal behavior achieves just the opposite. Children do their mistaken goal behavior and parents respond in mistaken ways (see the third column of the Mistaken Goals Chart), which only convinces the child that she doesn't

Mistaken Goals Chart

The Child's Goal Is:	If the Parent/ Teacher Feels:	And Tends to React by:	And if the Child's Response Is:
Undue Attention (to keep others busy or to get special service)	Annoyed Irritated Worried Guilty	Reminding Coaxing Doing things for the child he/she could do for him/herself	Stops temporarily, but later resumes same or another annoying behavior
Misguided Power (to be boss)	Challenged Threatened Defeated	Fighting Giving in Thinking: "You can't get away with it," or "I'll make you" Wanting to be right	Intensifies behavior Defiant compliance Feels he/she's won when parent/ teacher is upset Passive power
Revenge (to get even)	Hurt Disappointed Disbelieving Disgusted	Retaliating Getting even Thinking, "How could you do this to me?"	Retaliates Intensifies Escalates the same behavior or chooses another weapon
Assumed Inadequacy (to give up and be left alone)	Hopeless Helpless Inadequate	Giving up Doing for the child Helping too much	Retreats further Passive No improvement No response

The Belief Behind the Child's Behavior Is:	Coded Messages:	Parent/Teacher Proactive and Empowering Responses Include:
I count (belong) only when I'm being noticed or getting special service; I'm only important when I'm keeping you busy with me.	Notice me; involve me usefully.	"I love you and _____." (Example: "I care about you and will spend time with you later."); redirect by assigning a task so child can gain useful attention; avoid special service; plan special time; set up routines; use problem solving; encourage; use family/class meetings; touch without words; ignore; set up nonverbal signals.
I belong only when I'm boss, in control, or proving no one can boss me. "You can't make me."	Let me help; give me choices.	Redirect to positive power by asking for help; offer limited choices; don't fight and don't give in; withdraw from conflict; be firm and kind; act, don't talk; decide what you will do; let routines be the boss; leave and calm down; develop mutual respect; set a few reasonable limits; practice follow-through; encourage; use family/class meetings.
I don't think I belong so I'll hurt others as I feel hurt. I can't be liked or loved.	I'm hurting; validate my feelings.	Acknowledge hurt feelings; avoid feeling hurt; avoid punishment and retaliation; build trust; use reflective listening; share your feelings; make amends; show you care; act, don't talk; encourage strengths; put kids in same boat; use family/class meetings.
I can't belong because I'm not perfect, so I'll convince others not to expect anything of me; I am helpless and unable; it's no use trying because I won't do it right.	Don't give up on me; show me a small step.	Break task down to small steps; stop all criticism; encourage any positive attempt; have faith in child's ability; focus on assets; don't pity; don't give up; set up opportunities for success; teach skills—show how, but don't do for; enjoy the child; build on his/her interests; encourage, encourage, encourage; use family/class meetings.

belong. The coded message shows a way for parents to break this discouraging cycle and give children what they really need to stop the misbehavior.

Brad is a single father raising three children and working full time. As in many homes, his mornings are very hectic. One morning he could not find clean underwear for this three-year-old daughter, Emma. After a frantic search, he found a clean pair and gave them to Emma with the admonition, "Hurry and get dressed." The next thing he knew, Emma came into the living room stark naked. Brad asked, "Why aren't you dressed?"

Emma smiled sweetly and said, "My panties are wet." She had deliberately peed in them. Brad was flabbergasted.

When you understand mistaken goal behavior, it is easy to see how Emma could get the mistaken idea that she wasn't important (didn't feel a sense of belonging) as her father rushed around trying to get everyone out the door on time. Emma found a creative way to get some undue attention. It doesn't matter that Emma's father loves her very much and *knows* she belongs. He is doing a remarkable job of caring for his children all by himself while working full time. However, children base their behavior on their very unique perceptions—perceptions that often don't make sense to adults.

What could Brad have done to help Emma feel a sense of belonging, connection, and capability? It would not take much more time to take Emma by the hand and say, "I need your help to find some clean underwear. Where do you think they could be?" instead of searching by himself. Also, he realized that much of his morning hassles could be prevented by helping Emma lay out all of her clothes for the next morning as part of her evening routine. (See chapter 5.)

Once undue attention is determined as the goal of your child's misbehavior (because you feel annoyed, irritated, worried, or guilty), there are many things you can do to reduce the misbehavior. A few are listed in the limited space of the last column of the Mistaken Goals Chart. Please keep in mind that all the parenting tools in this book are designed to help children feel belonging, connection, and capability, and thus reduce misbehavior.

Misguided Power

When you feel challenged, threatened, or defeated, your child is involved in the mistaken goal of misguided power. Your child may have the mistaken idea that she will belong only if she is "the boss," or tries to show you, "You can't make me."

Children need a sense of power (or autonomy). In fact, they will use their power one way or another. It is the job of parents to guide them in the constructive use of power so they avoid the misguided use of power.

Just a few of the creative (though mistaken) ways children seek belonging when they have chosen the mistaken goal of misguided power are:

- Defiance
- Saying, "You can't make me"
- Saying, "Okay," but then not doing it
- Being bossy to others
- Complying just enough to "get you off my back," but not up to your satisfaction
- Bullying others
- Making disrespectful demands
- Pretending to forget

Notice that the last behavior (pretending to forget) is a behavior that was also listed under undue attention. Many behaviors can be for different goals. That is why you have to rely on your feelings to help you understand which one it is. A child who pretends to forget because she wants undue attention is likely to invite you to feel annoyed. A child who pretends to forget because she wants misguided power is likely to invite you to feel challenged.

When you are tired after working all day, it may seem easier to simply bark out orders. However, it would be much more effective and much less tiring to pay attention to the coded message. The coded message for the mistaken goal of misguided power is, "Let me help. Give me choices."

Too many parents "boss" their children around and then wonder why they rebel. It takes two to engage in a power struggle. Instead of doubling your efforts to make your child comply by using threats or punishment, you can defuse the situation by stepping out of the power struggle and using some of the suggestions in the last column of the Mistaken Goals Chart that respond to the coded message. Sometimes this requires what feels like a superhuman

> The coded message for the mistaken goal of misguided power is, "Let me help. Give me choices."

effort and self-control. (Aha, you have an opportunity to model what you want your child to develop.)

Nine-year-old Scott was respectful and cooperative at school, but at home he was a little tyrant. He bullied his four-year-old brother and caused trouble just when his father, who worked at home for a dot.com firm, was under serious deadline pressure. He would stand on top of his bunk bed with his finger pointed at his mother and say, "Get my backpack out of the van now! Move it! I need it!"

In desperation Scott's family marched him to the family therapist's office for help. The parents were shocked to learn that Scott felt like an "alien" at home. During sand-play therapy Scott chose a small, silver alien to depict himself. He lined up his mother, father, and little brother across from him in angry, blaming positions. He confided to his therapist that he always felt like he was the one in trouble. He believed that his parents loved little Steven more than him and that they were always too busy for him. He felt blamed for all of the problems between himself and his little brother because his parents would say, "You are older and ought to know better."

Scott was a very unhappy boy. He was hurting terribly because his core need to belong was not being met at home. That is why the same child could behave so well in one setting (in his school where he felt encouraged) and be a little "monster" in another (at home where he felt so discouraged).

Parents who understand that a misbehaving child is a discouraged child know that the best way to deal with misbehavior is to help the child feel encouraged—to feel belonging, connection, and capability. When a child feels encouraged, the misbehavior will disappear.

Scott's parents were asked to spend daily one-on-one time with Scott every day for the next week, regardless of his behavior. The father was asked to take Scott on a date *without* little brother. The parents were also instructed to avoid taking sides when the boys fought, but to simply separate both of them.[2]

One week later the mother said to the therapist, "It is a miracle. Scott is a different child. He is helpful and fun to be around. How did this happen?"

When a child believes he belongs, positive behaviors follow. When a child feels discouraged and unloved, the misbehavior returns.

The adult finger is often pointed at children as the "cause" of power struggles. Parents complain, "Why won't he listen to me? Why won't he do what he knows he should do? Why does she say she'll do it, but doesn't?" In many instances, the finger could be pointed in the other direction—not in a sense of blame, but in a sense of awareness. The child could complain, "Why don't you listen to me? Why don't you talk to me respectfully? Why don't you involve me in decisions that affect me instead of giving orders?" We have never seen a power-drunk child without a power-drunk adult close by.

If you recognize that you are engaged in power struggles with a child, a good place to start is to *apologize for your part in the power struggle*. Remember,

2. For more information, see Jane Nelsen, Lynn Lott, and H. Stephen Glenn, "Fighting," in *Positive Discipline from A to Z*, 2nd Edition (Roseville, CA: Prima Publishing, 1999), pages 133–138.

a power struggle takes two. Be willing to look at your part. Maybe you have been too bossy or too controlling. Apologize and offer to work *with* your child to find more respectful solutions. Too often when parents insist on winning the power struggle, that makes the child the "loser." This hurts and often is an invitation for the child to seek revenge.

Revenge

When you least expect it, your child may do or say something that invites you to feel hurt, disbelieving, disappointed, or even disgusted. This is a pretty good clue that your child has been hurt and is seeking revenge. Some typical revenge behaviors are:

- Name calling (You are a bitch!)
- Put-downs (You are so stupid)
- Deliberate destruction of property
- Failing as a means to get even
- Lying
- Stealing
- Self-destructive behaviors

You may have hurt your child without even knowing it. (Sometimes children feel unloved or conditionally loved because of their parents' high expectations, "You love me only when I get good grades or live up to your many expectations," and that hurts.) Sometimes they may have been hurt by someone else. In any case, it can be very easy for parents to fall into a "revenge cycle" when the child does something hurtful, the parent punishes, the child feels more hurt and hurts back, the parent punishes more severely. When children feel hurt, and are hurting back, it can be extremely difficult to see the coded message, but it is the only way out of the revenge cycle.

> The coded message for the mistaken goal of revenge is "I'm hurting; validate my feelings."

The coded message for the mistaken goal of revenge is "I'm hurting; validate my feelings." Children who choose revenge have almost submerged their desire for belonging, connection, and capability. They are more focused on their need to "hurt back."

Nine-year-old Marina was being difficult. Her mother, Tamara, is a very busy woman with a full-time job and an active social life. Late one afternoon, Tamara took Marina to the golf and country club where Tamara was looking forward to a nine-hole game of golf with three of her girlfriends. Her intention was to spend time with Marina while also taking care of herself.

Marina was cooperative at first, and she enjoyed driving the golf cart between holes. After two hours, Marina's patience was gone. She started to scream and threw herself on the floor of the country club dining hall, pounding her fists and shrieking, "I hate you! You are the worst mother in the world!"

Tamara was dumbfounded. She tried to explain to her friends that Marina's behavior was not typical. In embarrassment, she dragged Marina to the car. On the way home, Tamara shamed and blamed Marina. "You're grounded for a week! How could you embarrass me like that in front of my friends?"

Several days later, Marina confided to her family counselor, "I was just trying to make my mom pay for giving her friends all of the attention when she should have been paying attention to me." Marina didn't know how to tell her mom what she really wanted. Instead she chose the mistaken goal of revenge.

Two days later Marina felt neglected and started screaming at her mom. This time her mom said, "Sounds to me as though you are feeling angry and neglected right now. I love you, and we'll talk about this as soon as you have calmed down." Tamara was actually surprised at how quickly Marina calmed down. She experienced, firsthand, that children who have chosen revenge usually feel some satisfaction just from having their feelings validated. They may need a little more time before they are ready for a rational discussion, but feeling understood is a huge first step. A few hours later, Tamara asked Marina if she was ready to talk. Marina agreed. Tamara validated her feelings again and together they brainstormed for some solutions to solve the problem.

Once again you are called upon to use superhuman self-control to avoid reacting to a child who is being hurtful. It is human nature that when hurt, you want to hurt back. But as in the previous story, retaliation and punishment will only reinforce your child's belief that she doesn't belong and will escalate her misbehavior. Validating feelings and then brainstorming for solutions diffuses the revenge cycle and helps the child feel belonging, connection, and capability—thus reducing the misbehavior.

Assumed Inadequacy

When you feel despair, hopeless, helpless, or inadequate, chances are that your child is feeling the same and has chosen the mistaken goal of assumed inadequacy. Dreikurs called this "assumed" inadequacy because the child isn't inadequate, but assuming inadequacy can have the same results. Children who have lost confidence in their ability to be successful defend themselves by not trying. They are very discouraged and may have deep reservoirs of perceived inadequacy. They often choose to "give up" in the following ways:

- Won't try
- Makes self-deprecating remarks
- Withdraws
- Seeks isolation from others

This child often says, "I can't," and you know she believes she can't. A child who has chosen the mistaken goal of undue attention often says, "I can't," but you both know she really can.

It is common for parents to mirror the feelings of the child who has chosen the mistaken goal of assumed inadequacy instead of understanding the coded message: The coded message for the mistaken goal of assumed inadequacy is "Don't give up on me. Have faith in me. Show me a small step."

You may feel very helpless and inadequate when trying to help your child who feels like a failure or wants to give up and be left alone. These children can be very convincing. They may convince you that they want to be left alone. The worst thing you can do with a severely discouraged child is to leave her alone. This tells your child she truly is as worthless as she feels. On the other hand, coaxing and nagging compounds her profound sense of inadequacy.

> The coded message for the mistaken goal of assumed inadequacy is "Don't give up on me. Have faith in me. Show me a small step."

Six-year-old Eppie was a very discouraged child who refused to try just about anything. All she wanted to do was cling to her parents and say, "I can't." Her parents bought into her helplessness and rescued her and did everything for her. Eppie didn't have a chance to practice being capable, which deepened her belief that she was inadequate. She had a very difficult time leaving her parents to go to school, and she spent much of her time sitting at her desk trying to avoid being noticed. The teacher recommended testing with the school psychologist, who discovered that Eppie was very capable, but had simply developed the belief that she wasn't. The school psychologist explained mistaken goal behavior to Eppie's parents and suggested a plan for helping Eppie feel encouraged.

Her parents had a difficult time grasping the possibility that Eppie didn't feel belonging, connection, and capability because they loved her so much. In fact, they had "loved" her so much that they didn't require much of Eppie. They did everything for her. They thought this would make her feel more loved, not inadequate.

When they understood how Eppie came to her conclusions of inadequacy they started the process of weaning her from her dependency on them. It would have been too much to stop doing anything for Eppie. Instead they took small steps and more time for training. For example, Eppie didn't even want to put on her own shoes and socks. Mom started by saying, I'll put on one sock and show you a few secrets such as scrunching up the sock, and you can put on the other sock." Dad would sit down with her during homework time and say, "I'll draw the first half of the circle, then you can draw the second half." As Eppie started doing more things for herself, she had to give up her belief that she was inadequate and slowly stopped acting so inadequate.

Many experiences could lead some children to decide they are inadequate. It is important to note that different children come to different conclusions from the same experiences. Children who feel that they have not met parental expectations in the past may develop defenses to avoid future expectations. They may be passive, pretend not to care about anything or anyone, and refuse to try. Others may decide to try harder.

Sometimes children are afraid to put forth their best effort. If they don't really try and then fail they can fall back on knowing that they didn't give it their best shot. If they truly try and still fail they confirm what they already suspect: "I'm a loser." Other children may feel challenged by failures and simply try again. Some children may develop perceptions of inadequacy because parents have done too much for them, and they haven't had the opportunity to develop faith in themselves. Others simply disregard their parents' efforts to do too much for them and insist on doing things for themselves. We point out these differences as a reminder that all children are unique and make different decisions under similar circumstances.

Children Are Always Making Decisions

MOST PARENTS DON'T realize that their children are always making decisions that affect their behavior. These decisions form the foundation of personality and future behavior.

> Children are always making decisions that affect their future behavior.

Children are not consciously aware of their decisions, but they are making them nonetheless. Children make decisions based on their perceptions of how they are treated by their parents (as well as their perceptions of other experiences in their lives). These life-shaping decisions often fit into the following categories:

I am _____ (good or bad, capable or incapable, fearful or confident, and so on).

Others are _____ (helpful or hurtful, nurturing or rejecting, encouraging or critical, and so on).

The world is _____ (threatening or friendly, safe or scary, and so on).

Therefore, I must _____ to survive or to thrive. (When children make decisions about *thriving,* they choose behaviors that help them develop into capable people. When they make decisions about how to behave based on their perceptions of how to *survive* they usually choose what adults call misbehavior.

Let's take a look at one of the most familiar examples of early childhood decisions. A three-year-old usually feels dethroned by the birth of a new baby. Now, this child has had three years to be "queen of the castle." She has received unlimited love and attention, and she rather likes it this way. Suddenly, without consulting her, Mom and Dad bring home a baby. This baby is cute and she does like it (sort of), especially when she gets to hold it or play with it. But she also has become, quite suddenly, less important. Or so it seems. People come to the house, walk right by her, and coo over the baby's crib. They bring the baby presents. Worst of all, Mom and Dad are infatuated. They hover around the baby; Mom nurses it, Dad bounces it, and they talk about it all the time. She pouts and no one even *notices*. Obviously, something must be done about this situation.

The three-year-old observes all the time and attention Mom gives the new baby and *believes* that "Mom doesn't love me as much as she loves that baby." The truth doesn't matter; the child's behavior will be based on what she believes is true and the decisions she makes as a result. It is typical for young children who believe they have been replaced by a new baby to act like babies. One three-year-old loses interest in the potty, wants her pacifier back, and insists on having milk in a bottle. She also finds that she "can't" fall asleep without being rocked and walked. This behavior makes sense to her and is based on the unconscious belief that "Mom will give me more time and attention if I act like the baby," but it sure looks like misbehavior to Mom and Dad!

Getting Into the Child's World

To help parents become more aware of the fact that children are always making decisions, we like to invite participants at our workshops to take the role of children. We ask them to take turns kneeling in front of a partner who is standing on a chair. The person standing on the chair (the "parent") then points a finger at the kneeling "child" while scolding and criticizing. At the end of the role-play, we ask them to share what they were thinking, feeling, and deciding while in the child's role.

Of course, the decisions vary. Some are feeling inadequate and decide they can never measure up. Some are thinking the adult is ridiculous and decide they will just lose respect and ignore the adult. Others are feeling angry and are deciding they will rebel or get even and are plotting how to do it, while some get so scared they just tune out.

This activity helps parents (and teachers) gain insights into the long-term effects of their behavior with their children. They gain a new level of awareness they have never had before. Once parents have used their feelings to understand the child's mistaken goal, it may be helpful to consider how their own behavior may invite a child to develop the perception, "I don't belong."

What Part Do Parents Play in Mistaken Goal Behavior?

Considering the part parents may play in their children's discouragement should not be done with a sense of blame, but with a sense of awareness. Remember that each child is unique and each may form a different perception from the same experience. Taking a look at these few possibilities (among many more possibilities) may increase your understanding of mistaken goal behavior.

1. When parents overprotect and overindulge, children may decide,
    a. "I belong only if I receive constant attention or special service."
    b. "I belong only if I'm the boss and others do what I want." (I haven't learned to problem-solve for win/win solutions.)
    c. "I don't belong because you don't have any faith in me, and that hurts so I'll get even." (Sometimes it seems as though you care more about my grades than me.)
    d. "I don't belong because I'm inadequate, so I'll just give up." (Everyone else does everything so much better.)

2. When parents are too controlling, children may decide,
    a. "I can't get attention in useful ways, so I'll get attention in whatever ways I can."
    b. "I don't have skills to use my power in useful ways, so I'll use it to defy or to dominate others."
    c. "I don't feel belonging when you hurt me, but I can use my power to hurt you back."
    d. "You don't believe I'm capable, so why should I believe I am?"

3. When parents use punishment, children may decide,
    a. "I don't feel belonging when you hurt me, but maybe getting you to pay even negative attention to me will prove that you love me."
    b. "I don't feel belonging when you hurt me, but maybe using power in disrespectful ways is the way to achieve a sense of belonging."

c. "I don't feel belonging when you hurt me, but at least I can hurt you back."

d. "I don't feel belonging when you hurt me, so I'll just give up and try to stay out of the way."

The range of possibilities illustrates again that children will make very different decisions depending on their perceptions. Hopefully, this information will help you understand what can happen even when parents try not to discourage their children. Being willing to see how you may be part of the equation may inspire you to change your behaviors in order to help your children change their behaviors.

> When parents are too controlling, children may decide, "I can't get attention in useful ways, so I'll get attention in whatever ways I can."

Also, it may help to remember that decisions children make are not made at a conscious level. For example, they don't consciously think, "I don't belong." Rather they have a vague feeling of not belonging. They don't consciously decide, "Therefore, I will . . . (misbehave in some way)." Because this is the case, you may ask, "Then how do you know children are making these decisions?"

Mistaken Goal Disclosure

People used to ask Dreikurs, "How can you keep putting children in these boxes?" Dreikurs would reply, "I don't keep putting them there, I keep finding them there." One way he would discover the child's mistaken goal was through goal disclosure. Dreikurs would ask, "Could it be that you do this (specific behavior) because this is a good way to get people to pay attention to you?" Dreikurs would look for the recognition reflex. If the child gave a spontaneous grin while saying, "No," Dreikurs would say, "Your voice is telling me no, but your grin is telling me yes."

If the child displayed a recognition reflex, Dreikurs would not continue with the goal disclosure questions, but would start brainstorming with the child on how to get attention in useful ways.

If the child said "no" without the grin, Dreikurs would go on to the next question, "Could it be that you do this to show that you are the boss?" Again,

Dreikurs would get either a straight no or a grin with the no. If the child displayed a recognition reflex, Dreikurs would say, "Your voice tells me no, while your grin says yes." Then he would help the child find ways to use his power in constructive ways.

If the answer was "no" without a recognition reflex, the next question would be, "Could it be that you do this behavior because you feel hurt and want to hurt back?" Again, there might be a sly grin while the child said, "No." However, some children feel understood and simply say, "Yes." If yes, Dreikurs would validate the child's feelings and then work with the child to find solutions.

If Dreikurs still didn't get a recognition reflex or a yes, he would ask, "Could it be that you do this behavior because you feel you can't do better and so you just want to give up?"

Dreikurs taught that goal disclosure is a way of "spitting in the child's soup"—that sometimes the behavior loses its appeal when it becomes conscious. Also, there is something about feeling understood that helps a child feel encouraged so that misbehavior also loses its appeal.

Of course, there are many other reasons why children may develop a belief that creates one of the mistaken goals, such as beliefs they develop based on their birth order or beliefs they develop through their interactions with others. (For example, peer rejection may cause them to feel they don't belong.)

Mistaken goal behavior is one way to understand why children misbehave. There are many other ways. Sometimes what seems like misbehavior in children under the age of four is really behavior that is developmentally appropriate. (More about this in chapter 7.)

The Importance of Effective Parenting Tools

YOU ARE TIRED after working all day, so wouldn't it be nice to have your interactions with your children be encouraging rather than discouraging? Most of the parenting tools we suggest do not take any more time than ineffective methods. What they require is replacing old attitudes and habits with different attitudes, skills, and habits. Achieving these new attitudes, skills, and habits is much easier when you understand why they are important to achieve positive long-term results for you and for your children. In the following chapters, you will see how ineffective parenting skills are a detriment to your children, while effective parenting skills are a benefit for children—whether or not their parents work.

Quick and Quality Parenting Tips

School Problems

My son keeps getting poor grades even when he knows how disappointed we are and have grounded him for weeks. Then he got a detention for throwing a spitwad. I wonder if these problems would be solved if I quit working outside the home.

Working Parents' Common Mistakes

1. Believing the propaganda that only children of working parents have school problems.

2. Creating a cycle of discouragement by thinking that control and punishment are the best ways to motivate a child to do better.

Discouraging Words and Actions

1. Punishment of any kind increased discouragement.

2. Focusing on grades can give your child the impression that his grades are more important than he is.

3. Trying to enforce compliance for your goals, instead of helping your child figure out his own goals.

Respectful and Encouraging Actions

1. Get into your child's world so you can understand things from his point of view. As you look at what he is discouraged about you might wonder, "If he doesn't want to get poor grades, why doesn't he study? If he doesn't want to disappoint me, why doesn't he do what I ask him to do? And, why can't he just be himself and to heck with anyone who doesn't like him?" Sounds logical, but human beings aren't logical when they are discouraged.

2. Because a misbehavior child is a discouraged child, use the Mistaken Goals Chart \to make some guesses about what your son is discouraged about,

and what mistaken goal is he choosing to deal with that discouragement? Could it be that he feels discouraged about getting poor grades and about disappointing you? (It really hurts to feel that you are a disappointment to your parents.)

3. Guide him through the process of thinking about his own life goals and a plan for accomplishing them. Help him start with the small step of creating his own schedule and making a routine chart or writing it down it his personal planner.

4. Set up some special times with him—dates that the two of you look forward to just spending time together. This can be a little tricky with adolescents who start thinking it isn't "cool" to be seen with their parents. You could joke with him and say, "We could go to McDonald's in the next town, so no one will see you with your mom." Of course this time could be an hour once a week when you sit down together and play a board game. Or, you could take him to the library once a week—whatever would be enjoyable to both of you. The point is to let him know you look forward to spending some time with him—just the two of you. (It would be nice if he had a similar arrangement with his father.)

5. Think back to your teen years. What did you receive from your parents that made you feel special—or what do you wish you had received? Give that to your son.

Respectful and Encouraging Words

1. Love and accept him unconditionally. Let him know, "I would love it if you got good grades, but I love you even more than my expectations. I hope you'll choose to get good grades, but if you don't I will love you anyway, and I have faith in you that you'll be successful in your life no matter what you do."

2. Validate his feelings. First you have to listen to find out what they are. You can also make some guesses. "I'll bet you feel disappointed about not getting better grades." (Notice that validating his feelings is much different than sharing your own disappointment.) "It must feel terrible to worry about how to make your friends like you, and to be afraid that they won't like you if you just be yourself." "It must hurt a lot if you think that your grades are more important to me than you are." You don't have to do anything more. Just having their feelings validated can be a very encouraging experience for kids—and it may take a while for it to sink in. (I want to point out that many kids today

feel so hurt by their parents' disappointment [conditional love] that they go into revenge and fail just to hurt their parents back.)

3. Help him explore the consequences of his choices and problem-solve through curiosity questions: "How do you feel about your grades?" "What would you like to accomplish?" "What do you think causes you to get poor grades?" "What do you think would solve the problem to help you get what you want?" This is a tough thing for most parents to do because they want their children to give the answers they want—and to lecture at them if they don't. Curiosity questions are effective only if your son "gets" that you really care about what he thinks. Here are some more: "I'm really curious about the spitwad incident. I'm wondering how you feel about it? I'm wondering what you hoped to accomplish." "Could it be that you think this is a good way to appear 'cool' to the other kids?" "How do you think the other kids feel about you when you do this?" "How do you feel about yourself?" (These questions will be very ineffective if there is any sense of accusation instead of curiosity on your part. That is one reason these questions should never be asked when either of you is upset.)

4. Decide what you will do, inform in advance, and follow through. This means letting him know things such as, "I'll take you to the library on Tuesday nights." I'll be available to help you with homework on Mondays and Fridays from 7:00 to 8:00 P.M. When he comes to you with last minute requests say, "Sorry you missed my scheduled times this week. I'll be available at the same times next week." Don't rescue or lecture. Allow him to learn from his choices.

Encouraging Attitudes

1. Understand that there is a lot more on his plate—as there is on the plates of all teenagers—as they go through the huge individuation process of trying to figure out who they are and what are their values separate from their parents' values.

2. Some people think these suggestions look like permissiveness. Remember that Positive Discipline is about kindness and firmness at the same time. There are many kind and firm things you can do *after* you establish a base of encouragement and trust. Try nothing but encouragement for two weeks and see for yourself how magical it can be.

5

Creating Cooperative Children

Pampering vs. Respectfully Involving Children

ARE YOU TRYING to do everything? Do you think it's your job to get your children out of bed, get them dressed, make sure they eat their breakfast, fix their school lunches, find their homework and everything else they have lost, settle their fights, get them out the door on time—all while trying to get yourself ready and to work on time? If so, you are creating unnecessary stress for yourself and pampered children who will become more demanding and less cooperative as they progress in their manipulative skills.

You are pampering if you are spoiling, overindulging, overprotecting, catering to, having low expectations, rescuing, and all the other parent behaviors that teach your children to expect more from you, and less from themselves. Pampering teaches your children the skills of manipulation, not cooperation.

Does this mean you can never do anything for your children? No. It means that you and your children will benefit if you increase your awareness about pampering and pay attention to your intuition. If you feel you are being manipulated, chances are that you are. If you are doing things for your children that increase their demands instead of their cooperation, it is likely that you are pampering. If you are doing so much for your children that you rob them of opportunities to develop a belief in their own capability, it is likely that you are pampering.

Many parents, in the name of love, pamper their children. Often, working parents pamper their children as penance for their perceived "sin" of working. They mistakenly believe that pampering will "make up" for the time they spend away from their children while earning a living. This is a huge mistake.

Hopefully, by now, you have changed your attitude about guilt. You know that if you have the attitude that you *should* feel guilty, your children will milk that for all it is worth and invite you to pamper them because you feel guilty. By now you know that many problems you experience as a working parent do not stem from what you do, but from how you do it. If you feel proud of what you do, you are less likely to pamper your children and more likely to use the tools for teaching cooperation that you will find in this chapter. Your children will mirror your attitude and will develop the skills that will make them proud of themselves. Pampering produces a very different outcome.

Long-term Consequences of Pampering

HAVE YOU EVER thought about the long-term consequences of pampering your children? Have you thought about what they are learning? Of course, you can't know for sure because every child is unique. However, it is very common for pampered children to develop some of the following beliefs:

"Love means getting others to take care of me."

"I'm not capable."

"The world owes me a living."

"If I just complain enough I can get others to feel sorry for me and I'll get what I want."

These are just a few possibilities. We know this is not what you intend for your children to learn. Our guess is that you hope they are learning, "My parents really love me." Because your intentions and reality may be very far apart, it is important to look at the long-range consequences of your actions— to become aware of the difference between what you intend and what really happens.

Just about everyone we talk to is appalled by the examples they see of children who demand instant gratification—"I want it now!"—and have temper tantrums until their parents give in. They are disgusted by the many examples they see of teenagers who destroy the property of others, just for the "fun" of it. We can all, unfortunately, tell stories of teens and preteens (and even younger children) who bash mailboxes, egg homes, run their cars over front lawns, smash Christmas lights, and so on. You are undoubtedly familiar with too many children who are unpleasant to be around because they are rude, demanding, thoughtless, and selfish. Surely you have heard comments (or may have made them yourself) about how sad it is to see children "run the household." Because everyone is talking about them and the sad state of the society that produces such children, who or what is responsible? Pampering. So why do parents pamper their children?

Giving in When Children Whine

IT'S FUN TO give children the things they want and see their faces light up with joy. It's the whining and coaxing part that isn't fun. As children, many parents went without the things they wanted or needed when they were growing up and honestly want their children to have more than they had. So, they give in. Others just hate dealing with tantrums and public disapproval in the toy store or supermarket. So, they give in. The biggest mistake is thinking that giving children everything they want is the best way to let them know they are loved.

> The biggest mistake is thinking that giving children everything they want is the best way to let them know they are loved.

Of course you love your children. The question is, how to show your love in ways that help your children develop beliefs such as, "I'm capable. I can contribute in meaningful ways. I am needed. I feel confident. I have skills. I respect myself and others." Not by pampering. Parents need to consider the decisions children make when they are pampered and the decisions they make when they are not pampered. Let's take a look at that common family battleground, getting dressed in the morning.

Morning Hassles

MOST MORNING HASSLES are created because parents try to do everything, including dressing their children. During our parenting lectures we often ask parents, "At what age are children capable of dressing themselves?" It is amazing how many parents believe children can't do this task until they are four or five. We happen to know, from our own experience and the experience of many other parents, that children are quite capable of dressing themselves from the time they are three years old (and sometimes younger) if parents take time for training, if they establish a consistent routine, and if they buy the kind of clothing that is easy to pull over or slip on. (Fancy buckles, buttons, and bows are too difficult for small children because their fine-motor skills are not yet fully developed.)

We then ask, "Why do you think your neighbors are still dressing their children—because we know none of you would rob your children of the feelings of capability they have when they dress themselves?" After laughing at the joke, parents admit to three reasons they are still dressing their children when they are old enough to do it themselves:

1. It is more expedient—faster and easier.

2. Children look better. (Who hasn't cringed at the appearance of a proud and happy toddler clad in red pants, an orange shirt—

backward—of course, and shoes on the wrong feet? Instead of a return trip to the bedroom, celebrate your child's very real accomplishment—and take a photograph for posterity.)

3. Working parents don't want their children to have any extra hardships (as though dressing themselves is a real hardship) because they already feel guilty about working. Many working parents are held hostage to their guilt while their children get away with overt manipulation.

Of course, there is another reason. Once children become used to having you dress them, they may insist that you continue this service and whine, cry, or just plain stall until you do it.

After parents explore why they dress their children, we break the news to them that in the name of expediency, looking good for the neighbors, and/or feeding their working parent guilt, they are robbing their children of the opportunity to develop the belief that they are capable. How can they possibly feel capable if someone else does everything for them? Think about it. What decisions are children likely to make when their parents dress them when they are capable of dressing themselves? Consider these possibilities: "I'm not capable." "Love means getting others to take care of me." "I deserve special service." "I can use this situation to get undue attention or to use my power to get others to do what I want." We can't think of any healthy decisions that children might make from being served and waited on. Can you?

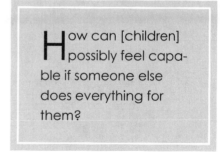

How can [children] possibly feel capable if someone else does everything for them?

Many parents are shocked when they hear that their good intentions are producing the opposite of what they want. They feel guilty that they have been "doing it all wrong."

There it is again. Will we ever be able to staunch that pesky guilt? This is not the time for more guilt. It is a time for awareness. And awareness is the golden key to making change happen. As we say over and over, mistakes are wonderful opportunities for learning—for you and your children. If you have been dressing your children and you now see that it is not the most loving thing you can do for them, there is one more catch: Do you think it will be easy to stop?

Weaning Is Never Easy for the Weanee or the Weanor

IT IS EASY to understand why weaning is not easy for children. But why is it so difficult for parents? Why is it so difficult to grasp the fact that weaning is beneficial to children even when they don't like it at the time? (They will thank you for it later, we promise.) The unfortunate paradox in loving children so much that you fail to wean them is that children inevitably resent you for it later on. Haven't you noticed that the more you do for children and the more you give them, the more they want and demand? Parents really think their children will appreciate all they do for them, but parents are continually hurt and disappointed when they see their children becoming spoiled brats instead of grateful. The reverse, fortunately, is also true: Children will respect and appreciate you (eventually) when you love them enough to wean them and teach

THE EIGHT-STEP WEANING PROCESS

1. Understand that creating dependence is disrespectful.

2. Expect to feel uncomfortable.

3. Apologize for your mistakes.

4. Do what is right with kindness and firmness at the same time.

5. Prepare a plan together and take time for training in new skills.

   a. No-conflict time.

   b. Involve children in the creation of routine charts.

   c. Avoid rewards and praise.

6. Expect resistance and let children have their feelings.

7. Follow through with confidence and consistency.

8. Allow time for the change process.

them self-reliance and self-confidence, even though they don't like it in the moment.

If you need more convincing, consider this: If it was not disrespectful and immoral, wouldn't you love to have a slave to do your every bidding? And, after getting used to such service, wouldn't you feel resentful if your slave decided to quit?

It is time for parents to stand up and stop being the family slave! As you learn to honor yourself, your children will respect you more, learn valuable skills, and you will spend more time feeling love for them, rather than resentment. Weaning is never easy for the *weanee* or the *weanor,* but it is essential to the ultimate growth and progress of each.

"But, my child won't dress himself and I have to get to work on time," you may cry. Of course your child won't want to dress herself—she has never had to. Weaning is a process that will take time.

Understand that Creating Dependence Is Disrespectful

BECAUSE SLAVERY IS disrespectful and immoral, being a slave to your children is teaching them to be disrespectful and it gives them an unhealthy sense of entitlement. Children learn what they live, and your actions speak much louder than your words.

How can you teach cooperation to your children if you do everything for them? Perhaps you are a parent who nags or pleads with your children to help and cooperate, but then gives in because it is *easier* to just do it yourself. What have you taught your children? Most likely, they have learned to simply wait you out (ignore the nagging and pleading) until you give in.

> Being a slave to your children is teaching them to be disrespectful and it gives them an unhealthy sense of entitlement.

Experience and practice are the keys to effective learning. It is essential to take a close look at the experiences you are providing for your children. Are your children practicing cooperation or manipulation?

We know that you don't mean to rob your child of the opportunity to learn self-reliance, cooperation, concern for others, and all the other skills for respectful relationships; but that is what you do when you pamper.

Every animal in the animal kingdom, except humans, knows the importance of weaning. They instinctively know that young animals will not become adult animals (and won't survive long as adults should they be lucky enough to make it that far) unless they are weaned. Mother animals are not influenced at all by the fact that their offspring do not enjoy the weaning process (actually, the mothers don't enjoy it much, either). Have you ever watched a young animal try to nurse after its mother has decided it is time to wean? Every time a colt or calf tries to suckle, the mother animal uses her head to butt him away. It does not matter how hard the young animal tries; the mother knows that weaning is essential to self-reliance and survival.

Differences and Similarities

Yes, humans are different, but there are some similarities. The similarities are that human children also need to be weaned to develop the self-reliance that will help them survive more successfully in society. The essential weaning isn't only from the breast or bottle (although most mothers can tell you that process can be tough enough); human parents must wean their children—gradually and lovingly—from emotional and physical dependence.

> A primary difference between animal and human mothers is that humans sometimes allow emotions to take precedence over the long-term good of their children.

A primary difference between animal mothers and human mothers is that humans often allow their emotions to take precedence over the long-term good of their children. A human mother tries to wean her child. The child cries. The mother can't stand it, so she gives in. This mother has just made a huge mistake in the name of love. She has loved her child "too much" to let that child suffer for the moment—and has just ensured greater suffering (for both of them) later on.

Too often human mothers (and fathers) give their children what they want instead of what they need. They would be unlikely to do this if they understood that they were hurting their children instead of helping them. On the following page is a list of just a few of the things that children want, followed by a list of what they actually need.

The animal kingdom provides more examples of the importance of allowing your children to experience and practice the skills that will serve them

Wants	Needs
Mommy to help me get to sleep	To learn to go to sleep by myself
To dress me	Teach me to dress myself and then don't give in and do it for me
Every toy I see on TV and in the store	To empathize with my feelings while not giving in and to show me how I can earn and save money to buy my own
Mommy and Daddy to solve my problems	To learn to solve my own problems (with support from Mommy and Daddy)
Mommy and Daddy to protect me from experiencing problems or being upset	Mommy and Daddy to have faith in me to handle and survive problems
To rescue me when I make financial mistakes	To show empathy while brainstorming with me about what I learned and how I can fix it
To buy me a car	Help me figure out how to buy my own car
To rescue me when I can't make car insurance payments	To hold my car keys until I can make the insurance payments again
To let me do whatever I want	To work with me on setting limits that are respectful to all concerned
No lectures, blame, shame, or punishment	No lectures, blame, shame, or punishment, but respectful discussions (family meetings or one-on-one) for joint problem solving
To borrow money	To have a good track record of repayment or to hear (in a kind but firm voice) no

throughout their lives. A mother bird knows by instinct when it is time to push the baby bird out of the nest. She knows that if she doesn't, her baby will not have the experience and practice to build the strength and the skills to survive.

You may have heard the story about the little boy who couldn't stand to watch the butterfly struggle as it tried to emerge from its chrysalis. He felt sorry for the butterfly and decided to "help." After the little boy opened the chrysalis for the butterfly, he watched it flutter a few feet before it drifted to the ground and died. The little boy did not realize that he had "robbed" the butterfly of the opportunity to develop its muscle strength through its struggle, just as you may not have been aware of the damage you were doing by pampering your children. Once you know, it is time for the next step.

Expect to Feel Uncomfortable

IT MAY NOT make sense to you that loving in healthy ways is sometimes very uncomfortable, but this is a very important concept to grasp. It is much more comfortable to rescue children, give in to them, or help them feel better when they are upset. Weaning is essential to healthy growth and development. If what you are doing in the process of weaning your child *feels* good, it may be an unhealthy thing to do. If it feels uncomfortable, it just may be the most loving thing you can do for your child.

For example, it may feel very uncomfortable for you to say no. After all, your child will be unhappy if he can't have that toy. However, if you think your child will ever have to deal with disappointment as an adult, wouldn't it be a good thing to help him learn now that he can deal with and survive disappointment?

It is important to note here that we are not talking about abandoning children or ignoring their safety, health, or genuine needs. As mentioned above, there is a simple way to know whether your child is trying to manipulate you: If you feel manipulated, you are! And feeling manipulated is solid evidence that it's time to begin the weaning process.

When your children get older, it is very uncomfortable to have them think you are the meanest parent in the world. ("All the *other* kids get to do it! You never let me do *any*thing!") You may fear that the only way to keep your children's love is to give in and do whatever they want. But think about that for a minute. Is real love based only on "getting what I want"?

Apologize for Your Mistakes

REALIZING YOU HAVE made a mistake does not mean you should feel guilty. Your mistakes give you the chance to model for your children that mistakes are wonderful opportunities to learn. Children will feel encouraged to hear you take responsibility for your mistake and to let them know a change will take place. Children are by nature eager to forgive you when you apologize and it shows them profound respect and caring.

With an attitude of wonder (at your discovery) and confidence in the value of learning from mistakes, you might say, "Honey, I have made a mistake. I didn't realize that I was being disrespectful to you by doing too much for you. I thought that was a way of showing you how much I love you. Now I realize that it is much more loving for me to have faith in you and to let you experience how capable you are."

If your child is old enough, tell her the stories of the mother bird and the butterfly. If your child isn't old enough to understand these stories, she may not comprehend what you are saying, but it is good to say it anyway—for yourself. Your child will feel the strength of your attitude and confidence even if she doesn't understand the words, and your actions will teach more than your words.

> Your mistakes give you the chance to model for your children that mistakes are wonderful opportunities to learn.

It is important to know that breaking old habits is difficult. It is almost impossible to break old habits unless you learn new behaviors to replace the old. That is why it is so important to take time for training.

Do What Is Right with Kindness and Firmness

ATTITUDE IS EVERYTHING. Even the wisest actions done with an attitude of shaming or humiliation will fail to have the desired effect. Many parents lack the courage to do what is right (weaning) without using blame, shame, and pain in the form of lectures, martyrdom, or punishment. See

whether you recognize any of these lectures: "Do you think I'm made of money?" "You are so selfish. Do you think the world revolves around you?" "Can't you ever take no for an answer?" "After all I have done for you, all you want is more, more, more!"

Parents should listen to their own lectures from time to time. Why would a child believe you are made of money unless you have given them that impression? Why shouldn't they be selfish when they get everything they want? Why wouldn't they think the world revolves around them when it usually does? How can they learn to take no for an answer when they don't get any practice at it? Why wouldn't they want more, more, more? If you haven't absorbed this yet, here is another bulletin: The more you do for children, the more they expect, and the less capable and confident they become. Does it surprise you that instead of feeling gratitude, children just want more? What other decisions could they make about themselves, others, the world, and what to do, based on the experiences you are giving them?

When you are kind and firm at the same time, you and your children may feel uncomfortable at first. Your children may even be genuinely unhappy. But you will both feel better later on. Unless you are unkind and disrespectful, they will not hate you (forever) and they won't hold on to their anger forever. However, if you have been intentionally unkind, you will feel guilty and your children may have reason to hate you. Then, because of your guilt, you may give in to their demands to regain their love, thus creating a vicious cycle.

The longer weaning has been delayed, the more uncomfortable everyone will feel and the longer your children may hold on to their anger. When you respect the needs of the situation (that your children will not learn self-reliance unless weaned) and do what is right with kindness and firmness, your children will eventually learn to respect both you and themselves.

Plan Together and Take Time for Training

AS WE CONTINUE with the problem of teaching children to dress themselves, the first step is preparation. This means making sure they have the kinds of clothes that are easy to put on. Avoid clothes that are difficult to manage (until children get older and choose these things for themselves). Buy pants with elastic waistbands that are easy to pull on, and t-shirts or dresses that are easy to pull over the head (even if they do end up inside out and backward). Teach little children how to scrunch up their socks before putting them on, until it is easy to fit little toes into small openings. Teach them to put the label side of their pants on the floor before sticking their legs into them, and to put the label of their shirt face down on the bed before sticking their head and arms into it. Then let them practice during a no-conflict time.

No-Conflict Time

It is almost impossible to teach anything positive during times of conflict or stress, yet that is the time when most parents try to teach. They then wonder why their children don't "listen" or learn.

During times of conflict, people seem to revert to their reptilian (primitive) brains where the only option is fight or flight. Power struggles are a good example of the fight syndrome. You are upset and try to get some cooperation by scolding and lectures. "I've told you a hundred times to get dressed. Can't you just cooperate?" Your child feels scared, threatened, hurt, inadequate, rebellious (or other feelings generated from a lack of connection or perceived sense of not belonging), and whines for attention, asserts her misguided power, hurts back, or just gives up. Thus, the conflict continues and/or escalates into constant demands for undue attention, power struggles, revenge cycles, and just giving up.

Why do parents keep trying to teach during times when it just doesn't work? One reason is that they haven't understood the importance of waiting for a more peaceful and calm time to teach, what we call a *no-conflict time.* Parents may believe they are "letting the child get away with something" if they don't deal with the problem at the time of conflict.

> It is almost impossible to teach anything positive during times of conflict or stress.

To break self-defeating cycles, wait for a time of no conflict to teach and practice new skills. During a calm time with small children, you can make it a game to practice getting dressed. They can try to "beat the clock," or just simply feel good about their accomplishment as you say, "See, you can do it." (Avoid praise and rewards as discussed later in this chapter.)

Once children have the skills, their cooperation will increase tremendously if they are involved in the process of creating routine charts during a no-conflict time.

Involve Children in the Creation of Routine Charts

Before discussing routine charts, we want to emphasize the "involve children" part. Many parents spend too much time telling children what to do instead of involving them in the process of figuring out what to do. Cooperation will increase in direct proportion to how much the child is involved and decrease in direction proportion to how much they are simply told. Whenever we hear a parent complain, "My child just doesn't listen," we can predict that the parent is talking too much and involving their child too little, if at all.

Actually, the older your child, the less involved you need to be. You can say to an older child, "Would you be willing to write down a plan (the word *plan* is more effective than *routine* for older children) that works for you (regarding your homework, activity schedule, etc.) and show it to me so I can see how I can support you?"

> Most morning hassles can be avoided if a bedtime routine chart includes such things as choosing clothes for the next morning and making a pile of things that need to be taken to school.

With a younger child, sit down with her during a no-conflict time and work on a morning routine chart together. Ask her to make a list (or dictate to you) of all the things that need to be done in the morning. The list will include things such as waking up, getting dressed, helping with breakfast, brushing teeth, finding things that need to be taken to school, hugs goodbye, etc.

Most morning hassles can be avoided if a bedtime routine chart includes such things as choosing clothes for the next morning and making a pile of things that need to be taken to school in the morning. One family had an eight-year-old son who took medication at night that made him horribly sleepy in the morning. As they created a routine together, he suggested putting a brown paper bag by the front door with a snack and his school clothes in it. He dresses and eats on the way to school and the family now enjoys peaceful mornings.

Once the morning (or bedtime) routine list has been made, gather construction paper or other art supplies to create an interesting chart. Elementary-school-age children might enjoy drawing pictures to illustrate each item on their chart. Preschool children love it when you take Polaroid pictures of them doing each task so they can paste the picture next to that item on their list.

Six-year-old Gibson created a routine chart in the form of a big clock depicting one hour in the morning (6:30 to 7:30). He made a list of all the things he had to do to get ready for school, and then figured out how much time he needed for each task. His father took a picture of him doing each task, which was then pasted on the clock next to the time it would take. For example, Gibson used a paper plate to trace a large circle on a poster board. At the top of the clock he wrote 6:30 and pasted a picture of him waking up just above 6:30. Going clockwise, he wrote 6:34 because he decided he could get dressed in four minutes. A picture of him getting dressed was placed just outside the clock next to this time. Next was 6:36 and a picture of him making his bed. Between 6:36 and 6:46 was a picture of him eating breakfast. Next to 6:48 was a picture of him brushing his teeth. Between 6:48 and 6:53 was a picture of him making his own lunch. Gibson was delighted to discover that he then had from 6:53 to 7:22 to play with his toys. (Before he made this routine chart, it seemed as though the whole morning was spent with him trying to play with his toys between each task and listening to his dad nag him to hurry up and get dressed.) He got his dad to take several pictures of him playing with different toys. Gibson decided he could pick up his toys in three minutes or less. Because he figured it out, he enjoyed proving he was right—and he liked the picture his dad took of him rushing to pick his toys up. His dad loved the fact that Gibson enjoyed carrying out his plan and that the plan included clean up. The picture next to 7:25 showed him putting on his coat and backpack to leave for school. Gibson loved following his morning routine chart, and Dad thought he had gone to no-nag heaven.

High school kids may find it helpful to have a day planner to keep track of the many things they need to do. Because high school kids often are resistant to your involvement, you may want to see if they would be interested in taking a time-management class. They may be less resistant to advice from others than from you. A word of caution: Trying to "enforce" the use of a routine or plan with teenagers (and even younger children) is an invitation to a power struggle that you will lose. A routine chart is an invitation for cooperation, not a control weapon for parents.

Once the routine chart is created, let the routine chart be the boss. Instead of telling your children what to do, ask, "What is next on your routine chart?" Younger children love to tell you and will let you know if you try to deviate from their routine. Older children don't need reminders to check their plan. During a family meeting or some other calm time, however, you might ask how they think their plan is working and offer your help if they would like it.

If younger children lose interest in their routine chart, it may be time to create a new one. Or, you can focus on problem solving during a family meeting (discussed in chapter 9). Part of the taking-time-for-training process may be to create a plan for what will happen if a child doesn't get dressed.

> Once the routine chart is created, let the routine chart be the boss.

Mark was dressing himself from the time he was two and a half years old. Part of his morning routine was to get dressed and then come to the kitchen where he would do something to help with breakfast. It was obvious to his mother that Mark felt very capable and loved helping. However, she noticed the day he decided to test the system (a very normal part of the individuation process discussed at the beginning of chapter 4). Mark didn't get himself dressed, and he didn't come to the kitchen to help. He did manage to take off his pajamas. When it was time to leave for work and his preschool Mark was naked.

Mom and Dad were prepared with a plan for the inevitable time when Mark would decide not to cooperate. They put his clothes in a paper bag and Dad picked Mark up in one arm, and grabbed the bag of clothes with his other hand, and walked out into the pouring rain just as his neighbor was out picking up his newspaper. (Sometimes you need to ignore what the neighbors think while following through.) Mark cried and complained about being cold all the way to his school. His dad offered him the choice, "You can get dressed if you want to." But, Mark was testing. When they arrived at the school, the director saw Mark and said, "Oh, I see you decided not to get dressed today. You can take your clothes into my office and come out as soon as you are dressed." And that is what Mark did. The next morning he went back to his normal routine of getting himself dressed and coming to the kitchen to help. A month later, Mark decided to test again, but this time he was in his pajamas when his dad carried him and his clothes to the car, and he decided to get dressed in the car before arriving at school.

Some people have noted that it would be disrespectful and humiliating to take an older, naked child to school. This is true. Mark didn't care about being naked, but an older child might feel humiliated. Remember to tailor discipline tools to the age of your children to make sure they are respectful.

Another mother heard the principle of this story and found a respectful way to follow it. Her daughter wouldn't get dressed before going to school, so her mother got her pajama-clad daughter and her bag of clothes into the car. She said, "I hope you'll get dressed before we get to school, but I can't make you." When they arrived at the school, her daughter still wasn't dressed. Mom found a parking spot close to the front door of the school and told her daughter to come in as soon as she was dressed. Mom then stood just inside the school where she could watch the car from a window. It didn't take long for her daughter to get bored staying in the car by herself; so she got dressed and came in. All her mom said was, "I knew you could do it."

"But, I'll Be Late!"

"But," you protest, "I'll be late for work if I have to stand inside the school while I wait for my child to decide to get dressed." Good point. This is why you plan for that possibility, in advance, during the training period. Sometimes you have to get up earlier and leave earlier to allow time for training and follow-through.

The one thing we can promise is that if you take time for training and follow through consistently, with kindness and firmness at the same time, your children will learn cooperation. Then you will save time because you will avoid power struggles and all the time it takes to "do everything." And, getting up early (and even being late a few times) may be the price you have to pay to save time in the long run. You will experience frustration if you expect change

> If you take time for training and follow through consistently, with kindness and firmness at the same time, your children will learn cooperation.

to happen overnight, as discussed in the last step of allowing time for the change process.

Avoid Rewards and Praise

Many parents are so used to the erroneous idea of using rewards and praise to motivate cooperation that they want to add rewards and praise to the routine-chart process. If you want cooperation, avoid rewards and praise. Rewards teach manipulation, "How can I get more," or, "I won't do this unless I get a reward." Praise encourages children to become approval junkies and to depend on the evaluation of others instead of experiencing the inner good feelings that come from cooperation and contribution. Rewards and the error of connecting them to allowances are covered more fully in chapter 6.

Expect Resistance and Let Children Have Their Feelings

IF YOU WATCH closely, you will notice that the baby bird is very resistant to being kicked out of the nest. And your children will not be thrilled about giving up the benefits of being pampered. Even though, in the long run, children do not feel good about themselves when they discover that they have not learned to be capable and confident, they aren't thinking about that when they are being pushed out of their "comfortable nests" where they have been taken care of with no effort required of them.

Let them have their feelings. Validate their feelings. Have faith in them to handle their feelings and survive. Even if you could protect them from ever experiencing upset or disappointment, it wouldn't be a good idea. How will they ever develop their confidence and capability to survive disappointment if they never have a chance to learn from experience that they can?

We hope it will be a bit easier to watch your children suffer a little when you know it is a more loving thing to do than pampering. We are not saying that you should make them suffer, but that it is good for them when you allow them to experience some upset and disappointment from normal circumstances. Children who have become used to pampering are likely to feel very disappointed when you decide to follow through on breaking the pampering syndrome.

Follow Through with Confidence and Consistency

IT WILL BE easier to have confidence in the weaning process and to follow through when you know it is beneficial to your children long term. As we have said before, children feel and are affected by your attitude. If you feel insecure, your children will feel insecure. If you feel confident, your children may not like the weaning process, but it will be much less painful.

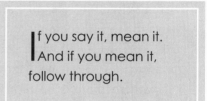

If you say it, mean it. And if you mean it, follow through.

Consistency is very important. If you say it, mean it. And if you mean it, follow through. If you say you will no longer dress your child, don't. Of course, this is effective only after following the other steps in the weaning process—especially involving children in plans and taking time for training. Consistency also requires being aware of the last step: allowing time for the process of change.

Allow Time for Change

BAD HABITS AREN'T created overnight and bad habits are not easily changed. In many ways allowing time for change is a culmination and natural outcome of the previous seven steps. You have to understand that creating dependence is disrespectful; that you'll only be more frustrated if you don't expect to be uncomfortable—both of you.; that apologizing for your mistakes is encouraging and a good model for your children; that the weaning process is much more difficult if you aren't kind and firm at the same time in all that you do; that you prepare (create a plan) and take time for training new skills; that you expect resistance and let children have their feelings; and that you have the courage to follow through with confidence and consistency.

We have used the example of children not getting dressed in the morning. We will now tackle another example to illustrate that these principles work for any issue that requires weaning before children can learn to cooperate.

Sleep Hassles

MANY PARENTS AREN'T aware that allowing children to sleep in their beds is usually an example of pampering, with all the negative side effects of manipulation, unreasonable demands, and bad feelings for everyone. (We are not talking about parents who choose the family bed and are comfortable with that choice. We refer to parents who find children in their bed even when they don't want them there and feel manipulated by the children.) Having children sleep with you when you do not want them in your bed is an unhappy experience for everyone. Many parents feel as though they are caught in a trap from which there is no escape. Let's follow the eight-step weaning process to stop pampering and allow children to experience cooperation and self-confidence.

First, understand that allowing children to sleep in your bed, when you don't want them there, is creating dependence and is disrespectful to you and your children. Accept the uncomfortable feelings you will both have about making a change. Apologize for your mistake and inform your children that from now on they will sleep in their own beds and that you have faith in them to handle this. Don't forget to be kind and firm at the same time as you help them get prepared by letting them know that whenever they get out of their bed and come into yours, you will kindly and firmly take them back to their own beds. Let them know you will give them a kiss and will leave, no matter how many times it takes. Take time for training by role-playing (small children might prefer "Let's pretend.") If your children are too small for this step, crying it out (allowing their feelings) may be the only option. This really isn't as cruel (remember crying is a language) as it may sound and usually doesn't take longer than three to five days. Some parents are concerned that their children will feel unloved if they take them back to their own beds, or if they let toddlers cry it out. This is not true if your children are getting plenty of love and attention during the day. It is a very loving thing to do. Your children will feel much better about themselves when they feel confident and capable than when they feel needy and manipulative. Many parents have discovered (and shared with us) that their children's behavior improved significantly during the day after they went through the three- to five-night weaning process. They noticed more co-operation, fewer demands, and a sunnier disposition in their children within a week or two. This does not sound like behavior you would expect from children who have been traumatized by a few nights of crying while they experienced the frustration of breaking a habit. The improved behavior is what you would ex-pect from children who feel more capable and confident within themselves.

If your children are old enough, involving them in the creation of a bed-time routine chart may ease the change a bit. Even creating the routine chart is the beginning of teaching them that they are capa-ble and can cooperate.

Expect resistance and let children have their feelings. Don't expect your children to like being weaned from your bed, but hang on to the knowl-edge that the goal is to help your children in the long term.

> Your children will feel much better about themselves when they feel confident and capable than when they feel needy and manipulative.

Following through with confidence and consis-tency takes practice. It means keeping your mouth shut while you kindly and firmly take your child back to bed, give her a kiss, and leave her room. The role-playing is as much for your benefit as for your children's. You may need to practice during a no-conflict time, because it will not be easy to be kind and firm when you are half-asleep and cranky. Practicing the skill during a no-conflict time makes it a little easier. Part of the skill of following through that you need to practice is to keep your mouth shut and let your actions do the speaking. Let your children know that you will not use words, just a kiss.

Many parents have told us that the first night they followed through on their plan to put their children back in their own beds required following through fifteen to twenty times. The second night required ten to fifteen times and the third night only three to five times. Most children get that you mean what you say in three to five nights if you follow through with confidence, kindness, and firmness. However, the worst thing you can do is give in on the second or third night. This teaches children that if they cry or hassle you long enough, you'll capitulate. The opportunity to learn cooperation is lost.

The Importance of Cooperation

COOPERATION IS SUCH an important skill for healthy families that we will continue this theme in the next five chapters as we discuss why punishment doesn't work, how effective discipline helps children develop social and life skills for good character, how to create even more cooperation and organization through family meetings, nonpunitive parenting skills to use with children under the age of four, and the long-term results of positive discipline for older children (four years old and older). You will also find the theme of cooperation in the last four chapters on taking time for self-care, balancing career, finances and family, prioritizing your marriage, and using positive discipline techniques for supervisors. For now, we hope you can see how much less you will have to do and how much better everyone in the family will feel when the underlying practice is cooperation.

Quick and Quality Parenting Tips

Whining

Whine, whine, whine. It drives me crazy. After working all day, I want to enjoy my children. Why do they whine?

Working Parents' Common Mistakes

1. Thinking their children whine because they work outside the home. Children will whine if whining gets them something they want; after all, children with stay-at-home parents whine, too.

2. Giving in to whining and doing what the child whines for because of the mistaken belief that they "owe it to the child" because they work.

3. Not taking time to deal with whining as an opportunity for teaching. Dealing effectively with whining doesn't take any more time than ineffective methods—and will save lots of time in the long run.

Discouraging Words and Actions

1. Lectures and put downs: "I can't stand it when you whine. Quit acting like a baby." This increases discouragement.

2. Giving in: "Okay, okay. I'll get it for you," reinforces the whining, whether you mean to or not.

3. Ignoring the whining completely may leave your child feeling totally frustrated and without options to get better results.

Respectful and Encouraging Actions

1. Your example is the best teacher. Speak to your children respectfully. They will learn what they live. When you make a mistake, show them how to make amends by apologizing and then speaking respectfully.

2. Take time for training. During a calm and happy time (a cooling off time may be necessary first), practice with your child ways to ask for things that feel respectful to others.

3. Ignore, but not completely. Ignore the whining and give your child a hug. This is a way to ignore the behavior, but not the child. Another way is to put your hand on your child's shoulder while ignoring the whining.

4. During a no-conflict time, create a signal with your child. Ask her, "What could I do that will help you remember to use your words instead of your whines?" It could be that the signal will be pulling on your ear or patting your heart. Then, when she whines, keep your mouth shut and smile while doing the action.

Respectful and Encouraging Words

1. Say, "I'll bet you can show me another way to ask for what you want."

2. Show appreciation when she remembers to speak respectfully. "Thank you for asking so nicely, and for remembering to say, 'please.'"

3. It is okay to give an option: "I'll respond as soon as I hear a respectful tone of voice." Do this only after taking time for training about what a respectful tone of voice sounds like.

4. Share your feelings: "I feel so annoyed when I hear whining."

5. Ask for help: "Please help me by using a friendly voice."

6. Decide what you will do: "I'm going to my positive time out area until I can stop feeling annoyed. I want to be with you as soon as I feel better."

Encouraging Attitudes

1. Remember that whining is another language. Children need to learn new language before they give up one that has been working for them.

2. Focus on the discouragement rather than the behavior. Then it will be easier to encourage the child.

3. Children do what works. When you quit getting hooked, the behavior will disappear.

6

Nonpunitive Parenting

Lack of Effective Parenting Skills vs. Effective Parenting Skills

W HAT? NO PUNISHMENT?" you may ask. "How will children learn? Won't they just keep misbehaving if they don't suffer a consequence? Are you advocating permissiveness? Do you think children should be allowed to do whatever they want?"

No. In the last chapter we discussed why pampering is not healthy for parents and children. Permissiveness, as we'll discuss later in this chapter, is similar to pampering with a few more twists. First, we hope to help you understand why punishment is not only not effective long term, but also very harmful.

Most people in our society believe that discipline and punishment are the same thing. They believe that the most loving thing parents can do is to "teach" their children through punishment. They recite memories from their own life to justify their position.

"I Was Punished, and I Turned Out Just Fine"

HOW FINE IS "fine"? Fine is relative. Yes, most of us turned out just "fine." We can laugh at some of the punishments we received as a child—and even say we deserved them. However, if we had been allowed to learn from our mistakes instead of being made to pay for them, is it possible we might be even better than "fine"?

Punishment is designed to make children "pay" for their mistakes. Discipline that teaches (the definition we prefer) is designed to help children learn from their mistakes in an atmosphere of encouragement and support. In the following story, Stan was led through a process that helped him understand the difference between punishment and nonpunitive discipline (positive discipline).

Stan told his parenting group about a time he cheated on a fifth-grade test. He said, "I was stupid enough to write some answers on the palm of my hand. The teacher saw me open my fist to find an answer." This teacher grabbed Stan's paper and, in front of everyone in the class, tore it up. He received an F on the test and was publicly called a cheater. The teacher told his parents. His father gave him a whipping and grounded him for a month. Stan said, "I never cheated again, and I certainly deserved the F."

The group leader helped him explore this experience to help everyone in the class see if there might be a more productive way to handle this situation.

Leader: Does everyone agree with Stan that he deserved the F?

Group: Yes.

Leader: Would that have been enough to teach him the consequences of his choices, or did he need the punishment also?

Group: Hmmmmm.

Leader: What do you think, Stan? How did you feel about getting the F for cheating?

Stan: I felt very guilty and very embarrassed.

Leader: What did you decide from that?

Stan: That I wouldn't do it again.

Leader: What did you decide after receiving the whipping?

Stan: That I was a disappointment to my parents. I still worry about disappointing them.

Leader: So how did the punishment help you?

Stan: Well, I had already decided I wouldn't cheat again. The guilt and embarrassment of getting caught in front of others was enough to teach me that lesson. Actually, the worry about disappointing my parents is a real burden.

Leader: If you had a magic wand and could change the script of that event, how would you change it? How would you change what anyone said or did?

Stan: Well, I wouldn't cheat.

Leader: And after that?

Stan: I don't know.

Leader: Who has any ideas you could give Stan? It is usually easier to see possibilities when you aren't emotionally involved. What could Stan's teacher or parents have done or said that would have demonstrated kind and firm discipline?

Group Member: I'm a teacher, and I'm learning a lot from this. The teacher could have taken Stan aside and asked him why he was cheating.

Leader: Stan, what would you have answered to that?

Stan: That I wanted to pass the test.

Group Member: Then I could appreciate his desire to pass and ask him how he felt about cheating as a way to accomplish that.

Stan: I would promise never to do it again.

Group Member: I would then tell him he would have to receive an F for this test but that I was glad he had learned to avoid cheating. I would then ask him to prepare a plan for me about what he would do to pass the next test.

Stan: I would still feel guilty and embarrassed about cheating, but I would also appreciate the kindness along with the firmness. Now I see what that means.

Leader: Now do you have any ideas how you could use your magic wand to change what your parents did?

Stan: It would have been nice if they had acknowledged how guilty and embarrassed I felt. They could have empathized about what a tough lesson that was for me to learn. Then they could express their faith in me to learn from my experience and to do the right thing in the future. They could reassure me that they would love me no matter what, but that they hoped I wouldn't disappoint myself in the future. Wow, what a concept—to worry more about disappointing myself than my parents. I find that very encouraging.

Several points are made by this discussion about nonpunitive parenting:

1. Nonpunitive parenting does not mean letting children "get away" with their behavior.

2. Nonpunitive parenting does mean helping children explore the consequences of their choices in a supportive and encouraging environment so that lasting growth and learning can take place.

3. Most people turned out "fine" even if they were punished—and they might have learned even more had they received both kindness and firmness to learn from mistakes.

Turning out "fine" isn't the issue. Are you satisfied with "fine," or do you want your children to have the kind of nurturing that helps them bloom into the best people they can possibly be? You nurture the best in your children when your methods meet the four criteria for effective discipline.

> Are you satisfied with "fine," or do you want your children to have the kind of nurturing that helps them bloom into the best people they can possibly be?

Yes, effective discipline can help children feel a sense of connection, belonging, and significance. Punishment doesn't. Kind and firm discipline is respectful. Punishment, permissiveness, rewards, praise, or rescuing aren't. Effective discipline has positive long-term results. Punitive methods may stop the behavior short term, but have negative long-term results. Last, but not least, you'll see how effective discipline methods teach your child important social and life skills for good character.

Keep the four criteria for effective discipline in mind as we continue to discuss what works and what doesn't.

FOUR CRITERIA FOR EFFECTIVE DISCIPLINE

1. Does it help children feel a sense of connection (belonging and significance)?

2. Is it respectful (kind and firm at the same time)?

3. Is it effective long term? (Does it consider what the child is thinking, feeling, deciding?)

4. Does it teach important social and life skills for good character (respect, concern for others, problem solving, cooperation)?

Good Intentions, Poor Results

PARENTS WHO USE punishment (excessive control) or rewards do so because they believe these methods will motivate their children to choose better behavior. It would take years to read all the research that has demonstrated that neither punishment nor rewards are effective motivators for long-term positive results. (Yes, now we will add rewards and praise to the list of methods that are not effective long term.) Alfie Kohn has summarized much of this research in *Punished by Rewards,* a book we highly recommend.[1] Kohn describes several research projects that demonstrate that rewards actually impaired performance and that children who tried to earn rewards actually made more mistakes than those who were simply told the results of their efforts at performing a task.

Praise, a form of reward, is a "golden calf" worshiped by thousands of loving adults who have not investigated the long-range results. Your own common sense will provide the answer to this important question: Does praise encourage children to appreciate their own self-worth, or does it encourage

---

1. Alfie Kohn, *Punished by Rewards* (Boston: Houghton Mifflin, 1993), 42–45.

them to depend on the opinions of others, turning them into "approval junkies"?[2]

Using punishment to manage children's behavior is as problematic as using rewards and praise, if not more so. Most parents who punish children do so because they truly love those children. They believe punishment will help their children learn better behavior. Again, Kohn eloquently states what we know to be true:

> *The unsettling news is that rewards and punishments are worthless at best, and destructive at worst, for helping children develop such values and skills. What rewards and punishment do produce is* temporary compliance. *They buy us obedience. If that's what we mean when we say they "work," then yes, they work wonders. But if we are ultimately concerned with the kind of people our children will become . . . no behavioral manipulation ever helped a child develop a commitment to becoming a caring and responsible person.* (p. 160)

What are the long-range results of punishment? Reams of research prove that punishment produces children who are more aggressive than children who do not experience punishment. The problem is that most of the research is buried in academic journals. Murray Straus of the University of New

---

2. Kohn takes a much more scientific approach in his chapter "The Praise Problem," taking the time to quote the research and explore, in depth, the long-range negative effects of praise.

Hampshire conducted a long-range study that followed families in which spanking was used by loving and conscientious parents to manage children's behavior. Straus discovered that over time, families that relied on spanking and other punishments reported ever-increasing incidences of misbehavior and disrespect in their children. Children who were spanked also are more likely to choose violent partners when they became adults. Physical punishment teaches children that violence is an acceptable way to express anger or dissatisfaction to people who are less powerful than you are.[3]

> Punishment produces children who are more aggressive than children who do not experience punishment.

Permissiveness Is Not a Good Alternative

PAMPERING (PERMISSIVENESS, OVERPROTECTION, rescuing), as discussed in the previous chapter, is at the other end of the spectrum. Parents who protect their children from experiencing the frustration and pain of disappointment by giving in to their demands for candy in the grocery store or for a car "because everyone else has one" hope their children are thinking, "Thanks for loving me so much that I will never have to suffer. I will be forever grateful and will make it up to you by being the best kid on the block." It is easy for working parents to fall into this trap. In fact, some parents say their reason for working is so their children can have more things (although they would prefer the word "advantages"). These are the parents who later can't understand why their children are so ungrateful and continue to demand more. When parents think about it, they realize that their children cannot develop survival and problem-solving skills (and, yes, they can survive disappointment) when they are never given the opportunity to practice.

Why are parents permissive? Besides the many reasons discussed in the previous chapter (such as wanting children to have happy childhoods), it is often just plain easier. Children hassle, hassle, hassle. Parents say no, no, no. Children hassle, hassle, hassle. Parents say no, no, no. Children hassle, hassle, hassle. Parents give in.

---

3. Straus, Sugarman, and Giles-Sims, "Corporal Punishment by Parents and Subsequent Anti-Social Behavior of Children." *Archives of Pediatrics & Adolescent Medicine* 151. 761–767, 1997.

This scene is repeated over and over—in grocery stores, at the mall, during bedtime, in the morning. Just as excessive control invites children to think and act "against" their parents, permissiveness invites children to think and act "for" themselves in selfish ways. Permissiveness invites children to adopt the belief, "The world owes me a living" or "Love means getting other people to give me everything I want." When children hassle and parents eventually give in, they teach their children that no doesn't mean no. It teaches them that no means "keep hassling until I give in." In essence, they train their children that the temper tantrums or other forms of misbehavior work, and assure that they will continue.

> Permissiveness invites children to adopt the belief, "The world owes me a living" or "Love means getting other people to give me everything I want."

Permissiveness and pampering go hand in hand, and parents do it because it seems to work at the moment. After all, most children do stop crying when they get their own way. Parents also claim they punish their children because the behavior stops, at least for the moment. In either case, parents are not considering the long-range results, the decisions their children are making, and how those decisions will affect future behavior.

"But I Would Never Do That"

Permissiveness is almost always something *other* parents do, and most parents recognize its ineffectiveness when they see other parents doing it. Millions of people watched, appalled, as a film crew for a popular TV newsmagazine followed parents who took their two children to a large discount store. One child wanted a toy. The parents talked to him very kindly and reasonably about why he couldn't have the toy. The child had a temper tantrum. He grabbed the toy from the shelf and put it in the cart. The mother took it out of the cart and put it back on the shelf while continuing to discuss the matter very firmly. But as the child's decibel level increased, Mom's willpower decreased. Finally, she gave in and bought the toy for the child.

This provoked a great deal of comment from viewers. Some said, "That kid should have received a spanking the minute he had a temper tantrum." Others said, "I can't believe those parents could be so wimpy" or "I would never let my child get away with that."

It is true that the parents were being wimpy in the name of love. (And chances are that these parents would have been horrified themselves had they been watching someone else!) It is very easy to judge others when you are not emotionally hooked and totally frustrated. It is true that the children were not served well by having their parents give in to them. However, is the only alternative a spanking or some other form of punishment? Of course not. Neither method produces effective long-range results when you consider what children might be deciding in response to either permissiveness or punishment.

What were these parents thinking? We can only guess. Were they thinking, "I can't stand it when my child has a temper tantrum?" Were they concerned about what others were thinking? Or did they finally give in because they just didn't know what else to do? All of these thoughts probably crossed their minds, but the latter may have had the greatest weight. Many loving parents simply don't have any other tools in their parenting toolbox than permissiveness or punishment. It is likely that these parents did not accept the punishment option and saw permissiveness as the only other choice.

> When children hassle and parents eventually give in, they teach their children that no doesn't mean no.

But there is good news: Many other options exist that are kind and firm *at the same time.* Kindness shows respect for the child, and firmness shows respect for the needs of the situation. What would this look like? There are several possibilities:

Option 1: When the child asked for the toy, the parents could say no only once. Then they could shut their mouths and act by kindly and firmly taking the child to the car where he could have his feelings in private. (We have talked about the importance of allowing children to have their feelings, which is not the same thing as allowing them to misbehave.) It is important to avoid conversation (children will use anything you say as fuel for an argument) except to say, "We'll go back to the store as soon as you are ready."

Option 2: When the child asked for a toy, the parents could ask, "Do you have enough money saved from your allowance?" When the child pouts and says no, they could say, "As soon as you have saved enough money, you can have the toy." (Some parents even offer to provide half. Most children do not want the toy badly enough to wait and save their own money, but they are happy to spend yours.)

Option 3: The parents could advise their children in advance that they will all leave the store immediately if there is any misbehavior. (Of course, it would be helpful if the parents had thoroughly described what misbehavior looks like during a family meeting and even allowed the children to learn by playing "let's pretend.") Parents could demonstrate appropriate behavior and what will happen when behavior is inappropriate. Then the parents could follow through and simply do what they promised.

> Children learn very quickly whether or not their parents mean what they say.

Children learn very quickly whether or not their parents mean what they say. The child in this story obviously knew his parents didn't mean it when they told him he couldn't have the toy. To children, parents are a lot like slot machines: They don't always pay out, but the odds are that they will eventually pay out something if the handle is pulled enough times. When children know you mean what you say, they soon stop hassling. The alternative is to fall into the trap of materialism and overindulgence.

The Harm of Materialism and Overindulgence

Every Christmas, advertising creates a shortage of the latest toy craze. In 1998, it was Furby; the year before, it was Tickle Me Elmo. Pokémon soon followed, and every Christmas brings another "must-have" toy. What do parents do? Sadly, many do anything they can to make sure their little darling is not deprived. Many have awakened before dawn to stand in line at a toy store with a limited supply or have paid ten times the retail price to scalpers who advertise on Internet auctions or in local newspapers.

In fact, the 1996 movie *Jingle All the Way* provides the perfect illustration of the buy-your-child's-love philosophy. In the movie, Arnold Schwarzenegger plays a distant, workaholic dad who reconnects with his son by managing to obtain for him the toy of the season. To do so, he fights an all-out battle with an equally dedicated mailman and, in a twisted transformation only too typical of Hollywood, reunites with his son by actually *becoming* the toy. That this

testament to commercialism should have become a popular holiday movie (a "family" movie, no less) speaks volumes about how our society has come to view parenting and what we believe we must do to earn the love and respect of our children.

Most American parents will confess that they have been known to over-indulge their children with material things, even when it means they must go without. Working parents are especially prone to this mistake when they feel guilty about being gone during the day and try to make up for it by purchas-ing "things" for their children. But then their chil-dren are robbed of the opportunity to develop many important life skills, such as resilience, pa-tience, concern for others, and problem solving. They don't develop the courage and self-confidence that comes from finding they can survive disap-pointment and recover from mistakes on their own.

When children are punished for or rescued from every mistake, they become less able (and less willing) to *learn* from their mistakes and may de-vote their considerable energy and creativity to defeating adults. How can chil-dren develop faith in themselves when their parents protect them from all suffering and rescue them whenever they make poor choices or lecture and

> How can children develop faith in themselves when their parents either protect them from all suffering and rescue them whenever they make poor choices or lecture and punish them?

punish them? How can they learn respect for self and others when they are not treated with respect? (Neither permissiveness nor punishment is respectful.) How can they figure out how to entertain themselves (or enjoy serenity) if their parents exhaust themselves ensuring that their children don't suffer a moment of boredom? Too many parents don't stop to think about these questions—or the answers.

The Problem with Punitive Time-Out

EVEN THE MOST loving, thoughtful parents (whether they work outside the home or not) have been known to react emotionally or out of habit. (The authors have done considerable parenting "research" in just this way.) Parents just don't think about the long-term results of what they do, especially when they are toe-to-toe with a defiant youngster. A typical example is the way parents impose punitive time-out. They say, "You go to your room and think about what you did!" When they stop to think about it, parents usually realize that this is a fairly ridiculous thing to say for a number of reasons. The most obvious is that they can't control what their child will think about.

Parents would like their children to be thinking, "Thank you *so* much for giving me this terrific opportunity to think about the error of my ways and to realize that from now on I must behave better." It is more likely that the child is thinking, "I'll show you. You can make me sit here, but you can't make me do or think what you want me to." Even more tragic is the child who thinks, "I really am a bad person."

We often invite parents to think about how they would feel and how they would respond if their spouse, boss, or friend said, "You go to time-out and think about what you did." They laugh and say something similar to "Excuse *me!*" or "I don't *think* so." If children made these comments to their parents, they would be accused of "talking back." However, when you think about it, why would a child respond favorably to a situation that would certainly not be motivating to you? (Positive time-out is discussed in chapter 10.) Parents want their children to "think" about what *they* do and to consider the long-term consequences of *their* actions; yet all too often, parents don't walk their own talk.

Parents Who Use Ineffective Parenting Methods	Parents Who Use Effective Parenting Methods
See children as possessions	See children as gifts
Try to mold children into what they want	Nurture children to be who they are
Are wimpy friends (or insist that a parent can't be a friend)	Are respectful and supportive friends
Give in or make child give in	Remain kind and firm
Control	Guide (copilot instead of pilot)
Try for perfection (in child and self)	Teach that mistakes are opportunities
Try to win over child	Try to win over child
Lecture or punish (for your own good)	Involve child in solutions
Treat as object or recipient	Treat as an asset
Overprotect	Offer appropriate supervision
Avoid feelings (try to prevent or rescue)	Allow feelings and empathize
Fix	Teach life skills
Bawl out and then bail out	Allow child to experience and then *explore* consequences of their choices
Take behavior personally	Help child learn from behavior
Think only of their point of view	Get into child's world
Are fearful	Have faith
Are child-centered	Are child-involved

Keeping the Long-Term Results in Mind

PARENTS NEED TO stop and think about these questions and the long-term results of what they do. When parents are indulgent and satisfy every demand, what are they teaching their children? Here are some possibilities:

1. If you want it, you should have it—now.
2. Material goods are the most important things in life.
3. Don't evaluate advertising and commercials. Just do whatever they suggest.

4. You can't deal with disappointment in life. I'll make sure you don't have to.

When parents overindulge, children get the toy, but they are deprived of an opportunity to learn valuable life lessons. When parents avoid overindulgence, children can learn the following:

1. What I feel is always okay, but what I do is not always okay. I can learn to feel what I feel and then decide on a respectful action.

2. It is okay to want, but I don't "have" to have.

3. I can deal with disappointment. I may not like it, but I will survive.

4. When a goal is worth pursuing, I can help create a plan to achieve the goal that involves my participation: to save my allowance, do odd jobs to earn money, and so on.

5. My parents will listen to me, but they won't indulge me.

6. My parents have faith in me to deal with life's problems and opportunities.

7. I am capable.

Perhaps the most important message of this book is the importance of long-term parenting. In chapter 8 we discuss a list of qualities parents hope their children will have as adults. The goal of parenting—and its greatest challenge—is handling each day's problems and crises in ways that promote those qualities we want our children to have in the long run. Parents are more effective when they consider, "What will my child decide if I do this?" "What will she learn—about herself, about me, about what 'works'?" "What are the long-term consequences of giving too much or controlling too much because I feel guilty about working outside the home or am simply too frazzled because I haven't learned to balance family and work?" In a world where parents feel torn between work and home, where they often feel they have too little time and too little energy, this sort of thinking is hard to do. Yet it is crucial that we do this thinking.

> When parents overindulge, children get the toy, but they are deprived of an opportunity to learn valuable life lessons.

By now you may be convinced that punishment and/or permissiveness are not effective methods to use for positive results with children—now and long term. We know, however, that it is almost impossible to give up old habits without new habits to take their place.

Alternatives to Punishment

THERE ARE MANY alternatives besides the extremes of permissiveness and excessive control. Parents occasionally find themselves swinging from one extreme to the other: They are permissive until they can't stand their kids, then controlling until they can't stand themselves. Positive discipline methods provide you with hundreds of alternatives that are respectful, kind, and firm at the same time and are effective long term.

It is important to mention that we are not advocating the other extreme— neglect. It is amazing how many parents are fearful that if they are not pampering or punishing, the only alternative is neglect. Neglect is never acceptable, but the big secret is that *many other alternatives are possible.* Over and over we hear, "I've tried everything." However, the "everything" these parents have tried usually falls under the headings of excessive control, punishment, permissiveness, or neglect. There is a whole world in between.

Effective Parenting Methods

PARENTS CAN HELP their children learn these important life lessons using nonpunitive parenting methods. The first is reflective listening.

Reflective Listening

Reflective listening means to listen without fixing. Validate your child's feelings by reflecting back everything she says until she feels understood. You can avoid sounding like a parrot by reflecting the feelings you are hearing as well as the words.

Child: I want a this toy.

Parent (with a smile): You would really like to have it. (You might be surprised how often this is enough, especially with younger children. The older children get, the longer the conversation might last.)

Child: This toy is so cute.

Parent: You really like this toy.

Child: Everyone is getting one.

Parent: You think all your friends will have one.

> Validate your child's feelings by reflecting back everything she says until she feels understood.

With reflective listening, the parent can empathize without rescuing. The parent can say, "This must be frustrating for you."

If reflective listening doesn't seem to be enough, you might try asking "what" and "how" questions. This can help your child enhance her thinking and problem-solving skills and can leave her with the belief, "I am capable."

What, Why, and How Questions

What, why, and how questions are curiosity questions and should not be asked unless you are truly curious about what your child thinks (instead of using the

questions to offer criticism or manipulate your child into thinking as you do). Your attitude and tone of voice are the keys to effectiveness with this parenting tool.

Child: I want this toy.

Parent: Why do you want one? (Children are very suspicious of why questions unless they perceive that you are really interested in their answer.)

Child: Because it is neat and cute and everyone is getting one.

Parent: How do you know that?

Child: I saw one on TV, and everyone is talking about them.

Parent: Lots of toys are neat. What do you think has made this one so special?

Child *(after a pause to think about it):* Maybe because of all the advertising, or maybe because everyone says they are so hard to find.

Parent: What is the purpose of advertising?

Child: To make people buy things. (Parent and child have had this particular conversation before.)

Parent: Can advertisers "make" people do things? Can they control people?

Child: They can't control me.

Of course, this conversation could go as many directions as there are children. One child we know concluded, "Last year another toy was hard to find. Now they are lots cheaper. I think I'll wait 'til next year to get this toy."

With curiosity questions, parents can be supportive and help children explore the consequences of their choices instead of heaping on *more* consequences (which usually are thinly disguised punishment).

Brainstorming for Solutions that Involve the Child

Another child concluded the process of what and how questions with "They can't make me buy one, but I still want one." His father then engaged his son in a brainstorming session to help him figure out what he needed to do to get one. After brainstorming several possibilities, he decided he would find extra jobs to earn the money and then get his twenty-three-year-old aunt to stand in a line with him. What do you think this child might learn about himself, about life? What would he learn if his working parents simply handed him the toy because they had more money than time?

> Brainstorming is effective only when the child is actively involved in the process and then chooses the suggestion that would work best for him.

It would not be helpful for a parent to say, "If you want this toy, get a job and buy it yourself." Brainstorming is effective only when the child is actively involved in the process and then chooses the suggestion that would work best for him. Parents can express faith in their children to solve whatever problem they may be having and offer to brainstorm with them if they are willing to put forth as much effort as their parents.

Decide What You Will and Won't Do

Too many parents have forgotten how to use this very simple, but important tool. They feel guilty when they aren't willing to spend more than they can afford and guilty when they say no if they can afford it. In either case, they make the mistake of overindulgence. If you decide buying a certain toy isn't in your child's best interests, follow through with dignity and respect—minus the guilt. (It is often helpful to have a conversation with your child explaining your decision in a kind but unapologetic way.) "Honey, I'm not willing to buy this toy. I am willing to help you figure out how to save for it, or to choose something else." For more on this parenting tool, see chapter 10.

"But It's Easier to Give In"

WHEN YOU CONSIDER the negative long-term results, the harm in overindulging becomes apparent. It is important to decide what you will and won't do and then to inform your children of your decisions kindly, firmly, and respectfully. If they feel angry or disappointed, use reflective listening to validate their feelings. This will probably be more uncomfortable for you than it is for your child! It's not easy to change old habits and beliefs. Like many parents, you may be hanging on to the belief that praise and letting children have what they want is a boost to their self-esteem.

What About Self-Esteem?

THE MOST DANGEROUS myths are those that have threads of truth. Self-esteem is one of those nebulous states of mind that seems to come and go. Have you noticed that there are days when your "self-esteem" is really good? You feel good about yourself and your abilities. Then someone criticizes you or you make a mistake, and your self-esteem thermometer drops to zero. Self-esteem *can't* be a permanent state of mind when a "bad hair day" can put such a dent in it!

The notion of being able to give children self-esteem doesn't make sense when scrutinized. Parents who use ineffective parenting are often too concerned about a child's self-esteem, while parents who engage in effective parenting are more concerned about helping their children develop skills that will help them handle the ups and downs of life. Children don't learn to handle the ups and downs of life when they don't have experiences that teach them how well they can cope and recover from disappointment.

Are Your Parenting Methods Hurting or Helping Your Child?

WHEN ALL IS said and done, this is the fundamental question we ask parents to consider. Your parenting methods are a much greater factor in your children's well-being than whether you work outside the home. You undoubtedly love your children and are concerned about their future, their success, and the problems they may face. We invite you to think about what you are doing, why you are doing it, and the long-term results of what you are doing.

The most important part of the learning process is your willingness to look inside, consider carefully and honestly the impact of your own decisions and beliefs about parenting, and be willing to change the ineffective parenting methods that aren't accomplishing long-term goals.

It is interesting to note that parents don't need training in the most popular parenting methods: punishment, permissiveness, rewards, praise, rescuing, and overindulgence. Those methods seem to come naturally. However, it does take awareness, training, and practice to use nonpunitive methods. This book provides the training. It is up to you to practice, make mistakes, learn from your mistakes, and keep practicing. Raising capable, confident, loving children takes time, energy, and patience, but it is possible and well worth the effort, even for working parents.

Quick and Quality Parenting Tips

Morning and Bedtime Hassles

My child won't get dressed in the morning and has a fit about getting her pajamas on at night. It is a constant battle. It the morning I'm rushed to get to work on time, and at night I'm too tired for these battles.

Working Parents' Common Mistakes

1. Lack of preplanning *with* their children.

2. Using their energy for power struggles instead of learning skills that invite cooperation.

Discouraging Words and Actions

1. "Hurry up, brush your teeth, get dressed." (Giving orders invites rebellion.)

2. "You are going to make me late." (Blaming children for your lack of preparation and skills.)

3. "I'll buy you a toy if you'll just cooperate." (Rewards invite manipulation.)

4. "If you make me late, you'll be grounded for a week." (Punishment invites revenge cycles.)

Respectful and Encouraging Actions

1. Plan in advance by creating morning and bedtime routine charts *with* your children.

2. Decide what you will do. For example, that you will leave on time no matter what. If the child isn't ready, she can take her clothes in a bag and get ready in the car or after arriving at child care. Go to your bedroom and tell your child to come get you as soon as she is ready for a story.

3. Hold regular family meetings where you and your children decide on solutions to solve problems.

4. Help children prepare for the next morning by getting everything ready the night before.

5. Give children their own alarm clock and help them learn how to use it. Let them decide how much time they need in the morning so they can set their alarm clock accordingly.

Respectful and Encouraging Words

1. "I need your help. Anything you can do will be appreciated."

2. "What is next on your routine chart?"

3. "What ideas do you have to solve this problem?"

4. "I have faith in you to handle this problem in a way that is helpful to you and me."

5. "I'll read you a story *as soon as* you have done everything on your bedtime routine chart."

Encouraging Attitudes:

1. Focus on solutions instead of blame and punishment.

2. Look forward to problems as opportunities for teaching valuable life skills.

7

Effective Parenting for Children Under Age Four

Inappropriate Methods vs. Age-Appropriate Discipline

A FATHER WHO lacked an understanding of basic child development and age-appropriateness thought he was being a good father when he took his two-and-a-half-year-old son to a basketball game. He most likely did not stop to consider whether such a young child would be interested in basketball for any length of time. Instead of understanding normal behavior for a child that age, he became annoyed when the only thing that interested his son was the treats that were being hawked up and down the aisles. After listening to his son whine for a few minutes and ordering him to "settle down" and "be quiet," Dad blew up. He grasped the child's hand firmly and proceeded down the wide cement steps at his own pace. The little boy, his face contorted with fear, seemed nearly to be flying as he was dragged along by his father.

This child couldn't understand what was happening. His "crime" was to be more interested in popcorn and soda than in basketball—a thoroughly appropriate (albeit irritating) response for a child his age. Although this father loved his son, he failed to understand his little boy's limitations, attempted to control his behavior, lost his own temper, and ultimately frightened his son badly. It will likely be a long time before this little boy wants to attend another sporting event with Dad.

Another father took his family, including a two-year-old son, to a drive-in movie. A week later the family drove past the drive-in theater. The two-year-old was bright enough to remember the place and said, "We went there last night." The father said, "It was last week, not last night," stopped the car, and spanked this child because he didn't want him to grow up to be a liar.

It is heartbreaking to consider how often parents' ignorance leads them to punish children for developmentally appropriate behavior.

Education for the World's Most Important Job

WE OFTEN ASK parents if they would consider trying to get the job of their dreams without an education or training. The answer is "Of course not." Everyone agrees that education and training are necessary whatever the goal, whether it is to be a bricklayer or a brain surgeon. We then ask, "What is the most important job in the world?" All agree that it is parenting. Is it then logical to think that this important job does not require education and training?

We strongly recommend that every parent take a basic child development class at a community college or read a book on child development.[1] However you do it, it is important to learn about child development because so many parenting mistakes are made when parents don't have an understanding of age-appropriate behavior. One of the most common mistakes parents make is the use of time-out with young children.

Time-Out Is Inappropriate for Children Under Four

TOO MANY PARENTS are sending their two-year-olds to time-out with the admonition, "Now you think about what you just did." Obviously, the hope is that these two-year-olds will think rationally about what they did, see the errors of their ways, and make a firm commitment to do better. If these parents

---

1. Two books that cover child development and how it applies to parenting methods are *Positive Discipline: The First Three Years* and *Positive Discipline for Preschoolers*, both by Jane Nelsen, Cheryl Erwin, and Roslyn Duffy (Roseville, CA: Prima Publishing, 1998, respectively).

understood basic child development, they would know this is unrealistic for a two-year-old who has not yet reached the age of reason. Time-out (even positive time-out) is rarely effective for children under the age of four, yet it is one of the most popular discipline methods used with children of all ages.

Most children cannot connect cause with effect—or behavior with consequences—in the way that adults can until they are closer to four years of age. If they cannot make this connection, time-out won't work. Few parents understand this until they learn about the discoveries of Jean Piaget.

> Time-out (even positive time-out) is rarely effective for children under the age of four.

Intellectual, Social, and Emotional Capabilities

JEAN PIAGET WAS one of the pioneers in understanding the cognitive development of children. He devised the following demonstrations to help adults understand how children's thinking ability differs from their own:

Find four glasses: two glasses that are of the same size, one glass that is taller and narrower, and one glass that is shorter and wider. Ask a three-year-old to watch as you fill the two glasses that are the same size with water until the three-year-old agrees they have the same amount of water in them. Then, ask her to watch closely as you pour the water from one of these glasses into the short, wide glass and the water from the other one into the tall, narrow glass. You can even verbalize what you are doing. "These glasses have the same amount of water. I'm going to pour the water from this glass into this tall, narrow glass, and the water from this other glass into the short, wide glass." Then ask her if they hold the same amount of water. She will say no and will tell you which glass she thinks contains the most water—almost always the tall glass.

Repeat the demonstration with a five-year-old. Most five-year-olds will tell you the glasses contain the same amount or water and can tell you why.

This example demonstrates the developmental thinking abilities identified by Piaget. A three-year-old has not yet developed *concrete thinking:* the ability to understand that the water is still the same amount even though it is poured into a different sized container. Adults often expect young children to understand things that their brains have not developed enough for them to understand.

You may think your young child understands she shouldn't touch something, but you need to know that she doesn't understand this means even when you aren't in the room. This child isn't being "disobedient" or "defiant." She simply doesn't have the developmental ability to comprehend at the level you may have assumed. Her understanding is further complicated when you combine intellectual development with what Erikson discovered about social and emotional development.

Erik Erikson, the child-development specialist, taught that the second year of life is when children are developing a sense of autonomy versus doubt and shame. When children are punished for what they are developmentally programmed to do, they are likely to develop a sense of doubt and shame rather than a sense of autonomy.[2]

When you understand that perceiving, interpreting, and comprehending an event are so markedly different for young children, your expectations as an adult will be altered. The meaning children attach to their experiences does not match the meaning adults attach to the same experiences.

Let's take what Piaget and Erikson discovered to explain why children under the age of three don't understand "no" the way you may believe they do.[3]

What Does Your Toddler Really "Know" About "No"?

Children under the age of three do not understand "no" in the way most parents think they do. (And a full understanding of "no" doesn't occur magically when the child turns three. It is a developmental process.) *No* is an abstract concept that is in direct opposition to the developmental need of young children to explore their world and to develop their sense of autonomy and initiative.

Oh, your child may *know* you don't want her to do something. She may even know she will get an angry reaction from you if she does it. However, she cannot understand why in the way you may think she can. Why else would she look at you before doing what she knows she shouldn't do, grin, and do it anyway?

---

2. For extensive information on how parents can use Erikson's information to be more effective with children of these ages, see Jane Nelsen, Cheryl Erwin, and Roslyn Duffy, *Positive Discipline: The First Three Years* (Roseville, CA: Prima Publishing, 1998).

3. Ibid., 110–112.

Knowing things as a toddler means something far different than *knowing* things as an adult. Her version of knowing lacks the internal controls necessary to halt her roving fingers. As Jean Piaget discovered long ago, toddlers lack the ability to understand cause and effect (an excellent reason not to try to lecture and argue a toddler into doing what you want). In fact, higher-order thinking like understanding consequences and ethics may not develop until children are as old as ten to twelve.

> Children under the age of three do not understand "no" in the way most parents think they do.

Students of developmentally and age-appropriate behavior know that the intellectual, social, and emotional capabilities of young children have not developed to the point where they can think like adults, yet many adults act as though they should. In addition to the inappropriate use of time-out, many parents try forcing a young child to "say you are sorry." As Bev Bos[4] said in a lecture for the California Association of Young Children, "Insisting that a two- or three-year-old say, 'I'm sorry,' makes as much sense as insisting that a Japanese child say, 'I'm Italian.'" They can say it, but it isn't true or meaningful.

Parents often cite the danger of a child running into the street as a justification for spanking a toddler. Reasons include the life-and-death nature of the situation, the need for immediate compliance, and the effectiveness of a spanking for getting a child's attention. The thing they forget is that to a toddler, an angry, shouting, spanking parent is probably far more frightening than any street. She may be watching out for you instead of watching out for cars.

Even when parents believe punishment effectively *teaches* a two-year-old child to avoid running into the street, would they let her play near a busy street unsupervised? No. They know, spanking or no spanking, that they can't expect her to have the maturity to understand what she has learned well enough to have that responsibility. Why then do they think their child has the maturity to understand "don't touch"? With young children it is important to take time for training—over and over—until their *understanding* catches up with the learning.

---

4. Bev Bos is the director of the Roseville Community Preschool, and author of *Together We're Better: Establishing Coactive Environments for Young Children* (Roseville, CA: Turn the Page Press, 1990).

Take Time for Training

THIS IS A very important tool for young children (as well as older children). Take your little one by the hand when you are walking and want to cross a street. Ask her to look each way and tell you if a car is coming. Ask her what might happen if the car is coming. (It is amazing how many parents think their children can understand the meaning of a spanking when they don't even understand what would happen if a car would hit them.) You repeat this process over and over. Still, you don't let your child cross a street by herself until she is much older. At some level, you know she doesn't have the maturity to handle such a task; so why is it that you expect her to remember not to touch things you think she knows she shouldn't touch? Continue to take time for training. Eventually she will be developmentally ready to understand and act on what she knows.

Just because your young child does not have the capability to understand all you teach is no excuse to stop training. Training must take place over and over until your children are developmentally capable of absorbing all this training. Hopefully, by now you understand that spanking is not an effective part of training.

Some parents insist that they can train toddlers not to touch things. Not only is this a mistake, it is very sad. Touching, exploring, and experimenting are part of the developmental programming for toddlers. It is heartbreaking to know that children are being punished (scolded, hands slapped, spanked) for things they are developmentally programmed to do. In fact, brain research demonstrates that when children are not allowed to explore, touch, and experiment, their brain development is hindered.

> It is heartbreaking to know that children are being punished (scolded, hands slapped, spanked) for things they are developmentally programmed to do.

Even when children learn to repeat, "Don't touch," they have learned it at the intellectual level of a parrot. When Dad put his feet on the coffee table, two-year-old Sage loved saying, "No," while she pushed his feet off the table. Everyone laughed and thought that was so cute. Later, they thought she was being defiant when she wanted to climb on the coffee table. Actually, she had learned how to get approval (like a trained puppy) when pushing her dad's feet off the table, but was in her exploring mode when she wanted to climb on the table. She didn't really *know* she should stay off the table any more than she would *know* she should stay out of the street if she was all by herself.

"But, How Do I Make My Toddler Mind?"

YOU MAY BE experiencing the frustration of so many parents who have a difficult time absorbing what we have been presenting in this chapter. Over and over, we hear the question, "How do I make my toddler mind?" You don't. If you don't understand why it is impossible to make a toddler mind, please read the previous pages again. We don't mean to be patronizing, but we know how difficult it can be for parents to grasp the facts and meaning of developmentally and age-appropriate behavior.

This doesn't mean you let your child do whatever he or she wants. It is so easy to fall into the trap of thinking the only alternative to punitive control is permissiveness. See the previous chapter for why neither punishment nor permissiveness is healthy for children.

For children under the age of four, it is the parent who must be responsible, not the child. Just as you can't expect a child to have the maturity to be safe near a busy street, even after spankings to *teach* him not to run into the street, it does not make sense to expect a child to *mind,* even after you have told him to mind and punished him for not minding. The primary alternatives to punishment and permissiveness for young children are supervision, supervision, supervision—and a little distraction and/or redirection.

Supervision, Distraction, and Redirection

WHEN YOU KNOW that young children are not capable of the kind of maturity and understanding you may have believed they were capable of in the past, it makes sense to accept that it is your job to supervise. Instead of expecting them to understand, "Don't touch," supervise closely and intervene when they go to touch something you don't want them to touch. Kindly and firmly show them what they can touch and know that you will have to do this many times.

One thing that amazes parents, when they think about it, is that supervising, distracting, and redirecting doesn't take any more time than punishment. Most parents find that they spank or send children to time-out for the same things over and over. Even though what they are doing doesn't work, they keep doing it because they are afraid they aren't being good parents if they don't try to stop the "bad" behavior.

Hopefully, you now know that it isn't bad behavior. Even though the behavior isn't bad, it also is not appropriate to let children climb on tables or run into the street. So, you stop the behavior through kind and firm supervision, distraction, and redirection, not by expecting your child to learn to stop because of your punishments.

Distraction can take many forms. One mother combined distraction and redirection in dramatic ways when her child would do something inappropriate such as playing in the fireplace. She would say something like—"I hear batman calling. Run to the living room to give batman the help he needs." Another way to distract is to simply remove a child who is climbing on a coffee table. Adding redirection means to show a child what he can do instead. Instead of saying. "No. No. Don't climb on the table," remove the child and say, "You can climb on your tricycle." Don't expect your child to never climb on the table again until he is much older. Supervision, distraction, and redirection are constant tasks for parents of young children.

The amount of supervision required will decrease dramatically and your child will be safer if you childproof your home.

Childproofing for Young Children

THIS IS A good time to decorate "garage-sale" style, so you don't have to worry about damage to expensive furniture. Put away those sentimental, delicate table decorations and anything else precious to you so that you minimize the number of times you are tempted to utter "no, no." Get plastic plugs for outlets, avoid cords hanging down off blinds, don't leave plastic bags lying in reach of children, keep pot handles on the stove turned toward the stove, and keep anything dangerous (knives, medicines, cleaning supplies) securely locked away from your child. You can find more information on childproofing from your pediatrician, parenting magazines, etc.

Some days does it seem as if "no" is the only word you say? Is it any wonder children learn to say "no" long before they understand what it means? Distraction, redirection, and childproofing can help you eliminate "no" from your vocabulary.

Parents of a two-year-old learned about age-appropriate behavior and decided they would childproof their home so their child would not be hampered in exploring and touching. They also decided they would not say "no" to their child. (This does not mean they were permissive. They read *Positive Discipline: The First Three Years* and were using the kind and firm discipline outlined in that book.) Their theory was that their child would not go through the "no, no" stage if she didn't hear that word.

> The amount of supervision required will decrease dramatically and your child will be safer if you childproof your home.

One day they were shocked to hear their two-and-a-half-year-old say, "No, no. Bad dog." They forgot that she would hear what they said to the dog. This was a powerful reminder that children learn from everything they experience—even when the lessons are not intended for them. They learn from words, actions, attitudes, experiences, and their environment. And they are more likely to develop a sense of autonomy in a childproofed environment.

Cooperation from Young Children— Forget It (Almost)

YOU MAY HAVE noticed that sometimes your little one seems very cooperative and loves to help. Other times she absolutely refuses to cooperate. Perhaps it is because *cooperation* is the wrong word to use. What adults think of as cooperation may be part of a fun game for a toddler who acts proud of herself as she fetches a diaper for the new baby. At other times she just isn't interested in the "game."

You can increase the chances of cooperation with your young children through many of the positive discipline methods, such as routine charts, but you will drive yourself crazy if you expect more than their brains are capable of delivering. Inviting cooperation from two- and three-year-olds (even when it is a game to them) increases the chances that they will continue to cooperate as they get older.

> "Me do it" is a common phrase for your two-year-old. At this age, they want to help. Yet too often they are told, "No, you are too little. Go play with your toys."

"Me Do It"

As children grow, they become more and more capable of contributing. However, you may have noticed that "me do it" is a common phrase for your two-year-old. At this age, they want to help. Yet too often they are told, "No, you are too little. Go play with your toys." These same parents then wonder why their children don't want to help as they get older and instead say, "No, I'm busy. I'm playing."

Let small children help. Give them a dust buster when you are vacuuming, a small dust rag when you are dusting, a safe chair to stand on while they help you tear lettuce.[5] Take time for training them in these chores, over and over and over. Toddlers are practicing cooperation as they help.

Routines

WE DISCUSSED ROUTINE charts in chapter 5. Even two-year-olds love routine charts with pictures of them doing their routine tasks, but even more important for this age is daily routines they can count on. Young children feel secure when they know what is going to happen on a regular basis such as sleeping in their own beds and having meals and naps at the same time every day.

You have probably noticed what happens when you go on vacation and routines get all messed up. Children get cranky and misbehave much more fre-

---

5. For age-appropriate chores, see *Positive Discipline: The First Three Years,* by Jane Nelsen, Cheryl Erwin, and Roslyn Duffy (Roseville, CA: Prima Publishing, 1998), 115.

quently. As soon as they get back to their regular routines, they settle down and are as cooperative as a young child of this age can be.

An Example to Illustrate Use of Parenting Tools

THE FOLLOWING QUESTION from a frustrated mother helps summarize what we have said so far about how to use effective parenting tools.

Question:
My twenty-two-month-old has been having a lot of outbursts that I know are related mostly to boredom and frustration, and we are working on changing our daily routine to get into more of a rhythm that I think might make a difference with this. But, what I need is some advice on what to do when these outbursts happen again, as they inevitably do.

Specifically, my daughter will throw everything on the floor, empty boxes of crayons onto the floor, and refuse to help pick them up. We take the things away when she dumps them, but she's at it again later with something else. She hits Mommy or Daddy even though we always say things like, "soft touches," "be gentle please," "hands are for drawing, tickling, stroking, etc., not hitting," and other such positive comments. She screams *loudly* when she can't have what she wants *now*. She just generally has tantrums, throwing herself on the floor and screaming and crying so frequently these days. I am torn between ignoring her and comforting her because I know that she is overwhelmed with emotions and things that are out of her control when she loses it like this. She's so little, and so much of what she's doing I know is developmentally appropriate, but what is the proper way to positively respond? She's very verbal, but she doesn't seem to really get it when you try to explain things to her like why it's not okay to hit. And redirecting doesn't really do much when she's upset. I am exhausted and my behavior is starting to get as out of control as hers! I find myself snapping at her and not being at all the loving mommy I know I am, and I am very disappointed in myself and want to change the direction things are going. *Help!*

Answer:

Dear Help!,

I'm exhausted just reading about your struggles. I remember those days. You are absolutely right—raising a toddler is the most difficult job in the world—and the most rewarding.

It sounds as though you already know so much, especially that everything she is doing is so age appropriate. And, so much of what you are doing is exactly the most effective thing you could do, saying things like, "soft touches;" "be gentle, please;" "hands are for drawing, tickling, stroking, not hitting." I hope some of the following suggestions will give you some relief:

1. Patience. I know it is difficult, but you only frustrate yourself if you think your daughter will "get" the positive statements after hearing them one hundred times. Maybe one thousand. Actually it has nothing to do with how many times you teach. It has to do with when she is developmentally ready to internalize what she has been learning.

2. Childproof your home. It drives me crazy when parents think they can leave things in reach of a toddler and "teach" her not to touch. Toddlers are programmed to touch, explore, and experiment. This doesn't mean they should be allowed to touch everything. However, instead of expecting them not to touch things, parents first should put things that should not be touched out of reach of toddlers. Then, second, if children get to things that should not be touched, parents need to supervise and gently guide toddlers away from what they can't touch. This is most effective if parents keep their mouths shut while kindly and firmly redirecting them to what they can do. Toddlers under-

stand actions better than words. So, to make it easier on yourself, keep things out of reach if you possibly can.

3. Don't expect a toddler to pick anything up unless you make it a game and do it with her. Even then, it will work only sometimes. Toddlers cannot think or understand the way adults do. They are not being irresponsible or defiant when they refuse to pick things up. Simply, they are not old enough to be responsible. And refusing to pick things up doesn't mean they will refuse forever. Well, they might, but after the age of four it is *a little* easier to find ways to invite cooperation. Even then it has to be done over and over. That is what raising children is all about—repetition.

Once you understand what I have said so far about picking up, try kind and firm persistence. This means taking her by the hand (kindly and firmly) and saying, "Let's pick these things up together." If she resists, let her go until she tries to get another toy, then kindly and firmly take her by the hand and say, "You can play with that toy as soon as we pick up what is on the floor." She may resist one hundred times (ten is more likely) until she realizes you are going to be consistently kind and firm. One thing young children do seem to understand is when you mean it and when you don't, so long as you are both kind and firm at the same time. If they have been used to manipulating you into giving in or reverting to punishment, they may push for the results they are used to, so it takes longer for them to understand that you will remain both kind and firm until they are willing to cooperate.

4. I'm glad you know the importance of routines. They are very important in the life of a toddler. Still, she will get bored and frustrated. It is not your job to protect her from all boredom and frustration. Allow her to be bored and to have her feelings about it. Empathy is fine, but she will benefit from learning to handle boredom and frustration and to know that she can. How else will she learn to handle disappointing situations?

5. Supervise, supervise, supervise. This is the most important suggestion of all. Toddlers require lots of supervision. Yes, it is hard. Yes, it takes lots of time. I wish more parents understood that before they had children, but it comes as a surprise to most of us.

6. Actually, as important as the supervision is, the point is to supervise with kindness and firmness at the same time. This requires follow-through. If

you don't want your child to touch something, *get up* and kindly and firmly remove her from what she can't touch and show her what she can touch. (This is also called *redirection*.) And, it must be done over and over. I know you are already doing this, but I'm not sure you understand the over and over part and that you keep your mouth shut and have a firm but friendly attitude.

> **D**on't expect a toddler to pick anything up unless you make it a game and do it with her. Even then, it will work only sometimes.

7. Don't be disappointed in yourself. I can tell you are doing an excellent job. All mothers of toddlers are exhausted, and all lose it at times. At least you are using this as an opportunity to learn, and mistakes are wonderful opportunities to learn. So make lots of them, and keep learning.

I know you have heard this repeatedly, and it is true. She will grow up so soon. It doesn't seem like that will ever happen when you are exhausted from the constant demands of a toddler, but it will happen. Patience, understanding age-appropriateness, and a few good parenting skills will make the journey smoother and much more pleasant.

Adapt Other Parenting Tools for Toddlers

AS WE PRESENT more parenting tools in the next chapters, you now have a basis to adapt them to the developmental level of your younger children or to know when the tools are too advanced.

You may want to read chapter 5 again for many other parenting tools that are effective with children under the age of four, such as choices that include the phrase, "You decide." You will want to do everything you can to help your children develop the belief, "I am capable," by taking time for training and avoiding pampering. You can use what and how questions as described in chapter 6 to help small children develop their thinking and problem-solving skills, so long as you know that their understanding will be at a very different level than that of older children.

For example, with a child who is having trouble getting his pants off, you could ask, "What would happen if you took your shoes off first?" This is much different than saying, "Take your shoes off first." The latter is a command that invites resistance. The former is a question that invites thinking, even though the question contains lots of clues.

This is a time of life when your child's personality is being formed, and you want him or her to make decisions that say, "I am competent. I can try, make mistakes, and learn. I am loved. I am a good person." Using discipline that is age appropriate, kind, and firm at the same time provides the foundation for the development of good character, which we discuss in the next chapter.

Quick and Quality Parenting Tips

Resistance to Toilet Training

Toilet training is like a roller coaster with my two-year-old. I know he can do it, because sometimes he uses the toilet and acts very proud of himself. Other times he simply refuses.

Working Parents' Common Mistakes

1. Thinking toilet training would be easier if they didn't work.

2. Thinking it is possible to "toilet train" children. (The truth is that adults train themselves, not their children.)

3. Being overly concerned about toilet training. (Most children use your overconcern as a way to seek undue attention or misguided power.)

Discouraging Words and Actions

1. "I'll give you some M&Ms if you'll use the potty." (Any kind of bribery or reward may have temporary results, but not lasting results other than teaching manipulation.)

2. "Do you need to go now? Do you need to go now? Do you need to go now? (This is giving the child too much undue attention.) (See number 3 below.)

3. Adding any kind of blame, shame, or disappointment when there are accidents.

Respectful and Encouraging Actions

1. Go ahead and engage in toilet training so long as you understand that you are the one being trained. (Most children reach an age when they want to do what "big" people do unless the issue has turned into a power struggle or a way to get undue attention.)

2. If possible, find a child care center or home where there are small toilets (or a potty chair for each child) and they all use the toilets during scheduled times. Provide several changes of clothing for accidents. Children become potty trained quicker when there is no pressure to do so.

3. If you want your child to be out of diapers, decide on a schedule for taking him to the toilet and keep your mouth shut while kindly and firmly taking him. Train yourself.

4. Because you are probably starting toilet training too soon, be responsible, with a kindly manner, for changing your child when he has accidents. (After your child reaches the age of three, and still hasn't displayed an interest in using the toilet consistently, teach him how to change his own clothes and put his soiled clothing in a special hamper. Let him help with the wash by dumping the soap in the washing machine and pushing the buttons.)

5. Become unconcerned about toilet training and have faith that it will happen before your child goes to college.

Respectful and Encouraging Words

1. "Let me know when you are ready to use the toilet."

2. "I have faith in you to handle the toilet when you are ready."

3. "Let me know if I need to pack diapers when you are ready to go to college." (This is a joke to give you perspective.)

Encouraging Attitudes

1. Accepting that children truly are unique and may not be ready to use the toilet on the same schedule as other children.

2. Understanding that children will train themselves when they are ready.

3. Understanding that just because a child is excited about using the toilet sometimes doesn't mean he has the emotional and social maturity to care about it all the time—until he does.

8

Good Character Education at Home

Lack of Life Skill Training vs. Life Skill Training for Good Character

IMAGINE YOUR CHILD is now eighteen years old and ready to leave your nest. What qualities, characteristics, and life skills do you hope your child has developed? What qualities, characteristics, and life skills will cause employers to put your child at the top of their list? What qualities, characteristics, and life skills will significantly increase the chances that your child will have a successful marriage and be a great parent? In other words, what kind of character do you hope your child has developed?

During our workshops, parents brainstorm a list of characteristics they believe will help their children become happy, contributing, successful members of society. No matter where we go in the world, the lists are very similar.

- Respect for self and others
- Honesty
- Integrity
- Enthusiasm for learning
- Hard working
- Self-discipline
- Problem-solving skills
- Responsibility
- Cooperation
- Communication skills
- Sense of humor
- Accountability
- Positive attitude
- Courage
- Resiliency
- Desire to contribute to the welfare of others and the community

Does this list represent the kind of character you would like your children to develop? If so, it helps to be aware of the experiences that develop good character.

Good Character Develops from Challenging Experiences

FIRST, LET'S SUMMARIZE the things we have already discussed that *don't* help children develop the social and life skills necessary for good character: lectures, scolding, punishment, lack of training, lack of practice, lack of encouragement, pampering, rescuing, and the lack of opportunities to make mistakes in a nonthreatening environment. Instead, character is learned and developed through experiences that allow children to practice developing the social and life skills for good character. The four criteria for effective discipline (page 89 in chapter 6) are designed to help children develop character.

Character is something every parent wants for their children; they recognize its importance to their future happiness and success. But when working parents feel guilty and compensate by doing too much for their children, character assassination is the result. Instead of developing the social and life skills required for good character, these children often develop traits such as self-centeredness, selfishness, and rebelliousness. They may develop a victim mentality and become demanding, dissatisfied, weak, and otherwise unattractive and ineffective.

Sometimes, character grows from the experiences we enjoy the least and from what we learn and decide about those experiences. Some famous people—people of great character—have spoken on the issue of how their character was developed. Here is a sampling of their wisdom.

The ultimate measure of a man is not where he stands in moments of comfort, but where he stands at times of challenge and controversy.

—MARTIN LUTHER KING, JR.

How can children develop character if they are protected from challenges and controversy? Instead they need to be encouraged to develop skills to deal with those challenges.

Our character is what we do when we think no one is looking.

—H. JACKSON BROWNE

Excessive control, punishment, or pampering often create an "external locus of control" in children. That is, children look outside themselves to find reasons and rewards for their actions. People with character have a strong *internal* locus of control—they choose an action because they know it is the right thing to do.

Nearly all men can stand adversity, but if you want to test a man's character, give him power.

—ABRAHAM LINCOLN

Will your children use their personal power in useful ways—to improve themselves and make a contribution to the world—or will they use it to hurt themselves and others? To which end are they being trained?

Character cannot be developed in ease and quiet. Only through experience of trial and suffering can the soul be strengthened, ambition inspired, and success achieved.

—HELEN KELLER

Helen Keller's parents were raising a spoiled brat until Annie Sullivan came into her life and cared enough to insist that she learn to be capable in spite of her physical challenges. And, Helen did not like it one bit—until she was older and appreciated the gift Annie Sullivan had given her with intense gratitude.

Children Are Not Born with Character

CHILDREN ARE BORN with temperaments and personality traits, but they are not born with character. Character must be taught and learned through experiences and practice. Lectures about being respectful, fair, responsible, and helpful just don't work. Lectures only "teach" defensiveness, avoidance, and possibly low self-esteem. The most likely result for children who have to endure shaming lectures are feelings of inadequacy, rebelliousness, or just plain boredom. In fact, children usually learn to tune out lecturing adults after about ten words!

> Too often, parents try to teach by stuffing in their wisdom through long lectures, and then wonder why it goes in and out.

Education comes from the Latin word *educarè*, which means "to draw forth." Adults can "draw forth" from their children by creating opportunities for them to learn from their own experiences as they discover for themselves how it feels to focus on solutions or to give service to others. Too often, parents try to teach their children by "stuffing in" their wisdom through long lectures. Then they wonder why it goes in and out.

Before pursuing the development of good character any further, it is important to restate the basic needs of children. We know what we want for them, but what are their basic needs?

1. A sense of belonging (connection) and significance.
2. Perceptions of capability.
3. Personal power and autonomy.
4. Social and life skills for good character.

These needs are the foundation for the development of character.

A Sense of Belonging (Connection) and Significance

ASK A GROUP of parents what they believe to be most important in raising healthy, happy children, and many will give you a simple answer: love. But love by itself is not enough. In fact, many parenting mistakes are made in the name of love. There are many definitions of *love,* and some of those definitions don't help children feel belonging and significance or learn the attitudes and skills they will need to live successful, happy lives.

Alfred Adler taught about the greatest core need human beings have—*to belong*—to have a place in the world that is ours alone, a place where we can be accepted and where we can believe in our own value and significance. If we were to condense into a few words all the complicated beliefs and attitudes that children need to grow into competent, confident adults, those words would be "a sense of belonging and significance."

All of us want to belong somewhere, to be accepted for who and what we are, and to be loved unconditionally. For children, the need to belong is even more powerful. Each child needs to know that there is a place in his family just for him, where he fits and is accepted unconditionally. As children grow, their peers often provide that sense of belonging. (If you doubt it, spend an hour or two in the halls of any middle school. Why do you suppose it matters to children what logo adorns their clothing, which athletic shoes they wear, or how their hair is styled?) The more self-confidence and skills they have, the less likely they are to be overly influenced by "the crowd."

> All of us want to belong somewhere, to be accepted for who and what we are, and to be loved unconditionally.

Children who don't believe they belong become discouraged, and discouraged children often misbehave, sometimes with violence.

Violence in Schools

Everyone is concerned about the violence that has taken place in our schools over the past few years. These horrifying incidents are a wake-up call for the great need to make serious changes in our homes and schools. Kids who are killing other kids and adults certainly do not feel belonging and significance. When kids do not feel a sense of belonging and significance, they usually choose one of four mistaken goals of behavior to compensate. They seek undue attention, misguided power, revenge, or they withdraw into assumed inadequacy. Students who engage in violence have chosen the most terrible kind of revenge.

Even the FBI has joined the search to find out what is at the root of the violence in schools today. They interviewed the young men who have committed these crimes and found that the core problem was their sense of rejection in the world—the antithesis of belonging. Not only did these young men believe that they didn't belong (that no one cared), but they also said that they were teased and bullied. They felt and eventually began to act like outcasts and aliens among their peers, which fueled the flames that led to revenge. This extreme example shows the power of the basic need to belong.

Fostering a Sense of Belonging (Connection) and Significance

Too many working parents try to help their children feel a sense of belonging and significance in ways that create just the opposite feeling. Children don't feel a sense of belonging and significance when parents coddle or control. Instead these children usually develop the belief, "I belong only when you do things for me, or give me constant attention, or rescue me, or order me around." Rather than helping children develop confidence in their own abilities and a sense of belonging that comes from within, working parents may foster dependence on others or rebellion.

One way that your family can create a sense of belonging and connection—and have a great time—is by creating family mottoes. All families have mottoes, although most are unwritten and unacknowledged. Mottoes can be positive and encouraging, or negative and discouraging. One woman in a workshop laughed and told the group that the motto in the family she grew up in was "Knock yourself out—and it still won't be good enough unless it's perfect." A recovering perfectionist in her 40s, this woman shared that her family's motto (and the decisions she and her siblings made about themselves as a result) was extremely powerful—especially because it remained unspoken.

What was the motto in the family you grew up in? What do you suppose the motto is in the family you have created? What beliefs do you want your children to adopt? Several examples of encouraging family mottoes are included here. You may want to use some of these and/or create your own:

1. One for all and all for one.
2. We love and support each other.
3. Anything worth doing is worth doing for the fun of it.
4. If it helps just one person, it is worth doing.
5. Mistakes are wonderful opportunities to learn.
6. We are good finders. (We focus on the positive and minimize the negative.)
7. We are problem solvers.
8. We look for solutions rather than blame.
9. We have an attitude of gratitude.
10. We count our blessings every day.
11. We work hard and play hard.

Your family might want to choose a different motto every month and do some activities together as a family that month that express the motto.

> All families have mottoes, although most are unwritten, unspoken and unacknowledged.

There are many other ways of creating a sense of belonging (or connection) for children; we have already explored the weaning process from pampering and many other tools. You will discover more tools in the chapters ahead. For the moment, consider that the greater your child's sense of belonging and significance, the less often she will need to resort to misbehavior and the more confidence and self-discipline she will have. Helping children develop a healthy sense of belonging and significance is the cornerstone of healthy love.

Perceptions of Capability

HOW CAN CHILDREN develop the belief that they are capable if they are not allowed to experience their capability? Many parents and teachers are

robbing children of opportunities to develop this important belief by doing too much for them and by trying to grant their every desire. There is a huge difference between what children need and what they want. Children always love special service (want parents to go beyond what is reasonable to meet their needs). But giving special service robs them of the opportunity to learn they are capable of helping themselves. Children want every toy they see. But granting them this desire teaches them materialism and robs them from learning they can handle disappointment or that they can work for what they want. Simply put, the more parents do *for* children, the less capable and motivated those children seem to feel. Merely *telling* children that they are capable doesn't work. Words alone are not powerful enough to build a sense of capability and competence in children. That perception can only come from experience.

Capability and Self-Esteem

Let's return for a moment to the subject of school violence. Many experts have focused on self-esteem—how children perceive their own worth and capability—as a cause of aggression. But is it *low* self-esteem that creates problems or self-esteem that is too *high?* In 1998, the American Psychological Association sponsored a study that unearthed an interesting fact. The young people most prone to aggression were those who had an excessive need to demonstrate their superiority, a trait sometimes called *narcissism.* When others didn't find these youngsters special or failed to praise them sufficiently, they were likely to react with anger or violence. Children who are pampered are falsely empowered by their parents, and this false empowerment leads to a profound sense of superiority and often aggression. Underneath their air of superiority these children actually feel very incapable. Conversely, children who are overly controlled and shamed feel completely disempowered, and they withdraw into feelings of inadequacy.

True self-esteem grows from perceptions of capability, from the skills and attitudes that allow children to learn that they are competent people. Parents help children develop perceptions of capability by teaching skills and expecting and accepting mistakes along the way.

Capability and Mistakes

Many parents (and many other adults) regard mistakes as catastrophes, experiences that must be eliminated. The typical response of many parents to their children's inevitable mistakes is to punish, rescue, or attempt to prevent the mistake from happening at all. Others believe they are letting their children "get away with something" if they don't at least impose a consequence. Perhaps the best way to respond to a mistake (and who hasn't made one or two in the process of growing up or learning a new skill?) is to kindly and firmly invite them to clean up the mess, whatever it is, and then to kindly and firmly help them learn how to avoid making that particular mess again through what and how questions (explained following).

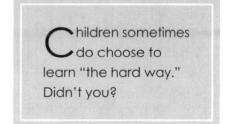

Children sometimes do choose to learn "the hard way." Didn't you?

Mark Twain once said, "Good judgment comes from experience. Experience comes from bad judgment." Children sometimes do choose to learn "the hard way." Didn't you?

Punishing for mistakes or rescuing children from ever making them will not help children develop perceptions of capability. Instead, teach your children that *mistakes are actually wonderful opportunities to learn.*

Capability and Consequences

Instead of *imposing* a consequence, which is usually an ineffective way to disguise punishment, parents can help children explore for themselves the consequences of their choices. This can be done through the respectful use of what and how questions (see page 100 in chapter 6 for more on these curiosity questions).

What happened?

What were you trying to accomplish?

How do you feel about what happened?

What did you learn from this experience?

How could you use what you learned in the future?

What ideas do you have to solve this problem now?

Remember, the point is to help children explore the consequences of their actions. This purpose is voided if you use a sarcastic tone of voice or if you are trying to get them to think what you think. They will know the difference. It is interesting that if you are sincerely curious in your questioning, your children often will end up with conclusions similar to yours. When children feel truly listened to and can see that you really do care what they think, they have the opportunity to *explore* the consequences of their choices by thinking it through, which also helps them become acquainted with positive uses for their personal power.

Personal Power and Autonomy

PARENTS MAY NOT like it, but the fact remains that children *do* have personal power and they will use it. The only question is *how* will they use that power? Will they use it in constructive or destructive ways? Will they engage in power struggles, or will they use their power for personal growth, social interest, cooperation, and contribution?

Working parents may love in permissive ways that teach children to use their personal power to manipulate. Others use exhaustion as an excuse to give controlling orders that invite their children to use their personal power for rebellion—or, worse, compliance. (Overly compliant children run the risk of becoming "people pleasers," putting them at the mercy of those who are stronger or more dominant than they are.)

Are you providing enough opportunities in your home for your children to use their power in constructive ways? Are you giving your children choices? (Limited choices for young children, and broader choices as they grow older.) Are you having family meetings (described in the next chapter) where children are respectfully involved in brainstorming for solutions and in creating limits and routines? Do you provide training in problem solving and then have faith in your children to solve their own problems (or to learn from the results of their occasional failures)? Are you providing opportunities for them to use their power to help others? Are you teaching them decision-making and problem-solving skills by involving them and providing them with opportunities to practice these skills? All of these skills will help your children develop good character that can lead to personal, social, and monetary success.

> Overly compliant children run the risk of becoming "people pleasers," putting them at the mercy of those who are stronger or more dominant than they are.

Personal and Monetary Success

Providing opportunities for children to develop good character is one of the best ways to help them achieve personal and monetary success. Dr. Thomas J. Stanley made some interesting discoveries when he interviewed "millionaires next door."[1] We certainly are not saying that acquiring lots of money is necessary to be a successful person. Yet it is interesting to examine the background and choices of people who have achieved a high level of the qualities society labels as "success." In fact, most of the millionaires interviewed by Stanley were also happy, contributing members of society who did not spend their considerable wealth in the flashy and self-serving ways you might expect (from examples of Enron and other scandalous executives). (Money is neutral; it can be used in positive and negative ways.)

Interestingly enough, high academic performance was not an important factor in predicting these millionaires' achievements. In fact, most of them were not scholars. Many had been told they were not intellectually gifted and

---

1. Thomas J. Stanley, *The Millionaire Next Door,* reprint edition (New York, NY: Pocket Books, 1998).

that they were not smart enough to succeed. What they *did* learn (but not from textbooks) was tenacity, the ability to get along with people, self-discipline, and discernment.[2] The five factors most significant to these millionaires' economic success are as follows:

1. Integrity—being honest with all people. (Character)

2. Discipline—applying self-control. (Capability)

3. Social skills—getting along with people. (Connection)

4. Having a supportive partner. (Intimacy)

5. Hard work—doing the things most people are unwilling to do. (Self-discipline)[3]

Obviously, school is important. But many parents spend a tremendous amount of time nagging their children about doing their homework and getting good grades. Sometimes the power struggles over schoolwork become so constant and ugly that the entire relationship is sacrificed. What is important is to create opportunities for children to develop integrity, self-discipline, social skills, and the ability to work hard to earn whatever they get. Most of the millionaires in Stanley's survey went to school and applied self-discipline to work hard. But that is the difference—*self*-discipline and hard work rather than too much external control from parents (the opposite of self-control) or rescuing from parents (the opposite of hard work).

> Sometimes the power struggles over schoolwork become so constant and ugly that the entire relationship is sacrificed.

Working parents can help their children develop self-discipline by involving them in the creation of plans and routines that work for the child, and then using what and how questions to help them explore the consequences of their own mistakes. Sometimes the best lesson children can experience is failure. What a great opportunity for them to explore what happened, what caused it to happen, how they feel about it, and what they want to do about it. (In fact, children are as-

---

2. Thomas J. Stanley, *The Millionaire Next Door,* reprint edition (New York, NY: Pocket Books, 1998).

3. Ibid., 11.

tonishingly resilient and are well equipped to learn from failure; it is parents who struggle with the concept!)

Personal Power and Money Management

TEACHING MONEY MANAGEMENT is an essential part of developing good character. In today's society it is too easy to become materialistic and become more focused on "getting" than on giving and receiving. Following is an excerpt from the book, *Positive Discipline A-Z,*[4] which illustrates how the issue of allowances can be used to teach money management and valuable life skills at the same time.

Allowances

Should I give my children allowances for doing their chores?

Understanding Your Child, Yourself, and the Situation

Allowances give children an opportunity to learn many valuable lessons about money. The amount given depends on your budget. If the money is used for punishment or reward, the lessons will be negative. This creates an arena for power struggles, revenge, and manipulation. The lessons are positive when children are allowed to have allowances so they can learn life skills. Chores are a separate issue and should not be connected to an allowance.

Suggestions

1. Do not rescue your children when they run out of money. Learn to say no with dignity and respect when they try to con you into rescuing them after they make mistakes with their money.

2. Be empathetic without trying to fix things. You might say, "I'm sure you feel disappointed that you don't have enough money left to go to the game."

3. Offer your services as a budgeting consultant, but do not give advice unless asked.

---

4. Jane Nelsen, Lynn Lott, H. Stephen Glenn (Roseville, CA: Prima Publishing, 1999, pages 40–44).

4. Help them explore what happened, what caused it to happen, what they learned from it, and how they will use this information in the future. This is effective only if they agree to explore and only if you are truly curious about the perceptions of your children. It is not effective to try disguising a lecture in the name of exploration.

5. It is okay to be reasonable and flexible. When children run out of money, offer them a loan and discuss the terms of how they will pay it back. (This is not the same as rescuing.) Show them how to set up a payment plan and agree together on an amount you can deduct from their allowance. Do not make the amount so high your child won't be able to manage during the week. Another possibility is to make a list of special jobs to earn money for extra items or to help pay back their loan. Don't make new loans until the first loan is repaid.

Planning Ahead to Prevent Future Problems

1. During family meetings, have periodic discussions about money where you share some of your mistakes with money and what you learned (without lecturing or moralizing). Allow others to do the same. Create a sense of fun so everyone can laugh while they learn.

2. For ages two to four, give children ten pennies, a nickel, a dime, and a piggy bank. For each year, add a few more pennies, nickels, dimes, and even quarters. They like putting money in the piggy bank and are starting a saving habit before they know it.

3. For ages four to six, take your child and the piggy bank to a big bank and open a savings account. Every one to three months, take your child to the bank to make a deposit. It can be fun to watch the balance grow in the bank book. Parents might even get excited about developing the saving habit themselves, if they haven't already done so.

4. At these ages, you might want to suggest two piggy banks: one for the savings account and one to save for items on a wish list.

5. Help your children start a wish list of things they would like to save money for. Whenever you are shopping and they say, "Can I have this?" You

can say, "Would you like to add this to your wish list and save your money for it?" (It is seldom that they want the item enough to save their money for it, but they want it enough for you to spend your money right now.) You can even offer to pay half if they will save half. It is amazing how many shopping hassles this stops when you are kind and firm in your offer.

6. For ages six to fourteen, schedule a planning session with your child for you to decide together how much money he needs and how it should be allocated for savings, weekly needs such as lunches, and fun. You might also encourage your child to save money to give to community organizations and those in need.

7. Set up guidelines, such as allowances will be given only once a week during family-meeting time. If you run out before then, you have an opportunity to learn what that feels like and what to do about it, such as go without or find a job to earn extra money.

8. Set up periodic times (once a year or every six months) when an allowance can be raised based on a child's thoughtful presentation of greater need. Some families raise the allowance of all the children on every child's birthday.

9. For ages fourteen to eighteen, add a clothing allowance so teenagers can learn how to plan. (Children who learn to handle money from an early age can handle a clothing allowance much sooner. In the beginning, instead of giving them money, tell them the total amount they can spend on clothing, and then deduct their purchases from a running total that you keep.) They quickly find out that if they spend too much on a few items of clothing, they don't have enough left for an adequate wardrobe. The clothing allowance can be given monthly, quarterly, or twice a year.

Life Skills Children Can Learn

Children can learn that they can develop their judgment skills by making good or poor decisions about money and learning from the consequences of their choices without punishment or humiliation. They can learn to budget, a skill they'll use all their lives.

Parenting Pointers

1. Using money for punishment or reward is a short-term solution. Giving allowances as an opportunity to teach children about money is long-range parenting that leaves children with life skills.

2. Keeping long-range parenting goals in mind, it is best to be kind and firm at the same time.

Booster Thought No. 1

One father says, When my daughter rushes up to me and says, "Dad, I need some designer jeans," I have learned to say, "Listen, kiddo, I got into this business to cover your body, not decorate it, and I can do that for $25 to $30 at many department stores. What you need is modesty and what you want is style. The difference will require some contribution on your part because I have a lot of other pressures and issues concerning finances to deal with."

There was a time in America when children wore jeans because parents were poor—now parents are poor because children wear jeans![5]

Booster Thought No. 2

The father of a six-year-old noticed that money was missing from his wallet and dresser top. His six-year-old brought in a container filled with money and said she found it. The father was very upset and wondered why his daughter would be stealing from him.

Upon further discussion, it was discovered that the parents told their daughter she could get a new bicycle when she earned $30 toward the purchase. Her weekly allowance was fifty cents, and it didn't take her long to figure out that she would have to wait forever for the bike. Using her ingenuity, she figured out a way to get the bike quicker.

Not wanting to start their six-year-old on a life of crime, the parents decided to raise her allowance to $2 a week. They told her that if she put half of her allowance away each week for the bike, they would match it. Then they sat down with a calendar and showed her how long it would take to save $30.

5. H. Stephen Glenn and Jane Nelsen, *Raising Self-Reliant Children in a Self Indulgent World,* 2nd edition (Roseville, CA, Prima Publishing, 2000).

They said that if she didn't want to wait that long, she could do special jobs for pay, which they posted on a list in the kitchen. Within a month, their industrious child had saved the $30 and the stealing never occurred again.

Social and Life Skills for Good Character

SOCIAL SKILLS, WHICH involve compassion, respect, empathy, communication, and old-fashioned good manners, appear third on Stanley's list. Most employees are fired because they lack good social skills, not because of a deficit in technical or intellectual skill. Social skills are among the most important skills children can learn, especially when those skills are used to contribute to society. What good are all the academic skills in the world if those skills are used in self-serving or hurtful ways? What good is self-discipline and hard work, if it is used only in destructive ways? Everyone benefits when children learn to treat others with dignity and respect. Children best learn social skills by watching your behaviors with your spouse, with your friends, and with them. Are you pleased with what you are teaching them? Are you teaching them to communicate directly with tact and respect? Are you teaching them to negotiate win-wins? What you do is what they will do. What you say has meaning only if you do what you say.

A few years ago, the newspaper *USA Today* introduced "All USA High School Academic Teams."[6] Each one of the amazing teens on the teams had initiated a project designed to contribute to society. Following is a list of some of their projects:

- Tutor disadvantaged children
- Tutor at public housing projects
- Tutor for Upward Bound
- Musical performances in nursing and convalescent homes
- Creator of a music stimulation program for Alzheimer's patients

6. "All USA High School Academic Teams," *USA Today*, 11 May 2000.

- Founder of "Read and Lead Foundation," a literacy mentoring program that expanded internationally
- Founder of America Online tutoring club
- Habitat for Humanity volunteer
- Hospital volunteer

The wonderful quality that these teens possess can be summed up in the word *Gemeinschaftsgefuhl,* a term coined by Adler when he wrote about the qualities healthy people possess. "Social interest" comes close to describing what it means: a feeling of community, a concern for one's fellow people, for the environment, and everything that is required for quality of life and relationships. It also implies the actions necessary to live a charactered life for one's self and for humanity. Social interest is the polar opposite of self-centeredness—one of the traits so frequently bemoaned in today's young people.

If our children develop the character required for *Gemeinschaftsgefühl,* just think what our families, neighborhoods, schools, communities, and world could become. It will be a challenge, but it is a challenge all parents must dare to accept.

As your awareness increases, you will find daily opportunities to use parenting skills that help your children develop social and life skills for good character—and to make a contribution to society.

Family Meetings Build Character

WHEN CHILDREN ARE respectfully involved in the creation of solutions to family concerns and problems, they take ownership. They have enthusiasm and motivation to follow rules and guidelines they helped create—at least for a while (more about this in chapter 9). When children are respectfully involved, they have many opportunities to develop the beliefs that they belong and are significant, that they are capable, that they can use their power and autonomy in constructive ways, and that they can develop the social and life skills for character that will lead them to become happy, contributing members of society.

Weekly family meetings are a way to involve children in creating solutions. They are the training ground on which children can learn the skills needed for

good character. Because family meetings are such an effective and important tool, we devote the next chapter to them.

Quick and Quality Parenting Tips

Strong-willed Child (and Parent)

Our child is very strong willed. He wants what we wants, now, *and he usually refuses to do what we want. We know we are too controlling, but after working all day, it is difficult to have patience; so we give orders and ultimately resort to punishment. How can we work all day and still be good parents?*

Working Parents' Common Mistakes

    1. Thinking it takes more time to use kind and firm parenting skills than it takes to give orders and use punishment. (Actually, the latter is simply a matter of habit and/or lack of skills. Kind and firm parenting takes less time, is less stressful, and is more respectful.)

    2. Thinking a strong-willed child is too challenging. (A weak-willed child would be more challenging.)

Discouraging Words and Actions

1. A power struggle takes at least two people. Be the first one to stop choosing power struggles. Choose instead to engage the child in cooperation.

2. Being strong willed yourself gives your child the very model of behavior you want him to stop.

Respectful and Encouraging Actions

1. Schedule regular family meetings: a great way to allow your child to use all his intelligence for problem solving. You may be surprised at how many of your problems will be solved when you get him involved in finding solutions.

2. Create routine charts (see page 74) with your child so he can learn to "plan in advance," and feel respectfully involved in the planning process. He will enjoy following a routine chart that he has helped create—one that has pictures of him doing his routine tasks.

3. Set up a positive time-out area for yourself where you can go every time you are tempted to be too controlling or punitive or to talk too much. Let him know in advance what you are doing, and that you will talk about the problem with him after you have calmed down and are feeling better.

4. Let him have his feelings. When he doesn't get his way, don't try to rescue him from feeling disappointed. My guess is that he won't be so revengeful when he is treated kindly and firmly at the same time. However, let him know, in advance, that if he gets angry and hurtful when he doesn't get his way you will go to your special place to respect yourself until he is ready to treat you respectfully. Later, you can ask him if we would like his own positive time-out area—because people do better when they feel better.

Respectful and Encouraging Words

1. Validate his feelings. "I can see that this is very upsetting. I would be upset too." But, don't rescue.

2. Set up "special time" with him for fifteen minutes a day at the same time. Several times a day say, "I'm looking forward to our 'special time' at 6:45 tonight." This can be very effective when he is demanding attention right now. You can say, "Not now, but I'm looking forward to our special time."

Encouraging Attitudes

1. Remember that mistakes are wonderful opportunities to learn. Since you are human, you will still make mistakes. When you accept this for yourself, you will accept it for your son. You and your child will also have an opportunity to stretch your character muscles.

2. Adopt an attitude of respect in all your interactions with your child. Adults treat children disrespectfully and then act surprised when children "learn what they live."

9

Family Meetings
for Organizing *with*
Your Children

Disorganization vs. Organization
with Your Children

Stress, disorganization, frustration, and anger—are these part of your morning routine? Getting sleepy, uncooperative children out the door on time in the morning can try any parent's patience, but is especially difficult when both parents have to get out the door and off to work themselves. Why is it that these same sleepy-eyed children are wide awake and full of energy after you've put in a full day's work and it's now time for bed?

Working parents often try to do "everything" for their children for unhealthy reasons such as guilt. But doing too much for children is a double-edged sword. While trying to "make up" for the deprivation many working parents believe their children feel, they create personal stress and feel overwhelmed and resentful toward their children and parenthood in general.

Have you ever muttered, "There's got to be a better way?" Well, there is. Picture this: Your children wake up on their own, get dressed by themselves, take turns fixing breakfast (including yours), get the lunches (that they fixed the night before) from the fridge, pick up their homework and gym clothes (from the place where they had them all laid out the night before), and give you a kiss as they leave for school—with time to spare. Sound like a *Leave It to Beaver* episode? This could be your home or very close to it.

> Family meetings . . . provide experiences for children to feel capable instead of pampered and to have all of their basic needs . . . met.

We aren't promising that you will never have morning hassles (or bedtime hassles), but we are promising that you can significantly reduce stress, power struggles, and chaos. In this chapter we focus on family meetings to help you find that "better way" through involving your children (four years of age and older) in creating an organized home. Family meetings also provide experiences for children to feel capable instead of pampered and to have all of their basic needs (page 128 in chapter 8) met.

Do's and Don'ts of Family Meetings

REGULAR FAMILY MEETINGS are a way to nurture a healthier and more positive home environment. It is extremely important to have family meetings on a weekly basis at a specified time. It is easy for the demands of our busy lifestyles to intrude on family time. Children need to know that they are as important as any business or social meeting their parents may schedule.

Before learning the family meeting format, it is helpful to be aware of the do's and don'ts for successful family meetings.

Do:

1. Remember the long-range purpose: to develop perceptions of connection (belonging, significance, and capability); to exercise power positively and allow everyone to be accountable; and to teach valuable social and life skills for good character such as communication, problem solving, decision making, and cooperation.

2. Post an agenda in a visible place and encourage family members to write problems on it—or anything that needs to be discussed by the family—as they occur.

3. Keep a family meeting notebook where you can record compliments, items that have been discussed, brainstorm ideas, and suggested solutions (circling the one that is chosen). Later you will have as much fun

looking at your old family meeting notebooks as you have when look-ing at family photo albums.

4. Rotate the jobs of chairperson and recorder. Of course, children who haven't learned to write can't be the recorder, but even a four-year-old can be a chairperson who calls on people to give their compliments, asks for an evaluation of past solutions, asks someone to read the next item on the agenda, etc. She may need help when something needs to be read and reminders of what is next, but she will feel a strong sense of belonging, significance, and capability when taking her turn as the family meeting chairperson.

5. Start with compliments to create a positive atmosphere from the be-ginning and to teach family members to look for and verbalize posi-tive things about each other. Compliments also serve to elevate the sense of belonging in the whole family, which guarantees more coop-eration and better behavior.

6. Focus on finding solutions, not on who is to blame, and teach that mistakes are wonderful opportunities to learn.

7. Brainstorm for solutions to problems. Start with wild and crazy ideas (for fun) and end with practical ideas that are useful and respectful to all concerned. Then choose by consensus one suggestion, circle it, and try it for a week.

8. Use the calendar to schedule a family fun activity for later in the week. Also write on the calendar all sports and other activities. Include a chauffeur schedule.

9. Keep family meetings short, fifteen to thirty minutes, depending on the ages of your children. End with a fun family activity, game, or dessert.

Don't:
1. Use family meetings as a platform for lectures and parental control.
2. Allow children or parents to dominate and control. Mutual respect is the key.
3. Skip weekly family meetings. They should be the most important date on your calendar.

4. Forget that mistakes are wonderful opportunities to learn.

5. Forget that a family meeting is a process that teaches valuable social and life skills, not an exercise in perfection. Learning the skills takes time (for parents and for children). Even solutions that don't work provide an opportunity to go back to the drawing board and try again, always focusing on respect and solutions.

6. Expect children under the age of four to participate in the process. If younger children are too distracting, wait until they are in bed.

Now that you understand the basis for positive family meetings, we will explain each step of the family meeting format (see box below).

FORMAT FOR FAMILY MEETINGS

1. Compliments

2. Evaluation of past solutions

3. Agenda items where the family member who wrote the item can choose to:
   a. Simply share feelings
   b. Invite a discussion for awareness (without brainstorming for solutions)
   c. Brainstorm for solutions and circle the one everyone is willing to try for a week

4. Calendar time: scheduling (write on the calendar upcoming events, family fun, need for rides, etc.)

5. Weekly meal planning

6. Fun activity and dessert

Compliments

COMPLIMENTS ARE NOT easy in the beginning—to give or to receive. We are not born with the ability to give and receive compliments. It takes education and practice. (We have to wonder why it is so easy to engage in put-downs without education and practice.) Part of the education for learning to give and receive compliments is to overcome past notions that it is immodest to receive a compliment—as though it is not okay to acknowledge good things about yourself.

Gracious receiving is easy to teach—a simple, "Thank you." Children learn this more quickly than adults who are used to saying things such as, "Oh, it's nothing." Teaching children to give compliments is a bit more difficult if they are more familiar with giving and receiving criticism.

> We are not born with the ability to give and receive compliments. It takes education and practice.

When teaching how to give compliments, point out that only respectful comments are allowed. During her first family meeting, four-year-old Mary said about her brother, "Mark is nice to me sometimes, but other times . . ." Dad quickly interrupted and said, "Whoops, no 'buts.'"

The next thing to teach is the importance of complimenting family members for efforts, accomplishments, helpfulness, and contributions. In the beginning it is helpful to use the words, "I would like to compliment _____ for _____."

COMPLIMENTS EXERCISE

1. Place blank compliment sheets on the refrigerator (or another spot) where everyone can write down compliments for others each day. (Young children can dictate their compliments to older members of the family.) This could be a ritual that takes place just before dinner.

2. When you see someone who deserves a compliment, write it down. If a child observes something someone else did, ask, "Would you like to write that on our compliment sheet?" Once children develop the habit of noticing compliments, they won't need reminders.

3. At the beginning of each family meeting, family members can read their compliments.

4. Ask for any verbal compliments that were not written down.

5. Make sure every family member receives at least one compliment.

6. Place this compliment sheet in a folder, and place another blank sheet on the refrigerator to be filled out during the week. Reading the compliments (saved in a folder) many years later can be as fun as looking at old picture albums.

The exercise above will help children get used to the "compliment habit" by providing them with daily practice during the week and culminating at the weekly family meeting.

Finding the Good

In his book *In Search of Excellence,* management consultant Tom Peters says that successful people are "good finders."[1] By this, Peters means that people

---

1. Tom Peters, *In Search of Excellence* (New York: Warner, 1988).

focus on the good instead of the bad, and they look for good things. In other words, they are people who see the glass as half full instead of half empty. You can help your children become good finders and create a positive atmosphere in your family by learning to look for the good in one another and to verbalize positive comments. But please, don't expect perfection! Some sibling squabbling is normal. However, when children (and parents) learn to give and receive compliments, negative tension in the family is reduced considerably.

Even though compliments may feel awkward in the beginning, it isn't long before families become compliment pros. Knowing how to compliment has been shown to help children be more accepted and well liked by their peers.

Evaluation of Past Solutions

EVALUATING PAST SOLUTIONS need not take long, yet it is an important piece to help the family evaluate their progress. Read over the solutions that were circled (more about that later) from the last family meeting. The meeting chairperson can ask, "How did it work?" If it worked well, it is nice to hear about it. If it didn't go well, the chairperson can suggest it be put back on the agenda for more brainstorming when it comes up in chronological order.

Often, it is a good idea to table a problem for another week if the solution didn't work. It could be that the item is too hot, and more cooling-off time is needed before family members can find a workable solution.

Agenda Items

THE FAMILY MEETING agenda can help to calm down arguing family members while ensuring that their concerns will be heard. Suppose your children are fighting. You can ask, "Which one of you would be willing to put this problem on the agenda?" Often that is enough to distract them from the fight while they focus on who is going to put it on the agenda. (If they fight about who gets to put the problem on the agenda, let them flip a coin to take turns writing their version.)

> The family meeting agenda can help to calm down arguing family members while ensuring that their concerns will be heard.

Suppose you are upset because you come home and find dirty dishes left in the sink. Instead of giving a nasty lecture, you can put the problem on the agenda. This becomes very satisfying when you see it as an opportunity for learning, and spotting such opportunities is the natural outcome when your family is in the habit of focusing on solutions. One mother came home to a sink full of dirty dishes and yelled, "Who left their dirty dishes in the sink?" Trey was quick to ask, "Are you looking for blame, or are you looking for solutions?" What could Mom say (since she had taught that slogan in the last family meeting) except, "Thanks for reminding me." She then put the problem on the family meeting agenda.

When it came time to work on solutions, none of the three children would admit to leaving their dishes in the sink. Since they were not interested in blame anyway, but only solutions, they proceeded to brainstorm for a solution to "nobody's" dirty dishes in the sink. The children came up with a great solution. Each family member would take turns (according to an elaborate chart Trey volunteered to design) cleaning up nobody's dishes. Trey had fun making the chart, but it didn't get a lot of use because everyone began taking care of their own dirty dishes after the discussion.

Think of all the things you and other family members complain about. Instead of complaining, everyone can put his or her problems on the agenda. When it is time to discuss the problem the family member can decide whether to simply share his or her feelings, invite a discussion for awareness, or brainstorm for solutions.

Calendar Time: Scheduling

Chaos results when children tell par-ents at the last minute about rides they need or events they have to attend. Much of this can be eliminated.

CHAOS RESULTS WHEN children tell parents at the last minute about rides they need or events they have to attend. Much of this can be eliminated when calendar time is part of your weekly family meeting. Each person can learn to come to the meeting prepared to share the important events for the upcoming week. If schedules clash, alternatives can be found for rides or event coverage. This is an important way for family members to learn to respect their own needs and the needs of others.

SIX STEPS FOR BRAINSTORMING

1. Define the problem (avoiding blame). You might teach the following slogans:

    a. We're looking for solutions, not blame.

    b. What's the problem? What's the solution?

2. Encourage everyone to think of as many solutions as possible. The recorder should write every one down. It can be fun to throw in a few wild and crazy ideas. No analyzing at this time.

3. After writing down as many ideas as possible go over the list and let your children practice analyzing which ones are disrespectful or impractical. (Most of the wild and crazy ideas have to be eliminated at this time, as well as anything that could be disrespectful.)

4. Choose and circle a solution that works for everyone if the problem concerns the whole family. If one family member is asking for help with a personal problem, he or she can choose and circle the one that works best. Sometimes a problem has to be "tabled" until the next meeting if it concerns the whole family and they can't come to a consensus.

5. Agree to try the solution for a week. When the chosen solution has been circled, it is easy to look back in the family meeting notebook and find it.

6. Evaluate how it worked (or didn't) at the next family meeting.

Weekly Meal Planning

ONE OF THE biggest complaints we hear from working parents is the hassle caused by mealtimes. Often it isn't finding time to cook that is the problem, but *what* to cook and having the necessary ingredients available.

Wouldn't it be nice to think about meal planning only once a week, have all meals decided upon, and have all the ingredients available? Even better, wouldn't it be nice if you didn't have to be responsible for every meal, but instead on some nights could come home to dinner already cooking on the stove or in the Crock-Pot or oven?

Mealtime provides a terrific opportunity to teach the character traits of cooperation and contribution. Even small children can take a turn (with supervision and a little help) cooking a simple meal such as soup, toasted cheese sandwiches, a vegetable, and Jell-O.

Meal planning during family meetings can eliminate the disorganization and stress from lack of planning. And it can make your dream of occasionally having healthy, homemade meals ready when you arrive home a reality.

1. At the family meeting, use a copy of the family meal plan (see next page) to ask every family member to help plan the meals for the week. Each family member can be in charge of the evening meal for one day. (If you have only one child old enough to cook, you may each take two days a week and go out or eat leftovers the seventh day.) Take a few minutes during the family meeting to have each family member choose the day or days he or she will cook. The family member should fill in the blanks for the evening meal on the appropriate day, then pass the family meal plan to the next person so that he or she can fill in the blanks for the evening meal on his or her day.]

Family Meal Plan

	Cook	Main Dish	Vegetable	Salad	Dessert
Mon.					
Tues.					
Wed.					
Thurs.					
Fri.					
Sat.					

2. Bring magazines that contain recipes to the family meeting. Let children (and parents) choose new recipes they might want to try. (It can be fun to make a family cookbook by cutting out the recipes and pictures and putting them in a binder. Family members might first want to rate the recipes for taste and save only the ones that receive a high rating.)

3. Use 3 by 5 index cards for your favorite recipes. On the back of the cards, write all the ingredients needed from the store. (Save these cards in a labeled index box so they can be used over and over.)

4. On shopping day, invite the whole family to the grocery store. (Teenagers may opt to skip this.) Children who are old enough can take a basket and find all the ingredients listed on the back of one or two recipe cards. Depending on how many children you have, each child may take one card or more than one. Check to see if you also need any of the staple items such as sugar, salt, and flour that may be listed on the back of the cards, and make sure only one person picks up these items. Younger children can help an older sibling or parent find the ingredients from other recipe cards.

> It is amazing how much better children eat when they are respectfully included in the meal planning and cooking process.

Periodically, you and your children may enjoy adding to your favorite recipe binder and the 3 by 5 cards. It is amazing how much better children eat when they are respectfully included in the meal planning and cooking process. If children still complain about the cooking or the food choices of other family members, see the Quick and Quality Parenting Tips on Picky Eaters at the end of this chapter.

Fun Activity and Dessert

END EACH FAMILY meeting with a fun activity. This could be something as simple as playing "button, button, whose got the button" or "hide and seek" with smaller children, to board games or popcorn and a video with older children. Dessert can be served during or after the fun activity. The important thing is that you are having scheduled fun as a family. You are providing your children with traditions and feelings of family closeness that they will talk about with affection for years to come.

Chore Hassles

WE DON'T KNOW of a single family, working parents or not, who don't complain about "chore hassles." Parents make all kinds of mistakes that invite lack of cooperation and rebellion among the ranks. They leave lists of chores that they expect their children to do before they get home. Then they lecture and scold them when they don't comply. Sometimes parents punish them by withdrawing privileges or deducting money from allowances. They offer bribes, which may achieve compliance for a short time. However, none of these tactics are effective long-term strategies and they don't help children develop responsibility.

Family meetings provide a great forum for creating chore charts that involve the whole family. Chore charts are similar to the routine charts explained in chapter 5. Discussing and planning for chores at the family meeting may not be a cure-all, but it will be more effective long term than punitive measures, and it teaches responsibility, decision making, and problem solving.

One mother shared, "We created a chore chart during a family meeting and the kids did their chores for about a week. Then they reverted to their old, slothful habits." She was asked, "Have you found anything else that got them to do their chores for a whole week?" She admitted that she hadn't. It was suggested that she keep doing what worked. Even if she had to do it once a week, it was better than the daily nagging that didn't work.

Why is it that parents are willing to use punitive measures over and over—even when they don't work in the long term—but refuse methods that are effective in the short term (and, with persistence, long term)? Dreikurs often said, "The solution for democracy that doesn't work is more democracy." In other words, when it works for a while and then stops, go back to the drawing board and come up with more solutions that will work for a while.

Jane Nelsen shares that in her family they had what they called the "three-week chore-plan syndrome." The family would create a chore routine that the kids would follow enthusiastically for about a week. They would follow the plan *un*enthusiastically for another week. By the third week, there was wailing and gnashing of teeth over the chore plan. So, back on the agenda chores would go. They would come up with another plan that would follow a similar three-week pattern. Jane said, "This three-week syndrome feels a whole lot better than the daily battles I used to engage in."

Some of the chore routines created by the children were as follows:

1. Draw two chores for the week out of a jar.

2. Make a wheel of chores and put a spinner in the middle. Spin for two chores for the week.

3. Create a chore chart with two slots for each child (a "to do" slot and a "done" slot). Make a card set of chores to be done by each child. The card sets go in the "to do" slot until the child does the chore and then moves it to the "done" slot.

Children can be very creative when they are treated respectfully and allowed the opportunity. Ask your children, perhaps over and over, for their ideas on solving the problem of organizing and getting chores done. You will be pleasantly surprised if you keep at it and allow time for children to learn

and practice the skills of problem solving. They will feel good about themselves and their ability to contribute, and so will you.

Be sure to discuss in advance your family's policy of building each other up rather than tearing each other down as each of you find your way in doing chores. Both children and adults must be asked to refrain from criticism and instead offer solutions or suggestions for how the chore can be done more effectively. It is important to seek improvement, not perfection.

The Role of Gratitude

> Ask your children, perhaps over and over, for their ideas on solving the problem of organizing and getting chores done.

A SENSE OF gratitude in a family gives the home a positive and uplifting atmosphere. And good character requires an attitude of gratitude, which does not come naturally. Gratitude must be learned and is one of the traits that parents can model effectively for their children. Regular practice and sharing will help all of you develop an attitude of gratitude. Some families include sharing two or three things that they are grateful for as part of their bedtime routine. At one of your next family meetings, you might try the following.

1. At the end of each family meeting, pass out sheets of paper that are blank except for the phrase, "I am grateful for . . ." written at the top. (We call this a *gratitude page*.) Encourage family members to put the page in a place where they can access it easily and write down the things for which they are grateful.

2. Allow time during family meals for people to share the things for which they are grateful.

3. During each family meeting, collect the gratitude pages and place them in a folder. Some families enjoy reading their gratitude pages once a year as part of a Thanksgiving ritual.

This exercise plus others that will come up in the course of planning and conducting family meetings will create traditions that increase family closeness.

Quick and Quality Parenting Tips

Picky Eaters

I don't use working as an excuse for not having well-balanced meals for my children. However, one of my children refuses to eat well. I don't know how to make her eat well.

Working Parents' Common Mistakes

1. Thinking you have to do all the cooking to make up for working.

2. Thinking you are not a good parent if your children don't eat well.

3. Becoming too concerned about how much your children eat gives them a "weapon" to seek undue attention or misguided power.

Discouraging Words and Actions

1. Trying to force your children to eat, "You aren't leaving the table until you clean your plate!"

2. Lecturing or nagging about the importance of good nutrition.

3. Bringing unhealthy snack foods into the house.

4. Giving in and letting your children eat unhealthy foods because they won't eat healthy foods.

Respectful and Encouraging Actions

1. Involve children in meal planning and meal preparation. (See pages 155–157 in this chapter on Family Meetings). Children are usually less picky when they have had a voice in planning, and when they take turns with meal preparation.

2. Take your children to a book store or library and help them find a cook book for children with lots of pictures.

3. Realize that different children have different needs for food amounts. So long as your children aren't filling themselves with sugary snacks, and have plenty of healthy food available, don't worry about how much they eat.

4. Allow everyone to dish up their own food and scrape what they don't eat into the garbage.

5. Let children know they don't have to eat what they don't want to eat, and they can still stay at the table for a reasonable amount of time to "be with the family." (During a family meeting let the whole family agree on what a reasonable amount would be.)

6. Let your children help you prepare healthy snacks (pieces of fruit, cheese, vegetables, etc.) for a special "snack shelf" in the refrigerator. If your children don't eat enough during their meals, and then complain about being hungry, let them know they can help themselves to the snack shelf anytime they want.

7. Get your children involved in ideas for making mealtime a fun time where everyone sits down together and shares happy times (which is good for digestion).

Respectful and Encouraging Words

1. "If you have a problem with what others are cooking, put it on our family meeting agenda. I'm sure we can find solutions that will work for everyone."

2. "You don't have to eat anything you don't want. I have faith in you to honor your hunger needs. If you get hungry later, you can go to the healthy snack shelf."

3. "It is so nice to have you at our family table even if you don't feel like eating. We love your company."

4. "How could you state your preferences in a way that is respectful to you and to the people who cooked this meal?"

5. Simply validate your child's feelings without getting emotionally involved. "Sounds as though you strongly dislike what we have for dinner tonight."

Encouraging Attitudes

1. Act in ways you expect your children to act. In other words, act respectfully so your children will have a model of respect to follow—eventually.

2. Become unconcerned about your children's complaints and how much they eat. People who lived during the great depression did not experience eating problems with their children. When there wasn't enough to eat, it was great if someone didn't want food so there would be more for those who did.

10

The Long-Term Results
of Positive Discipline

Short-Sighted Fixes vs.
Long-Term Success

I T H A S B E E N said that children need both roots and wings to be prepared for successful living in today's world. Very simply, your children may not develop the roots they need for stability and the wings they need to soar if you don't think about the long-term effects of your parenting methods.

One of the biggest mistakes parents make is their failure to consider the long-range results of what they do. It is so important to determine what your children are *really* thinking, what they are feeling, and what they are deciding about themselves, their relationship with you, and about life itself and how to live it. What behavior will these thoughts, feelings, and decisions produce in your child's future?

In this chapter we include several parenting tools that are designed to work in the short term and the long term. By long term, we mean tools that will invite your children to make good decisions about themselves and others, and that encourage the development of social and life skills for good character. Let's start with the most popular (though misused) discipline tool today—time-out.

Positive Time-Out

PARENTING IN OUR hectic world can create a sense of urgency where it seems imperative to deal with each behavior, each crisis, and each problem *right away*. Children have an impressive knack for frustrating, challenging, and angering their parents, but angry and frustrated parents can't do their best work. Thus, parents frequently find themselves *re*acting—doing what seems to work for the moment—instead of *acting* thoughtfully. Many parents have decided they do not want to use physical punishment, and they think time-out is a good alternative. In chapter 6 we asked you to consider how you would feel if your spouse or employer banished you to "time-out" to think about what you did. We usually hear how angry and disrespected you would feel. Since punitive (blaming) time-out wouldn't be effective for you, doesn't it make sense that it wouldn't be effective (long term) for your children? However, there is a nonpunitive form of time-out that is respectful and effective long term.

Positive time-out teaches children a very valuable life skill—the importance of taking time to calm down and wait until you have access to your rational brain before acting. You may think you are teaching that skill by demanding that children go to punitive time-out. But banishment to time-out invites resentment, rebellion, or, even worse, passive compliance based on the belief, "I am a bad person."

> Positive time-out teaches children a very valuable life skill—the importance of taking time to calm down and wait until you have access to your rational brain before acting.

On the other hand, you may find it very helpful if you agreed with your child in advance for both of you to take time-out by choice. It is even more helpful when you have decided in advance what kind of time-out would be most encouraging to you. Your children will appreciate the difference between punitive and positive time-out when you use the seven guidelines for positive time-out (see page 167). Each of the guidelines are explained in detail in the next sections. (Children who can't participate in these guidelines are not developmentally old enough for any kind of time-out—punitive or positive.)

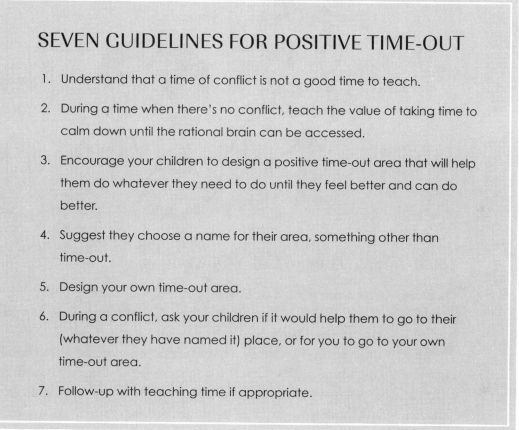

SEVEN GUIDELINES FOR POSITIVE TIME-OUT

1. Understand that a time of conflict is not a good time to teach.

2. During a time when there's no conflict, teach the value of taking time to calm down until the rational brain can be accessed.

3. Encourage your children to design a positive time-out area that will help them do whatever they need to do until they feel better and can do better.

4. Suggest they choose a name for their area, something other than time-out.

5. Design your own time-out area.

6. During a conflict, ask your children if it would help them to go to their (whatever they have named it) place, or for you to go to your own time-out area.

7. Follow-up with teaching time if appropriate.

A Time of Conflict Is Not a Time to Teach

Parents make a mistake when they try to teach children life lessons when they are both feeling upset. The feeling behind your teaching will more likely be one of frustration than kindness. You may think, "But, if I don't do something now, I'll be letting my children get away with bad behavior." This is not true. When you exercise self-control by waiting until you can be more calm and effective, you are teaching your children proper anger management by example. Sometimes, a positive time-out will be enough to stop your child's behavior. If not, you can follow up later, when you are both calm (a *no-conflict time*), with teaching time (see guideline 7).

Teach Taking Time to Calm Down

There are several ways to teach children about the value of time-out and the rational brain. The first way is to model taking time out yourself when you fall into using your irrational brain.

We are sure that you have certain buttons that when pushed send you into a tailspin. Your children know what those buttons are and exactly how to push them. Maybe you have a *fair* button. All your children have to do is say, "That's not fair," and you jump in to do everything you can to make sure everything is fair. Have you noticed that nothing you do seems to make it fair? You could bring out the finest weight scales to prove both children have the same amount of cake, and one would whine, "Well, his looks bigger." Your children aren't nearly as interested in what's fair as they are in the attention and reaction they get from pushing your fair button.

> You have certain buttons that when pushed send you into a tailspin. Your children know what those buttons are and exactly how to push them.

Perhaps you have a "peace" button. All your children have to do is start a little fight to get you to jump in and do your peace dance. You try to find out who started it and how to fix it, and then wonder why they don't award you the Nobel Peace Prize. They aren't interested in peace. They are interested in watching your peace dance! (Of course, there could be some mistaken goal behavior involved, but your efforts to create fairness and your peace dance won't address those issues.)

What happens when your buttons get pushed is that you go into your reptilian brain—and reptiles eat their young! In the reptilian (primitive) brain, the only option is fight or flight. If you are in a fight-or-flight state of mind, chances are your children will be right there too. Maybe they went to their primitive brains first and triggered you into yours. It doesn't matter. Nothing positive can be accomplished when either of you come from a fight-or-flight state of mind.

Where did we ever get the crazy idea that to help children do better, first we have to make them feel worse? Making children feel worse through shaming and blaming them (punishment of any kind) only prolongs the negative influence of the primitive brain. The truth is that children (and adults) do better when they feel better.

With some kids you could use the example of the reptilian brain. They usually enjoy this example. You can follow that example by saying, "We're not likely to solve the problem when we feel rotten. But when we both feel better, we'll be more able to think of ideas and solutions, so let's agree to take a break from each other when we are just too upset."

Another way to teach about positive time-out is to show your children the hand signal for time-out in sports and ask them what it means. If they are old enough to use positive time-out, they will know what time-out means in sports. They will also be able to tell you the purpose—to catch your breath, calm down, and come up with new strategies or plans after you are feeling better.

It takes training to help children understand that time-out can be a positive thing. The old adage is true, "Time heals all things." It is difficult to stay in the primitive brain when you take some time-out to do something you enjoy.

Children Can Design a Positive Area

After teaching the value of taking time to calm down, you can encourage children to design their own area that will help them do whatever it takes until they feel better and can do better. Involving children in the design is the key as is having this discussion during a no-conflict time. Encourage children to brainstorm things that help them feel better. You can ask some questions to get them started, but don't do this for them. "Does soft music help you feel better?

Encourage children to brainstorm things that help them feel better.

What about reading a book, stuffed animals, shooting basketball, jumping on the trampoline, talking with a friend, taking a shower. A time-out area could include a little corner where they have some soft cushions, books, and headphones for music. Or it could be something they do, such as shooting basketball or talking on the phone with a friend. It is a good exercise for them to think about what helps them feel better and to plan for times when they need it.

Children Can Choose a Name for Their Area

Punitive time-out has been used for so long that it is very difficult for both parents and children to adopt the new paradigm of time-out being a positive life skill. Suggest that your children come up with a positive name for their time-out area, a name other than "time-out." Doing this can shift the time-out concept from negative to positive.

Children (and parents) can have fun brainstorming for a new name for time-out. Some have decided to call it their "happy place," "cool-off spot," "Space" (with cardboard Planets and Stars in the area), or "Hawaii" (with posters of Hawaii on the wall). When a child creates a unique name for her positive time-out area, it makes the area her special place and gives her a sense of ownership.

Design Your Own Time-Out Area

Yes, your example is your child's best teacher. Positive time-out is good for you as well as for your children. Let your children know what you will do when you need to calm down because you find yourself acting from your reptilian brain. Perhaps a run or walk around the block (if your children are old enough) works for you. Maybe you feel refreshed after ten minutes of reading a good novel or your favorite magazine.

Whatever your time-out plan, let your children know in advance that you may go to your special place so you can behave better, not as a way to punish them. Sometimes posting everyone's positive time-out ideas on the refrigerator is a good way to keep the focus away from blaming the offender and more as a tool for everyone in the family when they are in need of self-soothing.

During Conflict, Ask About Going to the Positive Area

When it has been set up in advance, it can be effective to ask your angry (discouraged) child, "Would it help you to go to your positive, time-out place?" The language is very important—asking the child if he or she will find it helpful. If children don't choose it, it is punishment, not encouragement. If your child says, "No," you might ask, "Would you like for me to go with you?" Most children find it difficult to refuse this offer. Of course, it wouldn't be wise to offer this choice if you are as upset as your child. However, just seeing time-out in this positive way is enough to help adults make a paradigm shift away from their anger and into a desire to be encouraging to their children. Why not go with the child? Remember the purpose is to encourage and shift the mood, not punish. And you probably need the time-out as much as he does. If your child still says, "No," reply by saying, "Okay, I think I'll go." This will be a distracting shock (in a good way) to your child and an excellent model for them. Taking your own time-out is often the best place to start. Your children will learn the most from your example.

Follow Up, If Appropriate

Sometimes positive time-out is enough to stop the behavior and follow-up isn't necessary. Other times repairs or amends may be needed. Doesn't it make more sense to take time for teaching when you and your children are in a rational state of mind? It is almost impossible to be solution-oriented when any of you are in your reptilian brain. When your rational brain is restored after taking time to soothe yourself, then you can help your children find creative solutions. It will be easier to remember that mistakes are opportunities for learning, not for blame, shame, and pain.

There are many ways to follow up. Your child may want to put the problem on the family meeting agenda to get the whole family involved in brainstorming for solutions or you may want to do joint problem solving between the two of you. Sometimes curiosity questions, as discussed in chapter 6, are an excellent way to help children explore the consequences of their choices.

Exploring Consequences Instead of Imposing Them

IT IS A mistake to make children "pay" for their mistakes by imposing consequences. It isn't that consequences are wrong; consequences (both good and bad) happen as the natural and/or logical result of behavior.

Exploring consequences is much different from imposing consequences. Imposing a consequence might mean, "No more phone privileges until you do your homework." Exploration happens when you wait for a friendly moment and ask questions that help your child think for herself: "What do you think caused you to get that lower grade? How do you feel about it? What are your goals for yourself? What ideas do you have to solve the problem?" A friendly tone of voice is essential. A threatening tone of voice invites children to give the standard response: "I don't know." (Sound familiar?) Children can always tell the difference between when you are truly interested in what they think and when your real goal is to get them to do or say what you want. Children are much more likely to choose to apologize or to pay for repairs if you ask *them* to think of solutions. When you tell them what to do they feel resentful and will most likely resist or do it grudgingly.

> Children can always tell the difference between when you are truly interested in what they think and when your real goal is to get them to do or say what you want.

We have talked to many parents who have told us that most of their power struggles ended when they stopped imposing consequences and started focusing on solutions. Learn to think in terms of problem/solution instead of problem/ blame/punishment. It can be effective and empowering to help children explore the consequences of their choices by empathetically asking, "What do you think caused that to happen, and what ideas do you have to solve the problem?" This teaches them many valuable life skills: problem solving, communicating respectfully, decision making, conflict resolution, and negotiating. It also keeps their self-esteem in tact and teaches them how to voice their feelings and needs. Problem solving teaches so many of the life skills and characteristics that you want for your children in the long run that it should be your first-line offense in parenting. Most parents are programmed to think of punishment or consequences. Those who have made the paradigm shift to focusing on solutions rave about how much more effective they and their children become.

Of course, solutions don't always have to involve your children. Sometimes the most respectful thing you can do is stop trying to make your child do something and simply decide what you will do.

Decide What You Will Do

COUNTLESS POWER STRUGGLES could be avoided if parents would decide what they need to do under certain circumstances rather than trying to control what their children do. For example, it is fruitless to demand respect from a child. You can't control another person. You can control only yourself.

Let your children know in advance that you will treat them respectfully, and that you will treat yourself respectfully. Because you can't demand that they treat you respectfully, you will take care of yourself and leave the room if they choose to be disrespectful. Let them know that you want to be with them and will be available as soon as they let you know they are ready to interact with you respectfully.

Parents sometimes feel they are being permissive to "allow" a child to speak disrespectfully to them. So, what do they do? They talk disrespectfully to the child by saying, "Don't talk to me that way, young lady." In other words, they model the very thing they want their children to stop doing. It is much more effective to demonstrate your refusal to stay in a situation where you are being treated disrespectfully. Don't you hope your children will do that? Learning that you can't control what others do is a valuable life lesson.

Mark, a single father, dreaded laundry day. His daughter's clothes were rarely in the basket, and he found himself hunting in the closet and under her

> Countless power struggles could be avoided if parents would decide what they need to do under certain circumstances rather than trying to control what their children do.

bed for missing articles. Gwen, age ten, played a lot of sports and left her sweaty socks in damp wads. Mark detested turning them right side out. Mark believed he had tried everything: He'd lectured, threatened, and made huge heaps of Gwen's dirty clothes on her bedroom floor. Nothing fazed Gwen; she went right on leaving her clothes and wadded socks wherever she pleased. Eventually, Mark would gather everything up and wash it.

Mark was groaning about Gwen's habits to a friend one evening. "Why do you keep picking up after her?" his friend asked. Mark discovered that he didn't have a good answer. Gwen's behavior was certainly working well for her! It occurred to Mark that if his daughter was going to live on her own someday, she might need to know how to deal with her laundry.

That weekend, Mark sat down with his daughter and had a calm, friendly talk. "You know, Gwen, I get frustrated looking for your things and peeling your socks apart. From now on," he said kindly, "I'm only going to wash what's in the laundry basket, and if you put your socks in there in wads, that's how I'll wash them. Whatever doesn't get washed will be your responsibility. I'll show you how to run the washer and dryer." Gwen looked at her dad and rolled her eyes. "Whatever," she said with a shrug.

Mark stuck to his guns, and, as he had anticipated, trouble showed up right on schedule when Gwen stalked into his room on a Monday morning. "Where's my Abercrombie sweatshirt, Dad?" she said. "I want to wear it!"

"I don't know," Mark said. "Was it in the laundry basket?"

"I don't know," Gwen howled. "I don't know how to do this stuff. You've always done it all!" She went back to her room, where she discovered the missing sweatshirt behind her desk.

"Looks like you'll either have to wear it the way it is or wash it tonight," Mark said sympathetically and left the room to finish getting dressed. He heard Gwen muttering to herself in her room but resisted the urge to rescue her or solve the problem for her. Sure enough, that evening Gwen sat down at the counter while her dad fixed dinner.

"Sorry about this morning," Gwen said. "I sorta lost it. Could you show me again how to do the wash? I found my best jeans under the bed."

Mark smiled. "Sure. Come here and I'll show you how to cook pasta. You can tell me about your day. And after dinner we'll have another go at the washer and dryer."

As time passed, Mark discovered that although he and Gwen still battled occasionally over chores, teaching her skills and then having faith in her ability to work things out helped both of them. He was less grumpy, and Gwen began to take pride in her ability to master the everyday tasks of managing her life. The process required energy and patience from both of them, but the long-term results for Gwen promised to be worth the effort.

Take Time for Training

> Give your children opportunities to learn the skills they will need to be successful people in life.

ONE OF THE most encouraging things you can do as a parent is to *teach,* to give your children op-portunities to learn the skills they will need to be successful people in life. The problem is that teaching takes time and patience: Many parents find it easier—"just for now"—to do things *for* children or to punish them for their mistakes. When children learn that hassling and whining will make their parents give in and do the work for them or that punishment is a small price to pay for irresponsibility, they will have zero motivation to take responsibility.

In chapter 7, we explained how to use this tool with children under four. The example below shows how to use the tool with older children.

Mr. and Mrs. Jolson decided they wanted their children to have a different experience from what they experienced in their families of origin. In the Jolson family (Mom, Dad, Jill, Jeff, and Jeanne), everyone cooks dinner at least once a week. The parents get double duty because there are five cooks and seven days in the week. Each family member has clean-up chores, and once a week they spend an hour really cleaning the house together.

Hannah, a sixteen-year-old cousin from another country, came to live with the Jolsons for five months. Before Hannah came, Mom wrote and warned her, "Our family is a little different. We all share the work in the family." Mrs. Jolson wanted to warn Hannah so that she would know she would be part of the family and have family jobs, too.

When Hannah arrived, the kids decided that she should be a guest for a week and not have any jobs; that way she could see how things worked and get a little more comfortable.

The second week the family held a family meeting to arrange the chore schedule to include Hannah. She reluctantly picked her night to cook and was very nervous. She did not know what or how to cook. Her parents had "loved her too much" to require her to do any of the household chores. In the process Hannah lost the opportunity to learn skills and be a contributing member of the family. She did not have many skills and lacked confidence in herself. Mrs. Jolson kept encouraging Hannah by saying, "I have faith in you that you can do this."

Hannah was not at all happy. She had never had to cook at home and felt very picked on. After realizing they were not going to let her off the hook, Hannah chose spaghetti with sauce, because it seemed pretty easy. Mrs. Jolson stood by and helped her learn how to work the stove and taught her where everything was. Her children had been cooking for so long that she had forgotten that it takes some thinking to get everything organized so that all of the dinner is ready at about the same time.

When Hannah's turn came around the third week, she wanted Mrs. Jolson to "keep her company"—and help her. Mrs. Jolson declined, partly because she had a project she needed to finish, and partly because she had confidence (more than Hannah did) that she could do it on her own.

Hannah came to Mrs. Jolson to ask how to turn on the oven and for a preparation hint. She showed her how to turn on the oven (again) and answered her questions. At the very end, Mrs. Jolson joined her in the kitchen to help coordinate getting things on the table. After that, Mrs. Jolson stayed out of the kitchen while Hannah took her turn to cook.

For the next few weeks, choosing a menu was still hard for Hannah. Since she was inexperienced, figuring out how to make a balanced meal was a challenge. (Permissive parents don't think about how much they contribute to the lack of confidence and skills in their children.) As Hannah ate dinner with the family every night, though, she soon learned about the many possibilities for main dishes and side dishes.

By the seventh week, Hannah had learned how to choose a menu and make a balanced dinner *all* by herself! She was thrilled with what she had done. She told Mrs. Jolson that she wanted to have her family share cooking like this when she got home. She disclosed that her mom did all the cooking, but since she really doesn't like to cook she puts things together from packages. Hannah said, "It would be nice if everybody helped and could cook for each other, and the food would be better." That made Mrs. Jolson feel good, too, because she knew that Hannah felt like she was part of the family and felt good about participating and giving to her new family.

Conscious Irresponsibility

ONE OF THE best ways to help your children learn responsibility is for you to be "consciously irresponsible." Parents sometimes spend endless energy and time being responsible *for* their children. They set their alarm clocks for them, shake them out of bed in the morning, issue incessant reminders to get dressed, eat breakfast, find their shoes, pack their backpacks, and grab their lunch—and still find themselves driving children to school because they missed the bus. It's a good system—for the kids (at least on the surface). But children aren't learning self-discipline and motivation and often become discouraged about their own competence, and parents are becoming cranky, frustrated, and resentful.

What's the harm? Children will not learn to be responsible when their parents are responsible *for* them. In other words, ineffective parenting does not prepare children to be responsible adults or happy, contributing members of society. (It's not particularly healthy for parents, either, who also deserve a little serenity, sanity, and respect.)

So to be consciously irresponsible, let children know what they are capable of doing on their own, then don't do it for them. Don't set the alarm clock; don't remind them to get dressed or eat. As they experience natural consequences, they may choose to be more responsible themselves.

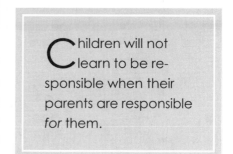

Children will not learn to be responsible when their parents are responsible *for* them.

You now have several examples of what "ineffective parenting" looks like, as well as some effective parenting methods. Many more examples of effective parenting are shared in the next chapter and are woven throughout this book. Hopefully, you will now consider the long-term effects of the parenting tools you use.

Spend One-on-One Time with Your Child

PARENTING FOR LONG-TERM results requires investing time now. It's important to have one-on-one time without distractions, noise, and crowds to spend with each child in your life. We call these moments *special time,* and children crave them. Special time need not cost money; it isn't always about enjoying your children and helping them feel belonging and significance. Special time can be as simple as doing a task together ("Hey, kiddo, want to see what a car engine looks like?"), reading a story, or going for a walk. Special time may be part of your bedtime routine, or it may happen in the car on the way to school or soccer practice. It may mean having a special lunch or shopping trip with each child. Special time is "just us, Mom" or "just us, Dad" time. It's probably obvious that it happens best when it's been planned and budgeted for. See the next chapter for more ideas on creating and spending special time.

Time and money tend to be the two things people never have enough of. Of the two, time is perhaps the most critical. Find a piece of paper and a pencil, and take a moment to consider:

What are the things in your life that you believe are most important? What do you value most? What has the greatest significance? How would you like to be remembered when your life has ended? Each of us has different values and priorities; there are no hard and fast rules about what should be most important. But it is a rare parent who doesn't list "children" and "family" somewhere near the top of the list.

Now make another list. What things require your attention each week? How do you spend your time? What are all the things you "have" to do? Most adults find they spend hours at work, driving, cleaning the house, working in the yard, shopping, cooking, doing laundry, and on, and on, and on. Many are shocked to find how little time they actually spend on the things they claim are most important to them—a situation that fuels much of the guilt we discovered in chapter 2. One man in a recent workshop stood up with tears in his eyes during a discussion of priorities. "If I spent half the time on my wife and children that I spend watching television," he said sadly, "we would have a much stronger family."

> If I spent half the time on my wife and children that I spend watching television . . . we would have a much stronger family."

Special time doesn't need to take hours and hours. A few minutes that happen regularly may be all you need. You may find that a few moments of special time have a powerful effect on your child's sense of belonging and significance and on your sense of connection to him. Listening, curiosity, and special time are not intended to increase your control over your child—control is not the answer. Connecting with children is about knowing who they are and what they are deciding, so that you can solve problems, set limits, and face the risks of the future *together*.

Have Faith in Your Children and Learn to Let Go

MANY LOVING PARENTS believe that effective parenting is about knowing *where* your children are—what they're doing, who they're with, and when, and where. We believe that it is more important to know *who* your children are than just *where* they are. Knowing who your children are gives you the security and the faith to let them learn, let them try new things (and make mistakes) in a supportive environment, and let them become the people they truly are. There will be times when you feel wonderfully close to your children—and other times when they seem distant and even hostile. For instance, understanding development will tell you that teenagers insist on privacy. It isn't personal; it's just what they need at that stage of their lives. What matters is keeping the door (and your ears) open, having the time to spend with them, and being genuinely interested in the way they see the world around them.

Being invited into a child's world is a fascinating and truly educational experience—and you can't force your way in. Like it or not, children determine whom they will trust, when they will speak, and what they will say. Wise parents learn to offer a little space, some understanding and encouragement, and the time to listen. You can find time to play with kids (yes—you, too, can play Barbies and Legos) and be available. You can remember that you get only one chance to share their childhood with the children you love so deeply.

Ultimately, a parent's job is to teach, guide, and encourage, and then to let go in loving, appropriate ways. The letting go is always a little scary; it becomes less so when you know who your children are and what they are capable of. You will know that far better when you take time to get into their world, stay a while, and truly connect with the interesting, capable people they are becoming. There's that word again. Parenting definitely takes a lot of time. The more special time you spend with your children, the less time you will spend dealing with the misbehaviors that result from discouragement.

Have the Courage to Allow Your Children to Experience Life's Difficulties

EFFECTIVE PARENTING REQUIRES that you recognize that your children need the opportunity to learn skills, make mistakes, and survive those mistakes. They need to stretch and grow a bit, to learn that they are capable of acquiring new abilities and taking risks. And children need to learn the sound judgment that comes from facing problems, exploring solutions, and learning from the results. Parents will not always be there to smooth the way for children. Effective parenting means equipping children to succeed in a challenging and difficult world. Offering emotional support and helping them brainstorm for solutions is much different from overprotecting and/or rescuing.

Take a moment to think yet again about your hopes and dreams for your children, about the qualities you want them to develop and the people you hope they will become. Let your love for them—that overwhelming, heart-melting feeling you get at unexpected moments when they catch your eye, hug you, or simply lay dreaming on their pillows—empower you to choose life, strength, and competence for them. Love them enough to make the tough decisions: to teach, to guide, to let them wrestle a bit with life, and in so doing, to learn how to live it well.

Quick and Quality Parenting Tips

Fighting, Sibling

After working all day, I would love to have a peaceful place to come home to. Instead I find my kids fighting with each other over every little thing.

Working Parents' Common Mistakes

1. Thinking their children would fight less if they didn't have working parents.

2. Thinking they should make up for their absence while working by controlling everything that happens when they are home.

Discouraging Words and Actions

1. Taking sides—thinking you know who started the fight.

2. Blaming the oldest, while protecting the youngest.

3. Trying to stop the fight by joining the fight.

Respectful and Encouraging Actions

1. Take time for training to focus on solutions during family meetings.

2. Create a Wheel of Choice (see next page) and ask the fighters to each choose from the wheel the choice that will help them right now.

3. Let kids have their feelings or their fun. Sometimes they are simply acting like bear cubs enjoying a good tussle.

4. Teach children about positive time-out and help each one create their own "special place." During a fight, ask which would help—one of the above suggestions or to go to their "special places" until they can focus on solutions.

Respectful and Encouraging Words

1. Instead of taking sides, treat them the same (give them the same choice), "Kids, would you like to stop fighting or go outside to fight." "Would you like to go to separate rooms until you are ready to stop fighting, or go to the same room until you have found a solution that works for both of you?"

2. Ask, "Which of you would like to put this on the family meeting agenda so we can work on a solution together later?"

3. Say, "I have faith in you to work this out." (Use this one only after you have taken plenty of time for training so they are familiar with problem-solving skills.)

4. Teach them to identify the problem and focus on solutions. "Let me know when you have identified the problem and have some ideas for solutions." Then go to your own time-out place.

Encouraging Attitudes

1. When you are consistently respectful to your children, it is more likely that they will learn to be respectful to each other.

2. Remember that a big reason children fight is to get you involved. (If you find this difficult to believe, try staying out of their fights (while teaching them how to handle fights during calm times) and see what happens.

11

How Busy Parents Can Help Children Feel Special

Neglecting Children vs. Planning Special Time with Children

D*O YOUR EYES light up when your child walks into the room?* Author Toni Morrison asked this profound question on a recent *Oprah* show. What could make a child feel more special than to watch your eyes light up when you see her? Even the busiest parents can find time for this. All it takes is an attitude of gratitude. Positive discipline requires both positive attitudes and effective skills to overcome the problems created in our speeded-up world.

For many parents today, work is only a "beep" away. Easy access to the Internet, laptops, cell phones, pagers, and Palm Pilots has blurred the boundaries between work and family. Families are going on vacation with cell phones and laptops so Mom and Dad will be available for any crises at work. Parents who opt for working in their homes to reduce the amount of time they spend away from their children face daily challenges to keep work and family separate.

We don't have an easy solution to the invasion of technology, but we do know it is critical to make time for your children. Children aren't impressed when you tell them you are working hard so they can have more *things*. They want *you*. As Galinsky found (see chapter 1) children don't want or need you full time. They do need you to be fully present and engaged when you are home. The greatest gift you can give your children is your time, and as we explained on pages 178–179 in chapter 10, the gift of time also helps children in

NINE WAYS PARENTS CAN HELP CHILDREN FEEL SPECIAL

1. Take time for hugs.

2. Spend regularly scheduled special time.

3. Try closet listening.

4. Write love notes to your children and tuck them in lunch boxes, on pillows, or on mirrors.

5. Invite children to run errands with you.

6. Share the day's sad and happy times during the bedtime routine.

7. Ask for help.

8. Hold weekly family meetings.

9. Take time for effective communication.

the long term. Even as a busy working parent, you can find many simple and meaningful ways to help your children feel special. Start with the nine suggestions we explain in this chapter.

Take Time for Hugs

NO MATTER HOW busy you are, there is always time for a three-second hug. A substantial hug can lift spirits and change attitudes—yours and your children's. Sometimes a hug can be the most effective method to stop misbehavior. Try it the next time you are feeling frazzled and your child is whining, and see for yourself how well it works.

Francine shared, "I remember the time I was so angry at my three-year-old son that I felt like hitting him. Instead, I stooped down and gave him a hug.

His whining stopped immediately and so did my anger. Later I realized that he was whining because he could feel the energy of my stress. Hugging him was enough to calm me down, even though I thought I was doing it to calm him down. Well, it takes two for a good hug, and both people benefit."

Don't wait until you are angry or your child is misbehaving. Give hugs in the morning, right after work, several during the evening, a longer one just before bed. When you offer that hug, whisper in your child's ear, "I feel so blessed (lucky or fortunate) to have you in my life. How do you suppose, of all the little boys in the world, I've got the best one?" You will both feel very special.

Spend Regularly Scheduled Special Time

THIS DOES NOT take very much time and can be comforting to parents and children when it is part of the schedule. Very young children need special time daily for ten to fifteen minutes. This doesn't mean you never spend more time than that. It does mean that it is a special time for you and your child to count on and look forward to.

One mother scheduled time with her daughter for reading books or playing games from 5:30 to 5:45. Her daughter loved helping her mother start dinner first while looking forward to their special time. If the phone rang during the special time, Mom would say, "I'm sorry, I can't talk right now. It's Tara's special time," or she would let the answering machine pick up the call. Tara would beam.

There were times when Mom really was busy with other important things when Tara would beg for attention. Mom could say, "Honey, right now I'm busy talking with your Dad, and I'm really looking forward to our special time." Usually, Tara would go to another task with a grin of satisfaction because she had something to look forward to.

After the age of six, thirty to sixty minutes a week works well. Take a few minutes at the end of each special time to decide what you will do during your next special time. It could be a bike ride, a ball game, a game of Monopoly, a trip to the library, or whatever you and your child like to do together. During one of your special times, you could brainstorm a list of fun things to do together.

Sadly, teenagers often lose interest in spending time with you, preferring their friends. They may feel especially embarrassed to be seen with you in a public place such as a shopping mall. However, you may be able to talk them into a *date night* for just the two of you, once a week. Or, take them skiing, or on some other trip long enough to spend time in the car. Make an agreement in advance that you will listen to your teen's music half the time if he or she will talk with you about important things the other half.

> Children feel special when they know that time with them is as important to you as all your other appointments and tasks.

The amount of time is not as important as the attitude it creates. Children feel special when they know that time with them is as important to you as all of your other appointments and tasks. During the times when you are just too busy or tired, children will not feel discounted (and you don't feel guilty) when you can say, "I'm too busy or too tired now, but I'm looking forward to our special time together." Once the date is made, honor that commitment every time unless there is an emergency.

Try Closet Listening

HAVE YOU EVER tried talking with your children only to be frustrated by one word, unenthusiastic, totally bored responses from your children? Many parents become discouraged when they ask their children, "How was your day?" and their children say, "Fine." Then they ask, "What did you do today?" The response is, "Nothing." Try closet listening.

Closet listening means you find times to be near your children, hoping they will talk with you, but not being obvious about it. Mrs. Escalante tried this with her teenage daughter, Maria. Mrs. Escalante woke up ten minutes early and got ready for work. While Maria was fixing her hair and makeup at the bathroom mirror, Mrs. Escalante would go in and sit on the edge of the tub. The first time she did this, Maria asked, "What do you want, Mama?" Mrs. Escalante said, "Nothing special, except that I think it is special just to spend a few minutes with you." Maria waited to see what would come next. Nothing did. She finished fixing her hair and makeup and said, "Bye, Mama."

Mrs. Escalante continued to do this every morning. It wasn't long before Maria got used to having her there. Mom didn't ask any questions, but before long, Maria would chat away about all the things that were going on in her life. With teenage boys it is helpful to get interested in what they're interested in. Watching sports together or listening to the same music really gets them talking.

Perhaps children who resist questions will respond when you make yourself available and keep your mouth shut.

Write Love Notes to Your Children

IT DOESN'T TAKE much time (only a few seconds) to write a note for your children's lunch bag, pillow, or mirror. One very busy working mom decided to put a note in her ten-year-old daughter's lunch bag every day for a year. She took time on airplanes or while waiting for an appointment to write several notes or silly rhymes in advance, such as "Roses are red, Violets are blue, Every day, I think about you." When she traveled, she gave her childcare provider notes to tuck into the lunch bag for each day she was gone. Her daughter's friends gathered around her at lunch in eager anticipation to hear the note of the day. Her daughter felt very special.

Invite Children to Run Errands with You

WHEN YOU NEED to run a short errand in the car, ask one of your children to ride along, just so you can spend as much time together as possible. You might make a big deal of this by creating a chart during a family meeting so

> You may be surprised at how much your children open up and start talking when there is no "inquisition."

you can check whose turn it is. During these rides, become a closet listener (don't ask questions). You may be surprised at how much your children open up and start talking when there is no "inquisition" that invites them to clam up. Simply let them know how glad you are to have a few minutes to be with them, and share special moments from your own life or day. Kids feel special when you share yourself.

Share the Day's Sad and Happy Moments at Bedtime

WHEN TUCKING YOUR child into bed at night, take a few minutes to let her share the saddest thing that happened to her that day. Just listen respectfully without trying to solve the problem. Then share your saddest time of the day. Follow this by taking turns sharing your happiest event of the day. You may be surprised at the things you hear when your children have your undivided attention to evaluate their day and hear about yours.

Mr. Sutter decided to try sharing sad and happy times while tucking his children in bed at night. At first, four-year-old Jesse really got into the sad times and went on and on. Soon she was crying for sympathy and Mr. Sutter wondered if this was such a good idea. However, he listened patiently without trying to solve the problem. (He did ask Jesse if she would like to put the problem on the family meeting agenda.) Jesse finally stopped crying. When Mr. Sutter asked Jesse to share her happy time, she pouted and said, "I didn't have a happy time today." Mr. Sutter knew this wasn't true. He had seen his daughter laughing many times during the day. He was wise enough to say, "Okay, I'll tell you mine. Actually, my happiest time is about to happen. I can't wait for my butterfly kisses." Soon Jesse was laughing as they exchanged butterfly kisses.

Even though sharing sad and happy times with his other two children had been successful, Mr. Sutter wondered if he should skip it with Jesse. He decided to give it another try. The second night Jesse tried again to get more sympathy from her sad story. When it didn't work any better than it had the night before, she went ahead and shared her happiest time. It wasn't long before Jesse often wanted to skip her saddest thing and share two happy things.

Ask for Help

CHILDREN LOVE TO feel needed, and you, as a busy working parent, need help. What a great combination. You might say to your child, "I need your help so I can get to work on time. How could you help me?" Notice the wording. Hopefully you remember from past chapters how much more effective it is to ask than to tell. Most children are much more willing when they are empowered to use their ideas about how to help than when they are told what to do.

It is much different when you ask for help in an inviting manner instead of lecturing and scolding. "I would appreciate anything you can do to spruce up the family room before dinner," usually invites much more cooperation than, "How many times have I told you not to leave all your stuff all over the family room."

Asking works better when it is done during a no-conflict time than when everyone is upset. However, sometimes asking for help can be a distraction from a conflict, especially with young children.

Little Lisa didn't want to leave the swings when it was time to leave. Mom said, "I need your help. Do you want to carry my keys, or are you big enough to carry my purse to the car? You decide." Suddenly, helping became more appealing to Lisa than the swings. She wanted to carry the keys.

With older children, it is usually more effective to get them involved in advance during family meetings about how to be helpful.

Hold Weekly Family Meetings

EVEN THOUGH WE have devoted a whole chapter to family meetings, we want to mention them again in the context of helping children feel special. Twenty to thirty minutes a week is a small investment of time with huge payoffs. Children feel very special when they are listened to, taken seriously, and have their thoughts and ideas validated. That is the immediate payoff of family meetings.

The near-future payoff is that you can handle many daily hassles during a family meeting. The kids can help you create morning and bedtime routines and come up with creative ways for handling chores. They can find solutions to any family problem. It is amazing how much more willing children are to follow rules and plans they have helped create.

> It takes much less time to hold weekly family meetings where children learn to cooperate and solve problems than it takes to nag, lecture, and scold every day.

The long-range payoff is that children learn important life skills such as communication and problem solving. Think how much this will help them in future jobs and relationships. It takes much less time to hold weekly family meetings where children learn to cooperate and solve problems than it takes to nag, lecture, and scold every day. During busy times, parents often find relief or create a diversion from a problem by simply inviting the child to put the problem on the family meeting agenda. Everyone learns to trust that a respectful solution will be found soon.

Take Time for Effective Communication

AS A RESULT of demanding responsibilities and hectic schedules, parents often fall into the trap of maintenance talk—questioning, stating facts, gathering information, and giving a solution. Effective communication needs to be

more than just conveying facts and information; it needs to go to a deeper level of communicating feelings and ideas from the heart. It is impossible to accomplish this deeper level of communication until your children feel they are truly special and valued.

When your children have something to say to you, give them your undivided attention. Make eye contact. Listen without trying to fix their problem for them. Ask what, where, and how questions to help them think things through. In other words, communicate with your children as though they are special. Before you know it they will feel special. All it takes is commitment, and even busy parents can help their children feel special.

You Will Feel More Effective

THE BONUS BENEFIT of making it a habit to help your child feel special is that you will feel more effective as a parent. Helping your child feel special is a matter of planning and habit, not a lack of time. Children interact differently when they are one-on-one with you than they do when they are competing with their siblings or others for your attention. These special times will help you get to know your child better and forge a strong connection.

Quick and Quality Parenting Tips

Won't Listen, Won't Talk

My children seem to ignore me when I talk to them, and their vocabulary when talking to me usually consists of mono-syllables, "Nothing," "Fine," "Yeah," or a shrug. I really love my children. How do I get them to listen and to talk?

Working Parents' Common Mistakes

1. Thinking they will get results by talking too much.

2. Trying to make up for lost time by talking too much.

3. Taking it personally when children don't talk or listen. "Maybe they would talk more if I was home more."

Discouraging Words and Actions

1. "Why won't you listen to me?" "Why won't you talk to me?"

2. Talking too much, giving lectures, barking orders.

Respectful and Encouraging Actions

1. Talk less and listen more.

2. Become a closet listener (which means you listen without letting them know that is what you are doing). Just hang out without saying a word. You'll be surprised at how much they talk when you create silence.

3. When they do talk validate their feelings instead of giving your opinion and/or advice every time they talk.

4. Have regular family meetings where every member of the family has an opportunity to give and get compliments and to brainstorm on solutions. To make sure family meetings don't become another platform for you to lecture and give orders, have a *talking stick* that is passed around the table. Only the person with the talking stick gets to talk.

5. With small children, use action instead of words. Take them by the hand and show them what needs to be done instead of telling them what needs to be done.

6. Create a sense of fun by whispering so they have to strain to listen.

Respectful and Encouraging Words

1. "I have some information about that. Would you like to hear it?" (Children are more likely to listen if you ask them first. If they say no, at least their intention is out in the open.)

2. When they do talk, respond with, "Anything else? Anything else? Is there more?"

3. "Do you want my opinion, or do you just want to share and have me listen."

4. Stop telling and start asking, "What happened? What do you think caused it to happen? How do you feel about it? What do you want to do now?"

5. Instead of lectures, use one word. "Towels," "Clean-up time," "Dishes," "Naptime." Or use non-verbal signals that have been decided upon in advance with your children.

6. Be respectful when you make requests. Don't expect children to do something when you are interrupting something they are doing. Ask, "Would you like to take a break and do this now, or in twenty minutes?" You decide. Adding, "You decide is very empowering." If they choose twenty minutes, ask, "Would you like to set the timer or do you want me to?"

Encouraging Attitudes

1. Children will listen to you *after* they feel listened to.

2. Give up control and teach and practice cooperation.

12

Honoring Your
Needs First

Miserable Martyrs vs. Happy and
Healthy Parents Who Take
Care of Themselves

HERE IS THE bottom line: "If momma or daddy ain't happy, ain't nobody happy!" Unhappiness oozes over everyone you care about—your children, your mate, your co-workers, and your friends. Unhappy people are less effective parents and employees and make depressing company.

There is nothing attractive about hardworking martyrs. Children know intuitively if you are happy and enjoying life as a parent. One mother was shocked to realize that her stressful, overloaded schedule was teaching her son that being a working parent was miserable. She overheard him tell a friend, "I'm never having kids. It's way too much work, and it looks like a total pain in the rear."

Far too many working parents feel like the proverbial "hamster on the treadmill," running as hard as they can just to keep up with the sheer volume of responsibilities at work and at home. But they aren't getting what they want out of life. They feel trapped in an endless cycle of duty and responsibility. What typically gets cut from the "to do" list are the very things that make their lives worthwhile and joyful, things like bike riding, golfing, a night out with the girls or the guys, a weekend away with your partner, or a barbeque with couples from the neighborhood. Contrary to popular belief, the pursuit of your individual happiness is a worthy and honorable goal.

Family therapists frequently ask the unhappy couples they work with, "Did you used to have fun together and enjoy each other's company?" The following response is typical, "Well, that was before we had kids and responsibilities. Those days are over. We're not kids anymore." This is a tragic belief, both for the adults, who have renounced enjoying life as a worthy pursuit, and for their children, who learn by their parents' example that commitment to parenthood also requires a vow of poverty in the fun and self-care departments.

Find What "Spins Your Beanie"

ONE WORKING MOTHER of three teenagers loved to play tennis. But as her children's extracurricular activities became more time-intensive and finances required she spend more time at work, she decided that her two weekly tennis games with girlfriends would have to go. Several weeks later her youngest daughter noticed something was different and said, "Mom, you aren't singing in the car anymore, and you aren't making those weird, little happy noises you used to make. Those noises really bug me but it's kind of sad that you don't do them anymore."

The following Saturday the kids were all gone, so this busy mother arranged a spontaneous game of tennis. Afterwards she found herself singing "La Bamba" at the top of her lungs while she showered. Her daughter's words came ringing back to her. She realized that tennis was somehow essential to her joy. It provided a much-needed respite from the weighty responsibilities she carried for her work, her family, and her home. It filled a deep need for social connection and physical exertion, and this mom decided it was no longer negotiable.

> You ... must find what "spins your beanie"—the things that will put spark back in your life.

This woman realized that tennis "spun her beanie"—in other words, tennis unleashed passion and energy that carried into every area of her life. You also must find what "spins your beanie"—the things that will put spark back in your life. Finding the formula that is uniquely right for you will allow you to claim your God-given birthright: a joyful and meaningful life. As television self-help guru Dr. Phil says, "I want you to get excited about your life! You, and you alone, can make the choice to be happy and you and you alone can choose to sabotage it."

Discover Where You Are Out of Sync

THE FIRST STEP in achieving joy in life is to correctly diagnose where the problem really lies. The Wheel of Life (below) will help you identify the trouble zones in eight very important aspects of your life.

Take a moment to rate your current level of satisfaction in each area from zero to ten, with ten meaning you are completely content and satisfied. View the center of the wheel as zero and the outside edge as ten. Draw a line in each section that correlates with your current level of satisfaction to create a new outer edge. (See the example on the next page.) When you are finished, you will have a graphic, visual depiction of where you are most out of balance. If you've ever driven a car with a tire that is uneven and low on air, you'll know it creates a bumpy, difficult, and uncomfortable ride. The lowest scoring sections in your wheel are most likely the sources of your greatest unhappiness.

The Wheel of Life

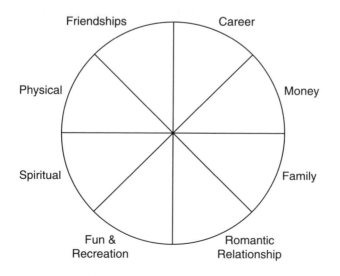

The Wheel of Life Example

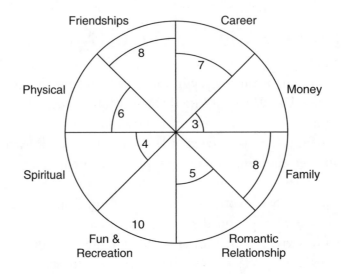

The left half of the wheel addresses four critical areas of self-care: your physical health, friendships, fun and recreation, and spirituality or personal growth. (We will cover the right half of the wheel in chapters 13 and 14.)

You are always free to neglect self-care, but you are likely to experience the unhappy consequences, such as feelings of emptiness, depression, loneliness, exhaustion, and apathy. When you dishonor yourself by ignoring your core needs, unhappiness and dissatisfaction (for you and those around you) are the guaranteed results.

Physical Exercise

PHYSICAL EXERCISE IS unequivocally the *best vaccination* of all time. It inoculates us from a host of life's evils. It staves off obesity, heart disease, diabetes, stroke, and stress. It is a natural antidepressant and reduces anxiety by offering a powerful "endorphin cocktail" that can cure our foulest moods in twenty minutes. It elevates our body image, enhances our sexual vitality, and produces an overall sense of well-being. One mother confessed, "When I am particularly grouchy, my kids beg me to go on a run. They know I'll come home a more patient and tolerant mom."

With the media heralding the benefits of exercise ad nauseam, why aren't more of us committed to a regular exercise program? The cry of most working parents is, "It's impossible—there is so much to do and so little time!" One father of two toddlers said, "I used to be in great shape before we had kids. I ran marathons and lifted weights three times a week. But that all changed when I had to juggle the kids and work. I hate my body now, and I miss how great it felt physically and emotionally to be in good shape."

Many working parents have to get creative to find time to exercise without feeling guilty about cheating their kids or their employers. You don't have to join a gym or exercise for hours. Twenty minutes of walking three times a week is often enough, and small amounts of time may be easier to find. Here are a few suggestions.

- Find an exercise you love. You will never stick with it if you hate it.

- Put your small children in a double running stroller and walk or run with them after work. (Bring snacks for them.)

- Let older children ride bikes or scooters while you walk or jog. You can visit with them and get your exercise in.

- Buy a treadmill or other piece of exercise equipment and use it at home when the kids are asleep or while they are watching a show on television.

- Exercise during lunch. Combine walking or going to the gym with friends from work and you meet two core needs: social connection and exercise. You will find you have far more energy for the rest of the afternoon.

- Work as a "tag team" with your partner. For example, he can help with the children's homework while you exercise, and then you can start dinner while he exercises.

- Get up a half hour earlier and sneak to the gym before the kids are up.

- If you carry work stress home, take half an hour before coming home to exercise and "sweat to forget." On particularly stressful days, one mother called her in-home babysitter to ask her to put her exercise clothes outside the front door so she could get them, go to the gym, and come home in a better frame of mind before interacting with the kids.

Adequate Rest

AMERICANS ARE MORE sleep-deprived today than at any other time in history. In 1850, for example, the average American got nine and a half hours of sleep per night. By 1950, the rate was down to eight hours. Currently, it is seven hours and still declining. Sleep deprivation leads to fatigue. Prolonged fatigue causes lethargy and irritability. Exhaustion and burn-out are well-known contributors to depression and anxiety. In short, tiredness impairs our coping skills in all walks of life. And when we are less able to cope, we become less effective parents, mates, and professionals.

> Tiredness impairs our coping skills in all walks of life.

One mother relayed an incident when she was exhausted and lectured her children with her periodic "martyr tape" that sounded like this: "I work so hard around here. I work forty hours a week, come home exhausted, and all I want is a clean kitchen—and you can't even do that for me. After all I do for the three of you, cleaning up your own messes shouldn't be too much to ask. I am sick and tired of being the family maid." Her fifteen-year-old interrupted her litany of self-pity by saying, "Mom, I think things would look a whole lot better if you'd go and take a nap." She admitted, "His comment infuriated me but the truth hurts. I was exhausted, and I was becoming a royal pain to be around." (See page 159 in chapter 9 for how to get the kitchen cleaned up!)

Here are some suggestions for getting adequate sleep:

- Renounce the cultural bias that says you are more worthy if you sleep less. Don't take pride in sleeping only six hours a night if you would function best at eight. Have the courage to honor the sleep requirements appropriate for you. Listen to your body and allow it to tell you when it is time for bed.

- Tell your children when you have "hit the wall" with exhaustion and are no longer fit to be around other humans. If it is a weekend nap or an 8:30 bedtime that is needed, ask your kids and your partner to support you. It is your responsibility not to burden your family with your bad mood. Often the culprit is exhaustion.

- Avoid caffeine and alcohol if you have difficulty sleeping. Alcohol may create the relaxation conducive to two to three hours of good sleep but it may then interrupt the sleep cycle and cause middle-of-the-night wakefulness. Caffeine and other stimulants like ephedra also interrupt sleep.

- If you are suffering from chronic insomnia, go to the nearest sleep disorders clinic and receive diagnostic testing. Over seventy million Americans suffer from sleep disorders that are treatable. One man with chronic fatigue and depression discovered he had sleep apnea. Surgery restored his energy and enthusiasm for life.

- Regular exercise reduces insomnia and deepens sleep.

- Stop all activities that require alertness (work, reading intellectually challenging material, or stimulating phone conversations) at least one hour before bedtime. Signal your mind and body that it is time to let go by turning the lights down low and quieting yourself. Read something easy or ask your partner for a back rub or some cuddling.

- Decide how much sleep you need to function at your best and make it a priority. Your co-workers and loved ones will thank you.

Nutrition

EATING WELL IS important to your overall sense of health and well-being. However, you may share Sondra's concern. "My mother stayed home full time when I was a kid. She cooked a home-made meal every night of the week. Half the time we are too exhausted to cook, or it is impossible to find the time between soccer practice and piano lessons. We order pizza or go through the drive-through more nights than not. I feel guilty about how I'm feeding the kids, and I'm embarrassed by my ever-widening girth."

The reality is that if you work, you probably don't have the time to cook like stay-at-home mothers do. Let go of the guilt on those unavoidable fast-food nights and try to plan some quick, easy, and healthy home meals for those nights when you are tired and busy. See chapter 9 for suggestions on meal planning, and make a point to save the recipes you use that are quick and easy.

> Having good friends who offer unconditional love and encouragement boosts your spirits and makes the challenges in life bearable.

Friendships

STUDIES CONSISTENTLY FIND a link between nurturing friendships and personal wellness. Having good friends who offer unconditional love and encouragement boosts your spirits and makes the challenges in life bearable. Attentive listening and empathy are therapeutic in and of themselves. It is sad that so many working parents stop making time for friendships.

Gary shares a common problem of working parents. "Before we were married with kids we had a lot of friends. We went to ball games, I'd play poker with the guys, and we'd go camping once in a while with other couples. Now there is only time for work and the kids." What a common and heartbreaking sentiment this is.

FITTING FRIENDSHIP INTO YOUR SCHEDULE

1. Try to combine social time with exercise time. Kill two birds with one stone. Jog, play tennis, or do an aerobics class with a friend.

2. Create rituals and traditions with your dearest friends that happen regularly, such as,
    a. Annual golf trip with your college buddies
    b. Annual birthday overnight with your best friend
    c. Lunch the first Tuesday of every month
    d. Annual fishing or camping trips
    e. Annual Cinco de Mayo or New Year's party
    f. Monday Night Football parties
    g. Monthly game or poker nights
    h. Weekly coffee

3. Make friends who have children with whom your children enjoy playing. This will allow you to meet some of your social and family needs at the same time.

4. Be proactive—take the initiative and invite someone you enjoy to do something fun. If you wait for the other person to make the first move you may be disappointed.

5. Limit your time with negative people. They can be toxic to your emotional health. If you are spending time with people who bring you down with their pessimism and criticism, it may be wise to keep your distance until they improve.

There is a huge correlation between depression and social isolation. It is not true that your spouse, children, and work are enough. You need good friends to help you through the ups and downs of life. Laughter with your girlfriends or guy friends is like "inner jogging"—it renews your soul and arms you with a fresh perspective on life.

Fun and Recreation

FUN AND LAUGHTER are good medicine. Laughter has been referred to as a "brain enema" because it purges the most jaundiced thoughts and perspectives. One of the areas of deepest resentment in many marriages is the couple's inability to negotiate time for personal fun and recreation. Paul angrily complained in therapy, "As soon as I walk in the door, I am barraged by Linda's demands and my children's needs. I fantasize about flying a plane again or playing golf, but I don't even ask. It would start World War Three."

> One of the areas of deepest resentment in many marriages is the couple's inability to negotiate time for personal fun and recreation.

Paul's sentiments are all too common. The solution to his problem is relatively simple through a tool we call, "Reveal Your Desired Agenda!" If you learn to use this tool with dignity and respect for your mate and your children, you will find a way to honor your personal needs without ugly power struggles. The following example illustrates how this tool works:

Paul and Linda had been fighting for months. Both of them worked full time and shared responsibility for three small children. There was no time allotted for personal fun. They both felt overwhelmed by the magnitude of their obligations, and they resented each other for their unhappiness. Their communication had descended into childish tit-for-tat retorts such as, "I changed the diaper last time. It's your turn!" Or, "I guess you expect me to help Bradley study for his spelling test!"

At the suggestion of their marriage counselor, they sat down to do the "Reveal Your Desired Agenda" exercise. The purpose was to find a way to meet their individual, couple, and family needs.

First, they individually brainstormed as many ideas as possible of things they would like to do in the following three categories: individual fun, couple fun, and family fun.

Next, Paul and Linda were asked to select one item from each of the three categories to put on the agenda for that particular weekend.

Linda's desired weekend agenda looked like this:

1. Individual fun: Go to lunch and shop with Carla.
2. Couple fun: Go out to dinner with Paul.
3. Family fun: Take the kids to the park.

Paul's desired weekend agenda looked like this:

1. Individual fun: Bike riding with the guys.
2. Couple fun: Romantic dinner with Linda.
3. Family fun: Movies with the kids.

Last (but not least), they were to create a weekend agenda that would work for both of them and the children. (There is usually more willingness to accommodate one another's individual needs if family commitments and couple commitments are scheduled at the same time.) The couple fun was easy—both of them wanted a nice dinner together. They scheduled dinner for Saturday night, and Paul agreed to call a babysitter.

Linda felt that going to the park with the kids would offer more quality time than the movies. (In order to be respectful to children, it is usually best to invite them to brainstorm their ideas.) As it turned out, the kids preferred going to the zoo, so that activity was scheduled for Sunday afternoon. Linda happily agreed to be with the kids while Paul went bike riding with his friends Saturday morning, and Paul was content to take over so Linda could enjoy lunch and the mall Saturday afternoon. For the first time, they both were free to have fun without guilt because they had respectfully involved and honored each family member in planning the weekend.

Linda was happy with the arrangement but worried that the fun would result in too many undone household chores which would spoil her peace of mind in the coming work week. She and Paul then listed the top four chores that needed to be done on the weekend and they divided the list. In this way they reduced the stress that could be caused by too much play (leaving work undone) or too much work (leaving no time for play.)

Can you imagine how much better Paul and Linda's marriage would be if they used this tool not only on weekends, but for the whole week? And can you see how much happier families would be if they gave up their guilt about having fun and asked for support in meeting their personal needs? This system is so simple and so effective, but sadly, few families know how to use it.

> Many families do not spend enough time together doing fun things.

Many families do not spend enough time together doing fun things. They have good intentions; but they don't take the time to plan and schedule events on a calendar—and then life gets in the way.

Spiritual and Personal Growth

MODERN LIFE INVITES us to run at a more frantic pace than ever. It is imperative that you find your own way to seek peace and refuge from the strain and pressure in your daily life. It is an integral part of self-care to clock out of your worldly life on a regular basis in order to find a broader, more enlightened viewpoint. This is what we refer to as seeking spirituality or personal growth. Often we are so busy climbing the ladder of life that we fail to notice that our ladder is leaning against the wrong wall.

We invite you to turn on some soothing music as you discover what matters most to you. As author Steven Covey so wisely counsels, "We must begin with the end in mind."

Your Tribute Statement

Pretend you have arrived at a beautiful funeral home. There is a hearse parked out front. As you walk down the aisle, you wave quietly to everyone you have known in your life. As you make your way to the front, you slowly glance into the casket and see yourself. It dawns on you that this funeral is for *you*. You settle into the nearest pew as the organ begins playing "Amazing Grace." The first speaker on the program is your child, who will tell the audience what your life meant to him or her. In the following space, please record what you wish your child would say about you as a parent:

The next speaker is your spouse. Please record what you wish your spouse or significant other would say about you as a romantic partner:

If you are like the parents in our workshops, you probably shed a few tears as you filled in the blanks. More importantly, we hope you have learned what is truly important to you in your life. During this exercise many are struck poignantly by the painful realization that they are out of step with the values they hold most dear. This exercise is a wake-up call for you to look at the eternal, long-range result of how you are living and loving today. Broadening your perspective in this way is an opportunity for spiritual growth; you have a chance to get in touch with your deepest-held personal truths. The following ideas can help you stay on course with your chosen path:

Suggestions for Rejuvenating Your Spiritual Self

1. Listen to spiritual music while you walk or drive.
2. Listen to inspirational works on tape.
3. Take a long hike in nature.
4. Meditate.
5. Do yoga.
6. Attend your preferred religious services.
7. Write your hopes, dreams, and disappointments in a journal.

8. Pray for direction in your life.

9. Serve others less fortunate than yourself.

10. Attend a personal growth workshop.

11. Read a self-help book.

12. Engage in personal, couple, or family therapy.

13. Work with the terminally ill.

14. Be alone and silent for an entire day.

Your Personal Wellness

THE FIRST STEP in creating a happy, well-functioning family is to make sure you are a happy and well-functioning individual. This will require you to rigorously guard your physical health, cultivate meaningful friendships, make time for fun and recreation, and regularly attend to your spiritual needs. These are the four cornerstones of your personal wellness.

Remember the Wheel of Life? If your scores were lower than five in any of these four important areas on the wheel, we urge you to implement the suggestions that will help you reach a higher level of contentment in that area. Once you have achieved higher scores in your self-care, you are ready for the romantic section of the wheel. Keeping your couple relationship close and connected is the subject of the next chapter.

13

Prioritizing
Your Marriage

Positive Discipline Skills for
Encouraging Your Spouse

THIS BOOK IS primarily a parenting book, so why would we dedicate an entire chapter to marriage? It is not easy to put your best foot forward as a parent if you are miserable in your marriage. This chapter is designed for couples who can use the positive discipline concepts to improve their marriage and thus present a better environment for their children.

If you are a single parent, please skip this chapter and refer to *Positive Discipline for Single Parents*.[1] Many single parents are doing an excellent job for many reasons, including the fact that they don't have to deal with an unhappy marriage.

The mother and father are the foundation of the family. If the marriage is weak and crumbling, the entire house could come crashing down. Marital strife increases misbehaviors in children. Angry and defiant children are often mirroring the behaviors they observe in their parents' relationship. Therapists have noticed that children in homes with unhappy and tension-filled marriages will intensify their misbehaviors in a subconscious attempt to bring the parents together. So, for the sake of the children, as well as your personal well-being,

---

1. Jane Nelsen and Cheryl Erwin, *Positive Discipline for Single Parents* (Roseville, CA: Prima Publishing, 1999).

creating a happy marriage is a worthwhile endeavor. You will find that many of the requirements for good parenting are necessary for a good marriage as well, starting with the primary goal of belonging.

A Sense of Belonging (Connected) in Marriage

THE PRIMARY CULPRIT in most unhappy marriages is that the most basic human need—to feel a sense of belonging—is not being met for one or both people. We have underscored the importance of giving your children a sense of

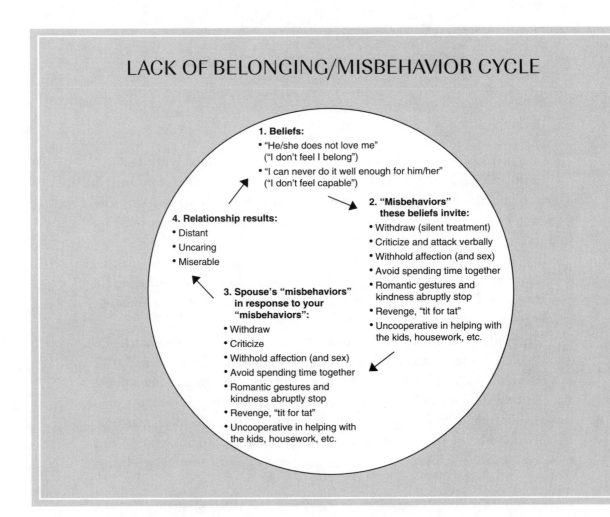

LACK OF BELONGING/MISBEHAVIOR CYCLE

1. Beliefs:
- "He/she does not love me" ("I don't feel I belong")
- "I can never do it well enough for him/her" ("I don't feel capable")

2. "Misbehaviors" these beliefs invite:
- Withdraw (silent treatment)
- Criticize and attack verbally
- Withhold affection (and sex)
- Avoid spending time together
- Romantic gestures and kindness abruptly stop
- Revenge, "tit for tat"
- Uncooperative in helping with the kids, housework, etc.

3. Spouse's "misbehaviors" in response to your "misbehaviors":
- Withdraw
- Criticize
- Withhold affection (and sex)
- Avoid spending time together
- Romantic gestures and kindness abruptly stop
- Revenge, "tit for tat"
- Uncooperative in helping with the kids, housework, etc.

4. Relationship results:
- Distant
- Uncaring
- Miserable

belonging through experiences that help them feel accepted, capable, valued, and connected. When children don't believe they belong, they misbehave. Likewise, when you don't feel loved, valued, and accepted by your spouse, you are unlikely to put forth your most kind and loving behavior. When you feel criticized and unappreciated don't you "misbehave"

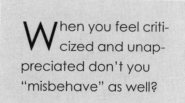

When you feel criticized and unappreciated don't you "misbehave" as well?

as well? The diagram that follows illustrates how your defensive behaviors (or "misbehaviors") show up when you get hurt and don't feel a sense of belonging with your spouse. Misbehavior based on a sense of not belonging creates a

The cycle progresses like this:

1. Beliefs:
   - "He/she does not love me" ("I don't feel I belong")
   - "I can never do it well enough for him/her" ("I don't feel capable")

2. "Misbehaviors" these beliefs invite:
   - Withdraw (silent treatment)
   - Criticize and attack verbally
   - Withhold affection (and sex)
   - Avoid spending time together
   - Romantic gestures and kindness abruptly stop
   - Revenge, "tit for tat"
   - Uncooperative in helping with the kids, housework, etc.

3. Spouse's "misbehaviors" in response to your "misbehaviors":
   - Withdraw
   - Criticize
   - Withhold affection (and sex)
   - Avoid spending time together
   - Romantic gestures and kindness abruptly stop
   - Revenge, "tit for tat"
   - Uncooperative in helping with the kids, housework, etc.

4. Relationship results:
   - Distant
   - Uncaring
   - Miserable

repetitive cycle of destructive feelings and behaviors, which, if left unchecked, will sabotage the marriage.

This unhappy cycle repeats itself over and over in a chain reaction in which both parties feel unloved, unappreciated, and hopeless. They feel hurt and disappointed, but don't know how to reclaim the love and passion they once shared. Why does this happen to so many couples who really loved each other in the beginning? How do so many well-meaning couples lose their connection?

Most courtships and marriages start off with the belief, "He or she really loves and admires me." These beliefs meet the greatest need of human beings—to belong (to feel connected and capable). These beliefs lead to loving and respectful behaviors such as affection, romantic gestures, special dates, regular fun and recreation, a lot of compliments, and frequent sex. These behaviors lead to a very close, connected, and loving relationship. The cycle is either going in a positive direction, which reinforces beliefs that support a sense of belonging and the attending positive behaviors, or in a negative direction, which reinforces beliefs of being unloved and the ugly behaviors that keep those beliefs in place. Relationships are always moving; they are never stagnant. At this moment your marriage is either in a positive or a negative feedback loop depending on whether you both perceive you are cherished and admired by your spouse.

> Relationships are always moving; they are never stagnant. At this moment your marriage is either in a positive or a negative feedback loop.

A Sense of Capability and Admiration in Marriage

A SENSE OF capability and the desire for admiration are essential parts of belonging (and significance). It is almost impossible to feel a sense of connection when you don't believe you are capable or admired, or when you are not seen as capable or admired by your spouse. When adults feel incompetent, they usually feel hurt and protect themselves with defensive "misbehaviors."

Morey's wife, Maureen, said, "Can't you do more than one thing at a time? I'm setting the table, making beans, a salad, dessert, and watching the baby, and all you're doing is barbequing the steaks!" Morey was furious. He threw the steaks down on the table and left the house. He felt that he could never please her. He resented the way she corrected him when he cleaned the house, bathed the children, and even chewed his food. Morey confided in his friend, "I fantasize about leaving her just so I can feel good about myself again." Morey loved Maureen and Maureen loved Morey. But Maureen was unaware that Morey did not think she saw him as a capable person. He longed to have her admiration—a deep and abiding need for everyone.

Once Maureen understood how important it was to demonstrate admiration for Morey, she was able to communicate in a more encouraging way. Morey's anger disappeared once his core need of feeling capable and admired was restored.

The following four behaviors are extremely damaging to a partner's sense of feeling capable and admired: controlling behavior, perfectionism, criticism, and refusing to allow participation. Each of these behaviors sends the messages, "I don't trust you to do it well enough" and "I don't respect or admire you." These messages are usually unintentional but they are hurtful and invite anger and withdrawal from the recipient.

Controlling Behavior

Ray seemed to do everything right, but in his haste to get the house looking clean and accomplishing other household tasks he began to tell his wife how to do everything. Years later, his wife had an affair with a vulnerable, single father who needed her and made her feel capable and important. After getting caught, she told Ray that he had repeatedly made her feel like a child who was being scolded and bossed around by a critical parent. She no longer felt admired by him. The underlying message Ray gave her was, "I am more capable than you, so you need to do it my way."

It is humiliating and disrespectful to insist that your spouse (or your children) do it "your" way. They need the autonomy to do things their own way, even if it is very different from how you operate and even if it is imperfect.

Perfectionism

Often people with a strong need to control have unrealistically high standards for themselves and everyone around them. They feel very tense and out of control when things are not done "perfectly." Perfectionism has destroyed many marriages and many parent-child relationships. The cure for perfectionism is to first learn to accept your own imperfections. When you can love yourself and give yourself "grace" when you make mistakes, you will be able to accept the imperfections in your loved ones. Perfectionists do not view mistakes as opportunities to learn. They view mistakes as opportunities to correct the idiot who should have known how to do it in the first place! Perfectionism is rooted in low self-esteem and a deep need to prove one's worth by doing things flawlessly.

> Perfectionism is rooted in low self-esteem and a deep need to prove one's worth by doing things flawlessly.

Perfectionists hurt their loved ones by questioning and criticizing their worth. Perfectionism guarantees that the ugly, self-perpetuating cycle of misbehavior will occur, and, without intervention, the relationship will be destroyed. If you are a perfectionist, we highly recommend you practice what Rudolf Dreikurs called "the courage to be imperfect" as well as the courage to allow your spouse to be imperfect.

Criticism, Put-Downs

Do you have the bad habit of chronically criticizing your spouse and children? Criticism destroys feelings of being cherished and admired. A critical spirit wreaks havoc on marriages and children.

If you grew up in a critical household and learned to be critical, decide now that this contagious habit will stop with you. If criticism continues, your children and your marriage will pay the price now and in the future.

Refusing to Allow Participation

It is discouraging to children and adults when they are not invited to help with household and other responsibilities. Many spouses stop trying to contribute because they are told they aren't doing it well enough or "right." It is so painful to feel incapable that they will soon stop trying to help. Their sentiments are, "I'm just going to do it wrong anyway so why should I try? I'm just setting myself up." If they feel unappreciated in their efforts to help, they may avoid being hurt by spending more time at the office or in solo activities.

THE FIVE STEPS OF ENCOURAGEMENT

1. Spend special time as a couple.

2. Convey a sense of belonging and significance through affection and sex.

3. Get into your spouse's world.

4. Give compliments and appreciations.

5. Give your spouse unconditional acceptance.

The Encouragement Anecdote

SINCE DISCOURAGEMENT IS the root cause of the pain and anger that lies beneath the destructive cycle of misbehavior in marriages, the obvious anecdote is encouragement. Both partners can learn how to strengthen the other's sense of belonging, connection, and capability by becoming experts in the art of encouragement.

Spend Special Time as a Couple

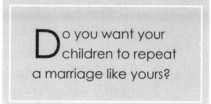

Do you want your children to repeat a marriage like yours?

Many marriages are taking a back seat to the urgent demands of work and children. Little to no time is carved out to honor the marriage. This is a huge mistake. Children benefit when they witness a happy and loving marriage. Your children learn about relationships by observing you. Do you want your children to repeat a marriage like yours?

Janie grew up in a home with parents who centered their entire lives on their children's needs, especially their youngest child who was severely handicapped. Her parents never did anything for themselves as individuals or as a couple. All recreation was family-centered and evenings out were always family outings. A nurse or babysitter was never brought in to care for Janie's handicapped brother.

Janie learned that "good" parents sacrificed everything for the needs of their children. At a very young age, Janie made a subconscious decision that only bad parents ever excluded their children.

In her twenties, Janie married Sam, a handsome, very social sales manager. Sam's parents were energetic, happy people who balanced time with Sam and his brother with time for them alone as a couple. They took ballroom dance lessons, went to dinner and the theater, and played bridge with other couples. Sam observed this and assumed (subconsciously) that this was the way parenting and marriage operated.

Janie and Sam were happily married until they had children.

One night Sam called his wife from the airport after a business trip and said, "I have missed you terribly. Can you put on a pretty dress and meet me downtown? I want to take you to a romantic dinner at a French restaurant."

Janie was furious, "How can you possibly not want to come home to your two little boys who have been missing you? What kind of father doesn't want to come home to see his kids?"

Depending on how you were raised, you may see Sam or Janie as being "right." Both of them have powerful internal "shoulds" operating around the appropriate way to honor the competing demands of self-care, marriage, and children. Sam believed that a romantic night with his wife would make her feel special and didn't have a moral issue with putting his wife first and enjoying time with the boys the next day. Janie's "should" caused an internal conflict for her. Her deeply rooted belief was that "good" parents put their time and energy into the children while they are living in the home while focus on the marriage was for after the children left the nest.

Janie believed that individual or couple time was only acceptable if it did not affect the children in any way. She believed it to be unfair and selfish to leave the children with a sitter so she and Sam could have fun together. Needless to say, this has caused conflict in their marriage.

Sam expressed his frustration, "I feel like I play second fiddle to the children every day. Any needs I have are viewed as 'selfish.' I'm embarrassed to admit that I feel jealous of her love and commitment to the boys. I am starting to feel like an unnecessary appendage that is good for only one thing—a paycheck."

Sam is suffering from a lack of special time with his wife. He knows his children belong to Janie. He just doesn't believe he does. In his hurt, he lashes out in criticism of Janie and the kids and then withdraws, feeling inadequate as both a husband and a father. Feeling unnecessary, he begins to spend more time away from home. Janie, stung by his withdrawal, and not understanding his hurt, responds by withholding affection and sex. She continues to make sarcastic remarks about his lack of involvement with the family.

They are stuck in the lack of the belonging/misbehavior cycle diagrammed earlier in this chapter. Their vastly different upbringings have caused them both to believe, "I do not belong." As soon as this belief has a foothold, defensive behaviors will escalate until both people no longer feel loved.

Janie is not alone in her beliefs. Many men and women allow their marriage to be put on the back burner behind work and children, especially if their parents modeled this. If you, like Janie, subscribe to this theory, we strongly urge you to rethink the cost to you, your marriage, and your children. It is imperative to carve out time with our mates. This time must be vigorously protected; it must be non-negotiable, carved in stone.

> Many men and women allow their marriage to be put on the back burner behind work and children, especially if their parents modeled this.

It is healthier for the couple relationship and for children when the marriage comes first. Ideally the children should be such a close second that they hardly know the difference, but the difference is important. Deep down, your children need to know that your spouse is "your one and only." It is great for them to see the two of you hugging and cuddling on the couch and going on dates together. This makes them feel safe and teaches them that a passionate, wholehearted commitment to marriage doesn't end when children come along.

There is too much at stake to let mistaken beliefs or urgent but less important tasks rob you of a vital and loving marriage. Regular quality time with your sweetheart will protect your sense of belonging and will create a loving cycle of behaviors to keep your marriage passionate and loving.

Take the time to sit down as a couple and brainstorm both of your ideas for your daily, weekly, quarterly, and annual time together. It is fun and exciting to dream about and plan sacred time for just the two of you. Make your dreams a reality by getting out your calendars and scheduling your special time together first. It is critical to prioritize and calendar time for your marriage before work,

PRESCRIPTION FOR A HEALTHY, LONG MARRIAGE

Daily special couple time

Weekly dates

Quarterly weekend getaways

Annual vacations

social, church, and extended family obligations rob you of the time you need to nurture and grow your relationship. Following through on your plans will pay huge dividends into your "belonging" bank account, which will bring forth the most loving behaviors of both of you.

If you find yourself objecting to the prescription for a healthy, long marriage, ask yourself why? Is it finances? Is it that you don't trust anyone other than yourself to watch your kids? Does it feel wrong to you? If so, consider the long-term consequences of your choices. You may be overprotective, which will rob your children of the opportunity to feel capable and teach them fear instead of confidence. If you were taught to make marriage a lower priority, consider making a decision that placing your marriage at the top of the family's priorities is not selfish, but is in every family member's best interest.

Convey Belonging Through Affection and Sex

"Affection," which we will define as caring, nonsexual touch, is one of the most powerful ways to make your partner feel cherished. Regular affection sends a powerful message of belonging, which summons our most loving behaviors. Affection meets the core need to feel special and deeply cared for. Holding your spouse on the couch, spooning him or her in bed, giving back rubs, holding hands, and frequent hugs will mean the world to your spouse. Affection and sex elevate the belief "I am loved," which always moves the relationship toward the positive cycle of behaviors.

Get Into Your Spouse's World

During courtship most couples recall how they would talk for hours about everything in their lives. Their sweetheart would listen to every last word. Later in marriage, the need for meaningful conversation continues and it is painful to both parties when the intimate sharing stops.

There is a special sense of connection when you share your innermost thoughts and feelings and hear the innermost thoughts and feelings of your spouse. When the conversational and emotionally intimate days of courtship are gone, the loss is acute. The cost to the relationship is high—loss of closeness and connection, and, you guessed it, belonging!

Listening Is Encouraging

When you think of the person in your life who has offered you the most encouragement and unconditional love, chances are you will recall a person who listened to you with real enthusiasm. Good listeners make you feel special. They send you a loud and clear message, "You matter to me. I care about everything that is going on in your life!"

Use What, Why, and How Questions

If you or your mate are feeling a lack of love and acceptance, listening and asking questions (as if you were Barbara Walters trying to get the scoop on a story) is a surefire way to elevate the sense of belonging in your marriage. Learn to become proficient in using the what, why, and how questions we have encouraged you to use with your children. Questions such as, "What is still missing from your career?" or "What specifically could I do to help you with your stress?" or "How can I be a better partner for you?" will help you know the internal thoughts, feelings, and needs of your partner.

Listen Without Fixing

Children and adults have a great need to be listened to without being "fixed." So does your spouse. It is important to listen attentively to your spouse and your children without trying to solve the problem, unless they invite brainstorming for solutions. You

> Listen attentively to your spouse and your children without trying to solve the problem, unless they invite brainstorming for solutions.

can provide comfort, caring, and a therapeutic benefit to your loved ones just from listening compassionately and allowing them to be heard.

One woman related a time when she cried in her husband's arms after her mother's death. "I wanted to cry and have him soothe me with hugs and words of understanding. But he immediately started giving me advice so I wouldn't get upset like, 'Stop torturing yourself by thinking about her. Just get busy so you can't think about it. Maybe you should try reading and exercising more, but stop dwelling on it!' I felt totally abandoned. I needed comfort, not to be told I was wrong to feel my pain. He made me feel worse than when I started."

Like many of us, this husband meant well. He hated to see his wife in pain and felt an urgent need to take it away. He failed to understand that she needed to share her feelings with an empathic and caring listener. While it wouldn't have brought back her mom, she would have felt understood, loved, and nurtured.

When you feel compelled to fix your partner or your children, remember to listen without fixing. It is a very loving and encouraging practice.

Give Compliments and Show Appreciation

Compliments and appreciation significantly bolster the sense of belonging and significance. It is much better to receive compliments without having to fish for them. Make it a daily habit to appreciate the little things. Compliments such as, "Thank you for working so hard day every day" or "I appreciate how you pitch in and help with the dishes every night" go a long way toward making the other one feel loved and appreciated. When people feel valued, the evil cycle of negativity is warded off and the positive cycle can flourish.

Give Your Spouse Unconditional Acceptance

Love and acceptance are a choice. To love well, you must decide that you will completely accept your partner as an imperfect human being. Some people have an easier time accepting their children's imperfections because they understand that young people are supposed to make mistakes. But the truth is that older people are also supposed to make mistakes.

If you want love and intimacy to thrive, you must make a conscious decision to give acceptance and grace to your partner. Your loved ones must be emotionally safe to make mistakes. If you decide to give your mate the gifts of unconditional love and acceptance, you will be blessed beyond your greatest expectations. The love and compassion you extend will come back to you a hundredfold in myriad loving and kind behaviors. It is your decision: Would you rather be happy or right?

If you become proficient in the art of encouragement, you will be well on your way toward bringing out the best behaviors in your partner and enjoying a close and intimate marriage. And you will notice a huge difference in your children.

Handling Conflict Positively

THE NEXT SECTION will give you tools to deal with the inevitable conflict and disagreements that occur in marriage.

Schedule Regular Couple Meetings

Just like family meetings, regularly scheduled couple meetings will prevent problems and resentments from building up and keep the lines of communication open. Here are a few suggestions:

SIX TOOLS FOR DEALING WITH COUPLE CONFLICT

1. Schedule regular couple meetings (problem-solving time).

2. Make agreements in advance; negotiate a fair division of labor.

3. Allow separate realities.

4. Balance kindness with firmness.

5. Decide what you will do, not what you will make your spouse do.

6. Take positive time-out when needed.

1. Have a regularly scheduled couple meeting each week.

2. Start with appreciations and compliments.

3. Brainstorm solutions for any problems.

4. Review upcoming events.

5. Plan your special recreational time as individuals, a couple, and family.

Make Agreements in Advance; Negotiate Labor

An excellent tool for avoiding conflict over who should be doing what with the children and the household tasks is to negotiate a plan that works for both of you. It is important for couples to proactively write down a "Desired Division of Labor" (similar to the desired agenda for fun and recreation), especially if both of you work outside the home. Agreeing in advance on the division of labor for taking care of the children and household maintenance and repair will avoid a lot of unnecessary arguments and hurt feelings. Both of your likes and dislikes should be taken into account. (For example if one of you hates taking out the garbage but enjoys weeding, make a deal!) This exercise will empower both of you to clearly understand your roles and responsibilities at home.

Finding a *fair* division of labor depends on what both of you think is fair. Make a list of all that needs to be done on a weekly basis and decide who in the family will do what. It is important that children are given age-appropriate tasks so that they can contribute in a meaningful way to the family as well.

Karen carried deep resentment that her husband, Fred, watched TV at night while she was doing homework with the kids, reading to them, and doing the dishes. One of the reasons Fred did not offer help more often is that Karen never voiced her needs, and when he did help, Karen would criticize his methods. She did the work herself and was angry that he didn't see her obvious need for help.

Karen made the following list of tasks for which she wanted Fred's help:

1. Helping the children with homework.

2. Co-facilitating family meetings.

3. Helping with the bedtime routine: baths, story time, etc.

4. Participating in family recreation at home and on outings.

5. Being aware of and attending the children's school activities—back-to-school nights, open houses, and the children's special events.

6. Attending religious services as a family.

7. Helping to organize family work and projects.

8. Assisting in preparation of and being home for family meals.

Fred said he would enjoy helping with homework and bedtime routines when Karen agreed to let him do these tasks in his own unique way without insisting he do it her way. They also agreed on who in the family would take responsibility for each household task on a weekly basis. They worked out the specifics in their family meeting. Because everyone hated taking out the trash and cleaning the cat box, they all took turns so that no one felt like the perpetual *garbage person*.

Appreciate Separate Realities

Many couples have conflict because one partner is unable to appreciate the separate reality of the other—individual thoughts, feelings, desires, and beliefs.

Or sometimes both partners deny the other his or her separate reality. The health of your marriage requires allowing each other to retain individuality and unique personhood. The attitude in your marriage must be "We can have different opinions and feelings and both of our viewpoints are valid."

> The attitude in your marriage must be, "We can have different opinions and feelings and both of our viewpoints are valid."

Misery is a foregone conclusion if the attitude in your marriage is "I know what is best, so you must do it my way!" Your marriage can be happy only if both of you seek to understand and accept your partner's different perceptions. It is a sacred duty for you to honor both your individual identity and reality and your partner's individual identity and reality. It is unhealthy to give up your own feelings and needs to please your partner just as it is unhealthy for you to force your partner to give up his or her feelings and needs.

Balance Kindness with Firmness

Too much kindness toward your partner can be dishonoring to yourself, while too much firmness can be dishonoring to your partner. A simple rule to remember in balancing kindness and firmness is "Always honor self and other at the same time." When we are kind, we are respectful to others, and when we are firm, we set boundaries that are respectful to ourselves. How can we do both? First, we'll advise you what *not* to do.

Many people are overly kind and generous to others. We define "overly kind" as doing for others even when it does not fit for you and may be detrimental to you. When you give too much, in that your giving is harmful to your well-being, you will ultimately feel resentful and taken advantage of.

Doug is the proverbial overly kind, placating husband. He cannot say "no" to anyone. He works two jobs so he could avoid saying no to his wife when she found her dream home in a great school district. He cannot say no to her when she wants to go on yet another trip to Disneyland that he knows they cannot afford. He is unable to say no to his mother when she asks for time-consuming favors like reroofing her home and replanting her yard. He is exhausted, deeply in debt, and angry that no one is looking out for his welfare.

Doug gives to everyone but does nothing for himself. He doesn't see friends, exercise, or goof off. He barely sees his family because he is so busy working to pay for a house he never enjoys and vacations they cannot afford. Like all overly kind, placating people, his motto is "I need you to value me so I'll give to you even if it kills me!"

Doug needs to balance his genuinely caring nature with the firmness to stand up for himself and his needs. He needs to learn how to go inside and give his true "yes" and his true "no." He is kind to everyone but himself. If he could learn to take care of himself, he would not feel so tired and resentful toward those to whom he gives too much. We train people how to treat us. Doug has trained his wife and everyone close to him that he will do whatever they ask of him, regardless of the cost to himself.

At the opposite extreme is the overly firm person—the blamer. Blamers are very firm in asserting their rights and needs. Their motto is "It's your fault. Why can't you get it right?" Overly firm individuals are very good at honoring their own needs while they trample on the needs, rights, and feelings of others. John is a classic blamer. When his wife makes a mistake, he is quick to point it out. When he makes a mistake, he is quick to defend himself by saying that she "made me do it." In short, it is always someone else's fault. John carries himself with a one up, superior aura.

In reality, his grandiosity is a cover for a deep sense of inadequacy and low self-esteem. He is overly firm to defend and protect himself from being hurt. Underneath his defensiveness, he is saying, "I feel vulnerable and hopeless." He wants to be close to people but finds himself very lonely because other people soon tire of his offensive behavior. John must learn to balance his assertiveness (firmness) with kindness and sensitivity for the needs of others.

You must learn how to balance kindness and firmness if you want to be a skilled marriage partner and parent. When you are kind to yourself by using boundaries to take care of your needs, you will be in a much better position to honor your partner as well. Overly kind behavior results in unhealthy enmeshment: One person gives up his or her individuality to be in the relationship. Doug is essentially saying, "I'm willing to give up me to be with you."

It is exciting to have two unique, whole individuals in the marriage. Differences are necessary to keep the marriage passionate and alive. If you can stand up for yourself without going overboard and dishonoring the other person through blame and shame, you will be in a position to have a healthy, exciting, and encouraging partnership. The correct motto is "I can be fully me and you can be fully you. I can freely share my thoughts, feelings, and needs in a way that is respectful to you, and you can freely share your thoughts, feelings, and needs in a way that respects me. We try as hard as we can to honor both of our needs."

> It is exciting to have two unique, whole individuals in the marriage. Differences are necessary to keep the marriage passionate and alive.

As you make a sincere effort to meet your partner's needs, he or she will feel loved and appreciated. A profound sense of belonging, connection, and capability is the result when you make the decision to honor yourself and your partner's needs.

Decide What You Will Do

Even though they have heard that you can't change anyone but yourself a million times, most couples are still trying to change each other. They really struggle with step 3 on the encouragement list—to allow and respect separate realities.

Matt and Molly, parents of two elementary school-age children, thought they had a marriage made in heaven until Molly discovered that Matt was "always" late. At first Molly was annoyed. She pleaded with Matt to be on time because she hated to be late for things. Molly was well organized and able to get her kids to cooperate with her need to be timely. But Matt continued to be late. Molly became very angry and started lecturing about how Matt was thoughtless and inconsiderate. Matt was still late. Then Molly became revengeful and started withholding sex. Matt could play this game. Not only did he continue being late, he sometimes wouldn't show up at all. Oh, he always had good excuses about having to work overtime or getting stuck in traffic, but his lateness got worse, not better.

Molly was almost ready for a divorce when a friend told her that the positive discipline principles work just as well with spouses as with children, and Molly might try deciding what she would do. And, her friend reminded her, "Don't forget the importance of being kind and firm at the same time."

Molly decided to give it a try. That evening she said, "Matt, I can't make you be on time. It is obvious that we have different values. I will no longer nag you about being late, but, also, I will no longer wait. When it is time to go to an event, I hope you will be home in time to leave with me. However, if you aren't, I will go by myself. We have two cars, and I hope you will join me as soon as you can because I prefer being with you to being by myself. I would rather have you join me late than to not come at all."

The next time they had an engagement to go to dinner at friends, Molly had picked up the babysitter, given hugs to the kids, and was in her car and ready to leave when Matt came driving up to the house and said, "It will take me just a few minutes to change my clothes." Molly said, "Oh good, I'm glad I won't have to be alone at the dinner for long," and she drove off.

Matt was annoyed. When he joined Molly at the dinner, he said, "Couldn't you wait even five minutes?" Molly kindly and firmly replied, "I respect your value to be late. I hope you'll respect my value to be on time. Even five minutes late is very upsetting to me. I don't want to take my upset out on you, so I avoid being upset by following my value to be on time." Then Molly joked, "Don't you just love it that I'm not on your case anymore?"

Matt realized he did love it, and he loved Molly. He started making an effort to be on time more often—and he was, about half the time. The rest of the time he was late and had to listen to his friends nag him about being late all the time.

Molly decided what she would do and allowed Matt to experience the consequences of his choices.

Positive Time-Out for Couples

Okay, so you have decided that everything we have discussed in this chapter makes sense—and you are going to do it. Unless you are a saint, you will make mistakes along the way. There is nothing like a marriage partner to bring up all the old, unresolved issues from your childhood. You are likely to become upset many times and revert to your reptilian brain.

The impossibility of resolving a conflict when upset (in the reptilian brain) is just as true for married couples as it is for children and parents. You will have a much more respectful and encouraging

> There is nothing like a marriage partner to bring up all the old, unresolved issues from your childhood.

marriage if you decide in advance that you will take positive time-out when you are upset.

Harry and Michelle used to argue all the time. The added stress of working full time and raising three children escalated their fighting. When they reached the boiling point, Harry would often slam the front door as he left and would be gone for several hours. Michelle would slam the bedroom door and lay in bed, fuming. Then she would have to get up and tend to the needs of their children while Harry was off by himself.

They often stayed angry at each other for days. They didn't think about the impact of their fighting on the children. It is no wonder that their children were always fighting. They had taught their children to take positive time-outs, but didn't think of taking time out for themselves until they attended a parenting workshop that included a component for how couples could improve their marriage by using the positive discipline principles.

When they went home that evening, the kids were already in bed so they sat down for a couple meeting and created their own ways to do positive time-out. Harry decided that getting out of the house still worked for him, but he told Michelle, "I won't be leaving to get away from you, but to walk around the block until I have calmed down and can talk with you respectfully."

Michelle said, "I still like going to the bedroom, but instead of fuming, I'll read a good book until I have calmed down. We'll let the kids know what we are doing, so we can be good role models for them and let them know that they can take care of themselves for a few minutes or join us in our "time-out" arrange-

ments to help us feel better. I have faith in us to find great solutions when we take some time-out until we can access our rational brains." And they did.

Each spouse should decide in advance what will help him or her feel better when upset and inform the partner of his or her plan. Their children were also invited to write a list of what helped them calm down when they found themselves in their reptilian brains. The whole family grew in the life skill of self-soothing.

Sometimes it is difficult to remember to take time-out when you are angry, but it will get easier with practice. Michelle and Harry and their kids decided to make it a contest to see who could catch himself or herself (not each other) in a reptilian state first. Often, the fun of being first was enough to make them laugh and the need for time-out would be gone. Other times, one or the other would say, "Okay, I can see what is happening, but I still need time-out." I'll get back to you when I feel better.

The Blessings of a Happy Marriage

THIS CHAPTER HAS explored the positive discipline principles and tools in the context of marriage. If you are diligent in applying them, you will find yourself in the self-perpetuating cycle of joy and contentment. As you become an expert at encouraging rather than discouraging your husband or wife, you will be blessed beyond your greatest expectations. These blessings will extend to your children and your children's children. It is well worth the effort.

The next chapter will focus on the three remaining sections on the right side of the wheel: your family life, career, and finances.

14

Family, Career, and Finances

Workaholism vs. Balancing Family and Work

THIS CHAPTER WILL focus on examining the three remaining sections of the Wheel of Life: career, finances, and family. Our purpose is to help you design a balanced plan of action between your work, finances, and family that will help you honor your long-term goals and bring you contentment. We will address the difficult decisions you must make in order to live true to your authentic self at work and at home.

If you are overly focused on your career and the pursuit of money, the cost may be emotional closeness and trust with your family. If you are deeply committed to your family, you may have to sacrifice some of your financial or professional goals for a time. These choices are not easy. It is difficult to truly have it all at the same time. Sometimes success in each area of our lives comes sequentially with an intense focus in one area for a season with a shift to a different arena during another season.

The tribute statement in chapter 12 was meant to help you get in touch with what you truly want your life to stand for when it is over. When you are living true to that vision, you will find peace and contentment. If you betray yourself by violating that vision, you will have stress, anxiety, and unhappiness. You cannot live out of step with your values and be happy. As the Greek philosopher Socrates stated, "An unexamined life is not worth living."

If you are like most people, you have a deep desire for a meaningful, close relationship with your children and mate. At the end of your life you want your children to be able to say that they felt connected to and loved by you. Achieving your family dreams as well as a measure of happiness and fulfillment in your career will require introspection and conscious decisions to support your internal truth.

Protect Your Family Time

POSITIVE DISCIPLINE TECHNIQUES require time and persistent effort. It will take time for you to achieve a deep connection with your children and time to teach them the life skills they need to become responsible and well-ad-

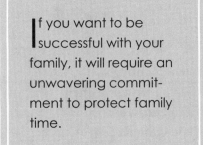

If you want to be successful with your family, it will require an unwavering commitment to protect family time.

justed adults. If you want to be successful with your family, it will require an unwavering commitment to protect family time. Without this commitment, the urgent demands from the office and the incessant beckoning of household tasks will steal precious relationship-building time. You must vehemently guard special time for your family or risk letting work and home responsibilities rob you of the precious years when your children want to spend time with you. The following Yiddish poem appeared in the *Wall Street Journal* and beautifully illustrates what can happen if you allow work to rob you of a meaningful connection with your child.

I have a son, a little son,
A boy completely fine
When I see him it seems to me
That all the world is mine.
But seldom, seldom do I see
My child awake and bright;
I only see him when he sleeps,
I'm only home at night.
It's early when I leave for work,
When I return it's late.

Unknown to me is my own flesh,
Unknown is my child's face.
When I come home so wearily
In the darkness after day,
My pale wife exclaims to me:
"You should have seen our child play."
I stand beside his little bed,
I look and try to hear.
In his dream he moves his lips:
Why isn't Papa here?"[1]

Become the Parent You Wish You Had

You may have grown up during a generation when mothers were home the majority of the time, and fathers who worked full time were home late in the evenings. As women have entered the workforce, increasing numbers of men are spending far more time with their children than their fathers ever did. Fathers are starting to know their kids in an everyday kind of way. Many are trying to become the fathers they never had by becoming totally invested in their children's lives. It is common to see men walking their children to and from school, helping with homework, coaching sports teams, and carpooling to myriad activities.

But often we unknowingly repeat the unhealthy parenting dynamics we observed in the families in which we grew up. It is important to "unlearn" what you learned from your parents if it is harmful. Kirk, a pool contractor, works ten to twelve hours a day, seven days a week. He doesn't remember seeing much of his father when he was growing up. Kirk, like his father, believes that it is his job to be a good provider and that his long work hours are for the greater good of his family. Kirk's wife, Margie, works forty hours a week as the office manager for his pool business and assumes full responsibility for raising their nine-year-old son, Connor. She helps him with homework, feeds him dinner, takes him to karate, and plans weekend activities for the two of them. Connor recently told his dad, "It's like I don't even have a father. It feels like I only have a mother." Kirk's response was, "But Connor, I am working hard for

---

1. Rabbi Jeffrey K. Salkin, "Smash the False Gods of Careerism," *Wall Street Journal,* 29 December 1994, A8.

you and Mom. If I didn't work this many hours we couldn't afford our nice house and all the activities you get to do, like karate." Connor's immediate response was, "I don't care about having a big house or karate. I just wish you'd play ball with me at the park like I see some of the other dads doing." Children hear what we do, not what we say.

Kirk and Margie had unconsciously fallen into the same lifestyle they experienced growing up. Doug measured his self-worth only in terms of his monetary achievements. He also defined his success as a husband and father in terms of monetary achievements, not time spent enjoying his family members. He did not understand that there are all kinds of currency to measure success, such as family success, marital success, social success, and physical success. Doug couldn't remember the last time he had played with Connor, taken his wife on a date, worked out, or had fun with friends. His scores in his Wheel of Life were extremely low in everything except career and finances.

Decide What Success Means to You

With input from Connor and Margie, Kirk decided that his focus in life was too narrow. He made a conscious decision to change his life to become successful not only at work and monetarily, but in meeting the needs of his wife and child as well. He decided that Sundays were to be set aside as sacred family time. He and his wife had to rework their budget and cut back on extras in order to buy him Sundays at home. Their long-term goal is to have the whole weekend reserved for family time.

Kirk also started coming home early on Fridays to take Margie on a date while Connor spent time with his cousins. Connor looks forward to Sundays all week. He and his dad made a list of fun activities they can enjoy together and they pick one from the list each week. They have played mud football, gone bowling, fishing, and bike riding. Kirk's relationships with his wife and Connor have improved dramatically. He now feels more successful at home and less exhausted on the job. An added bonus is that Connor's behavioral problems at school cleared up.

It is fine to be driven for success, but it is important that you seek a measure of success in every important and meaningful area in your life, not just in one or two. When you enlarge your definition of "success" to include accomplishments in your intimate relationship, your relationship with your children, and your ability to stay physically and emotionally fit, you will find yourself living a more balanced and fulfilling life. Ask yourself every week:

- How did I do at work?

- How well did I connect with my kids?

- How well did I connect with my mate?

- How well did I take care of myself?

- How did I do with my spending?

When you learn to proactively write down your goals and dreams in each area of your life and then set aside specific time to do them, you will be "successful" in the broadest sense of the word. Peace and happiness are the natural results when you live according to your most deeply held values.

> It is fine to be driven for success, but it is important that you seek a measure of success in every important and meaningful area in your life.

Block Distractions at Home

Larissa, a single mother of two small children, went back to work full time after an unexpected divorce. She realized that she would have only three waking hours a day with her children. She decided that she would not allow anything to infringe on the little bit of time she had to be with her kids between 5:00 and 8:00 P.M. She unplugged her phone and refused to open mail, pay bills, or check

e-mail until after 8:00. She made those evening hours count with her children by not allowing the outside world to encroach on their special time.

Larissa involved her children in all the tasks that had to be done. They helped her cook dinner (even if the little one took half an hour to peel one carrot!) and they helped her do dishes. She played a game with them each night and read stories. She made a firm commitment to be home for them after work and took care of her own needs on her lunch hour and when the children spent time with their father on the weekends. Larissa's children are grown now, and all of them cherish the memories that resulted from her unwavering decision to protect special family time when they were young. It was sacred time that forged an unbreakable bond.

Suggestions for Unplugging from the World

- Unhook from the electronic leash to work. Turn off work pagers, cell phones, and e-mail. Consecrate home time that cannot be disturbed. Let your supervisor and colleagues know you will be unavailable during certain hours. Unplug the phone and really talk with your children. If you absolutely have to do more work, wait until after you have eaten dinner and enjoyed some quality evening time with your children.

- Protect the family dinner hour as often as you can. The family dinner hour has been one of the casualties of our fast-paced world. It is an im-

portant tradition that has served to keep families connected for centuries. Attempt to eat together four times a week if possible—with the TV off.

- Use your calendar or planner to schedule non-negotiable family time. Schedule specific blocks of time for family meetings, evening family time, special one-on-one dates with your children, and couple time. It will empower you to say no when your boss or co-worker asks you to stay late or do extra work. You can say, "I'm sorry, I already have a very important meeting scheduled." They don't have to know it is a family meeting or an appointment to take your nine-year-old miniature golfing.

- Periodically prune activities that may be taking more from your family than they give. Try to have some evenings every week that are free from meetings and carpooling to extracurricular activities. Your family will benefit from some scheduled, unhurried time to play board games, watch a movie together, or just talk. Regularly reevaluate your lives to determine if you are too busy to enjoy each other.

Devise a Strategy to Stay in Touch with Your Kids

Dr. Phil, the no-nonsense, self-help guru, shares a decision he made to assure that he would stay close and connected to his two young boys.

I made a decision with my boys a long time ago that they would be able to reach me at any time, anywhere, for any reason. I've worked as a litigation consultant for many years. I was in a boardroom in New York on the 90th floor of a Fortune 100 company making a presentation to thirty executives and my cell phone rang. I looked at it and it was one of my boys and I said, "Gentlemen, can you excuse me for a second?" I came back and said, "I'd love to be able to tell you that I've been stamping out disease and suffering in Eastern Europe with that phone call but the truth is that that was my son and he couldn't find the pump for the basketball. But I just made a deal with them that they could reach their dad at any time so they don't feel they come second to my work." When I said it, thirty men stood up and applauded. They said that hearing about my decision with my boys was worth the meeting.[2]

> The greatest gift you can give your children is something that can't be purchased with money. It is the message, "You are important to me and your needs count."

The greatest gift you can give your children is something that can't be purchased with money. It is the message, "You are important to me and your needs count." Devise a strategy with your children for how to stay in touch.

Career

TO HAVE A high score in the career section of your wheel, you must really enjoy what you do. Are you in a career that makes your heart sing, or are you just trying to endure another day?

Finding a Career That Is Uniquely Right for You

Since half of your waking life is spent on the job, it is critical that you find fulfillment in what you do. It is almost impossible for you to be happy if you dislike your work. Your unhappiness at work will insidiously creep into the contentment in your home life and all areas of your life. It is essential that you honor yourself by having a career that is rewarding for you. It is not enough to have a high level of satisfaction in the financial arena if you hate what you do, day after day. *USA Today* reports that one in six workers think about quitting their jobs on a weekly basis.[3] It is doubtful that these workers have careers that are meaningful or fulfilling to them.

Lauren had been the sales manager for five years at a successful software company. She had an excellent salary, received hefty commissions and bonuses, drove a company car, had outstanding benefits, and an annual luxury vacation for her and her husband. She also enjoyed a fairly flexible work sched-

---

2. Dr. Phil show in January 2003 on workaholics.

3. Cindy Hall and Julie Stacey, "Quitting Time," *USA Today*, 10 February 1997, 1B.

ule so she could be with her two young children by 4:00 P.M. and care for them when they were sick. But there was one fundamental problem. Lauren hated what she did. She hated the constant cold calls to potential customers, the infighting among her sales staff, the detailed proposals she had to write, and the endless number crunching. She had wanted to be a psychologist for as long as she could remember. But the financial perks in sales kept her from following the desires of her heart year after year.

She dreaded work every day, but she and her family had become accustomed to her high income. She felt trapped, angry, and unfulfilled. While she scored the financial section of her wheel a "ten," her career section scored an unsatisfactory "two."

Lauren became increasingly unhappy with her work and life as a whole. She came home grouchy and was depressed Sunday evenings in anticipation of going back on Monday to a grind she despised. Desperate, she and her husband came up with a plan for Lauren to realize her dream of becoming a psychologist. They found a masters program that offered courses one evening a week and one Saturday a month for two years. They agreed she would stay with her current job while she completed her advanced degree. They significantly reduced their monthly budget so they could save for the time when Lauren would quit her job and work at a significantly reduced rate of pay.

Once Lauren had a plan in place to move into her preferred career, she stopped resenting her current position. She viewed her job as a means to a much-desired end. Lauren and her family have long since transitioned into her new career. She does not make as much money, but her life is infinitely more happy and meaningful.

If you know intuitively that you are in the wrong field, take a risk on your own behalf and find a career that uniquely suits you. If you don't know what that would be, see a career counselor or purchase the book *What Color Is Your Parachute* or *Cool Careers for Dummies*. It is also helpful to ask yourself what you would be willing to do for free. One woman parlayed her love of gardening into a full-time business creating beautiful flower gardens for the storefront businesses in her small town. A gourmet cook quit a job he found tedious to cater parties and weddings. Find out what career would be fun and meaningful to you. The effort will be well worth it. It will breathe new passion into your life and make you a more enjoyable person to be around.

Decide How Much You Are Willing to Work

Work expands to fill the time available.

—PARKINSON'S LAW

Just as it is important to be doing work you love, it is spiritually and emotionally essential to ask yourself how much work you are willing to do and then to guard that truth with all your might. Your life and the lives of your family depend upon it. Discover your optimum time for work that will allow you to stay passionate and interested in your work life while keeping you and your family happy and healthy.

Arlie Russell Hochschild, the author of *The Time Bind: When Work Becomes Home and Home Becomes Work,* notes women work an average of 41.7 hours and men, 48.8 hours.[4] The median husband and wife are on the job for a combined 90 hours per week. This is before you count the numerous hours spent working on the home front. Harvard economist Juliet Schor explains in the book, *Overworked Americans,* "In the last twenty years the average American worker added the equivalent of one month to the work year."[5]

This trend toward longer and longer work hours is having a devastating impact on most American workers and families. The effects of overwork include overwhelming stress, loss of intimacy with children, marital tension, increased physical illnesses, sleep disorders, anxiety, and depression. In spite of the harm caused by long hours on the job, there is tremendous resistance among American workers to buck the system by asking to work fewer hours.

While you may know that you need to work fewer hours to have the time and energy necessary for your family's well-being, you may be reluctant to seek the necessary changes. Some of this resistance is grounded in the practical realities of our work culture. Even the most *family friendly* organizations often expect you to perform as if you have no other life. You may fear the loss of respect or reprisals from your employer if you are forthright about your need to spend more time at home and less time at the office. It can be dangerous to behave in a way that suggests work is not far and away the top priority. So you are torn by two emotions—guilt for not spending enough time with your chil-

---

4. Arlie Russell Hochschild, *The Time Bind: When Work Becomes Home and Home Becomes Work* (New York City: Henry Holt and Company, 1997), interviewed on "The News Hour with Jim Lehrer," 15 July 1997.

5. Richard Swenson, *The Overload Syndrome,* (Colorado Springs, Co, NavPress, 1998, 172).

dren and worry about how less time at work will affect your career and your ability to make a living. You may find that you have to work two full-time jobs just to keep the lights on and put food on the table. Some jobs don't pay a living wage, so you may have to work overtime or have another job to make ends meet. This is not due to overspending—your family may be very frugal—but the cost of housing and health care are just too high to make it on one job that pays poorly. These are sad realities for many families.

> *Too many parents are working too many hours to collect "things," not to make ends meet. As these people look back at their lives, they often say, "My biggest regret is not spending more time with my kids." Making family your top priority means standing against a culture where materialism and workaholism are rampant. It means realizing that you may not advance as fast in your career as some of your colleagues—at least for a few years. It means being willing to accept a lower standard of living . . . knowing you're doing the right thing for your children.[6]*

Decide What You Will Do

Keith worked as an engineering supervisor in a fast-paced manufacturing firm in Silicon Valley. After adopting two infants a year apart, he decided that he was no longer willing to stay at the office until 7:00 P.M., the cultural norm in his company. By the time he commuted forty-five minutes home, he saw his little ones for only a half an hour before they fell asleep. He decided he was unwilling to miss every weekday evening with his family.

Keith switched his hours to an early start at 7:00 A.M. with a definite stop at 5:00 P.M. so he could enjoy dinner, play, bath time, and story time with his children. He communicated his decision to his supervisors and employees with kindness and firmness. He explained his need to commit evenings to his family and his reasons for preferring an early start.

Even though Keith consistently worked ten-hour days, he knew his colleagues typecast him as a slacker when he packed up to leave every day at 5:00 P.M. Keith said, "I would feel a lot worse about missing my kids growing-up years than I do about having my co-workers see me as less of a team player or being passed over for a promotion." Keith defined "success" for himself as giving a

---

6. Chuck Colson, *A Dangerous Grace* (Dallas, TX; Word Publishing, 1994, p. 198).

solid effort at work while spending quality evening hours with his wife and children. He has been unwavering in this commitment to balancing his work and family needs for the past five years. He enjoys a wonderfully close relationship with his two children. When he was passed over for a promotion at work, he was at peace because he viewed his worth and success in a holistic manner. He averaged his performance at work and at home and was willing to endure a temporary setback professionally in order to really be there for his children.

Are You Living to Work or Working to Live?

You may be unable to set the boundaries necessary to honor the needs of your family because your work defines you as a human being. If you consistently ignore your internal signals alerting you that you are hurting your family by working too many hours, you may be addicted to work. If you need to climb to the top of the career or financial ladder to feel valuable as a person, you will be unable to reduce your work time to honor what you know your family needs. You must first change how you get value as a human being. Until you realize that you have worth outside of your professional accomplishments, your efforts to scale back at work will be futile.

A workaholic is very different from someone with a solid work ethic. A workaholic receives a *fix* from the work itself. The work meets an intrinsic need that is so powerful it spirals beyond the person's control. A person with a good work ethic is in control of the schedule and has balance in his or her life. But a workaholic is controlled by the need for the high he or she gets from productivity, much like a drug addict craves his or her next high. This makes balance impossible.

> Your worth is based on so much more than how much money you make or how high you climb on the career ladder.

Workaholics, unlike other addicts, are socially and culturally sanctioned in our society. When you work long hours you receive praise and material rewards. This reinforces the need to continue the destructive addiction to work. The anecdote is to get a healthy relationship with yourself and realize that your worth is based on so much more than how much money you make or how high you climb on the career ladder. Many people must rewire their thought processes to find self-worth outside of work performance.

One successful attorney realized her parents had taught her at a very young age that her worth was contingent on financial success and prestigious work. When she was faced with losing her job due to a lack of compassion and respect toward her support staff, she had an opportunity to reevaluate what success really meant to her. She realized that success was so much bigger than money or prestige. She began to expand her definition of worth to include how she treated others, her relationship with her husband and daughter, and her quality of life and friendships. As she began to base her value on more than just money and career, she found herself able to detach from work in a healthy way. She no longer needs the praise from overwork to feel worthy as a person.

Ask yourself what you would do with your time if you had only six months to live. Your answer will reveal what truly matters most to you. Then you must confront the obstacles that stand in your way from claiming that truth for yourself.

Suggestions for Holding to Your Truth at Work

- Take responsibility for choosing how you are currently living. You have chosen your life at work and home and you can choose to change it, one step at a time.

- Think long and hard about promotions and the impact they will have on your family. You can refuse a promotion if the new role would not fit with the rest of your life and your goals.

- Begin with the end in mind. Reread your tribute statement from your kids (pages 206–207 in chapter 12) and think hard about how much time you are giving to work.

- If you live for work, *get a life!* Set goals for each section of the wheel and begin to take your partner and children on dates, find a new hobby, and make some friends! Learn to like yourself for all of you, not just your professional accomplishments.

- If the culture inherent in your company is workaholic, consider telling your employer about your long-term truth. If there is a total unwillingness to allow you a private life away from work, make a plan to get out. You and your family deserve better. The cost of denying your truth is too high.

- Attend Workaholics Anonymous meetings.

- Set boundaries to keep work, work and home, home.

- Consider working fewer hours.

- Cut down your commute time (the average is forty-five minutes per day).

- Be cautious about accepting a job with a lot of travel. It often requires weekends away from home to save on fares. Travel can take a real toll on the family.

Money

MANY PEOPLE OVERWORK for one simple reason—they overspend. Overspending pressures us to work more hours. If you, like most Americans, consume 110 percent or more of what you make, you will have little choice when it comes to changing to a less stressful profession or cutting back your hours—even if it is in your family's best interest. Overconsumption robs you of the freedom to honor your truth. Cutting back and living a simpler life will allow you to follow your heart. Money can be your master or you can master money.

> Many people overwork for one simple reason—they overspend.

Mary Anne was tired of being strapped by the huge house payment for her 3,000-square-foot home. She and her husband and son wanted more money available for vacations and fun. They sold their home and moved into a much smaller 1,800-square-foot home. They cut their house payment in half, and, with the savings, they purchased a motor home and three dirt bikes. Her family prioritized fun over a large house in an upscale neighborhood. They take several long vacations a year and spend one to two weekends a month camping in their motor home. They are thrilled with their choice. Some families downsize to allow one parent to work part time or not at all.

Personal indebtedness is the antithesis of freedom and is the major factor in determining people's willingness to reduce hours. Many of you would love to scale back at work and spend more time with your family, but high debt service makes it impossible. Interest payments are a cruel taskmaster.

Interest works night and day, in fair weather and in foul. It gnaws at a man's substance with invisible teeth.

—HENRY WARD BEECHER

Your children will learn how to manage money by watching what you do, not what you say. Do you like what you are teaching them? Use family meetings to teach your children financial principles by including them in decisions about how your family chooses to prioritize money. The most important thing about money is to make sure it accurately reflects your values and priorities. If you spend in a manner that allows you to live true to your ideals and goals, you will experience peace with your finances and in your life. It is sweet to enjoy the freedom that comes from consciously choosing your path.

Suggestions for Putting Your Financial House in Order

- Get out of debt. Determine why you got into debt in the first place and strategize to handle money differently in the future.

- Cut up your credit cards. Only use debit cards so you spend only what you have.

- Set goals as a family and budget together.

- Be willing to confront the reality of your financial situation if you are spending more than you make. Figure out how much less you need to spend and brainstorm with your family on how to make the cuts. Be willing to move your standard of living down if that is what you need to do to be financially solvent.

- Think long and hard about large purchases. Consult with your partner.

- Attend Debtors Anonymous if your spending is out of control.

- Seek credit counseling through the state if you are seriously in debt. They will help you consolidate and lower your debt payments so you can avoid bankruptcy.

- Teach your children how to manage money (as outlined in chapter 8).

Harmony and Balance Are Possible

PEACE COMES WHEN you live true to your personal values in each area of your life. If you valiantly protect family time, succeed in finding a career that is fulfilling to you, hold firm to your time boundaries at work to meet your family objectives, and manage your finances so they reflect your priorities, you will find that you are living a contented and meaningful life. When you work to bring harmony and balance to these three remaining sections of the Wheel of Life, you will possess the inner calm and happiness that comes when your external world accurately reflects the desires of your heart.

15

Positive Discipline
for Supervisors

Becoming an Encouraging Manager
with Positive Discipline Tools

T HE "LIGHT BULB" goes on for some parents when they realize that the positive management skills they use every day at work (if they already have these skills) are the same skills necessary to be an effective parent. Some parents have commented that the positive discipline skills they use with their children were also effective in the workplace. In short, effectiveness requires good people skills—at work and at home. And the art of encouragement is the foundation for good people skills.

Positive discipline provides you with tools of encouragement for your children. If you are a manager who applies these same principles in your work setting, you will become a very encouraging manager. You will succeed in meeting your employees' core human needs—to feel valued, a sense of belonging, capable, significant, and empowered. Your employees will love you for your efforts and will be more cooperative and productive. We include this chapter in the book because you can achieve the same positive results with positive discipline in the workplace that you can at home.

Encouragement

SOME PARENTS FIND it easier to be encouraging with their children than with employees. Others find it easy to be encouraging at work but difficult at home. One woman graded herself as an "A" mother, but a "C" supervisor because she was critical of her employees' mistakes but tolerant with her son's. One father confided to his parenting class that he was a respectful manager with healthy, equal relationships at work but was a punitive autocrat with his daughter. He was proud of his management abilities but ashamed of his parenting techniques. Most people recognize that they have room for improvement in at least one of the settings.

The following exercise will help you understand the traits of an encouraging supervisor from the employee's point of view. Please take a few minutes to fill out the traits of the worst supervisor(s) and best supervisor(s) you have had in your life. As you fill this out, remember what you experienced emotionally when you felt disrespected or unappreciated by your worst supervisor and what it was like to feel encouraged (valued and cared about) by your best supervisor. Recall one supervisor at a time and fill out the chart below.

Traits of My Worst Supervisor	Traits of My Best Supervisor

If you are like most people, you will be feeling some anger about how you were treated by your worst supervisor(s), even if it happened many years ago. On the other hand, it is likely that you remember your best supervisor(s) with fondness regardless of how much time has passed. What is it that separates them? How can you feel so vastly different toward them?

It is likely that your best supervisor treated you with dignity and respect and cared about you as a person. This supervisor knew how to bring out the best in you because he or she knew how to encourage you. You were treated in a way that met your deepest needs as a human being—to feel a sense of belonging, capable, significant, and empowered. Your worst supervisors may have treated you disrespectfully or did not value your unique contribution or you as a person, How does your list compare with the following compilation others have said about the traits they experienced from their worst and best supervisors?

Worst Supervisor	Best Supervisor
Enabling or controlling	Empowering
Unavailable	Open-door policy; available
Tears down through criticism	Builds up through appreciation
Micromanages	Gives autonomy
Rigid	Flexible
One up–One down relationship: "I'm right, you're wrong"	Equal relationship: "We both have a valid viewpoint"
Disrespectful	Respectful
Problem-solves alone and then tells you	Problem-solves with you
Creates rules alone and then tells you	Creates rules with you
Self-absorbed	Caring and empathetic
"I did it my way"	Team effort
Doesn't care about anything other than your output at work	Cares about all of you; honors you as a whole person
Blaming communication skills	Respectful communication skills
Instills the beliefs, "You are not valuable" and "You are not capable"	Instills the beliefs, "You are valuable" and "You are capable"

Encouragement is based on positive attitudes and actions. Following is a brief summary of the positive discipline attitude and action tools as they apply to being a positive parent and manager. It is uncanny how many parallels exist between being a skilled and encouraging parent and being a skilled and encouraging manager.

Attitude Tools for Positive Parenting and Positive Supervising

Core Principle	Parenting	Supervising
Love and caring	Make sure the message of love gets through	Make sure the message of respect and caring gets through
Constant encouragement will invite their best effort	Give your children a sense of belonging by encouraging them—it will invite cooperation	Give your employees a sense of being valued by encouraging them—it will invite their best work effort
Empower them	Don't do for your children what they can do for themselves	Don't micromanage your employees; give them autonomy to perform in their own way
Balance kindness and firmness	Show kindness for your child along with firmness to respect yourself and the needs of the situation	Show kindness for your employee while setting boundaries that respect you and the needs of the situation
Focus on long-range results	Think through your long-term goals for your kids; be careful of short-range methods that may hurt their character development	Think through your long-term organizational goals; avoid short-term management styles that sabotage long-term cooperation
Get into their world; seek to understand their view	Get into your child's world rather than lecturing them about your feelings	Seek first to understand where your employees are coming from rather than forcing your ideas or solutions
Seek solutions, not blame	Problem-solve with your children rather than spending time figuring out "who did it" and "why"	Problem-solve rather than focus on the mistake
Redefine the meaning of "success" in your role	Success is contingent on your ability to encourage your child and build his or her capability, not on your child's external performance	Success is contingent on how well you encourage and build capability in your employees; this will invite them to give their best
Mistakes are opportunities to learn	Instead of blaming or shaming your child for mistakes, problem-solve and teach new skills	Mistakes are your opportunity to better understand your employee and to work with the person to improve skills

Attitude Tools for Positive Parents and Positive Supervisors

Action Tools	Parent	Supervisor
Love and caring	Make sure the message of love gets through	Make sure the message of respect and caring gets through
Spend special time	Spend one-on-one time with your children to build a close connection	Spend one-on-one time with your employees to build a solid connection
Talk less, listen more	Ask what, why, and how questions to better understand their view	Ask what, why, and how questions to better understand their view
Use a cooling-off period when anyone is angry	Punishment is unnecessary but cooling off is critical prior to problem solving	Cooling off is necessary before communicating or problem solving
Take time for training	Teach your children how to clean, cook, study, etc.	Don't short-cut training; doing so causes headaches in the long run
Make agreements in advance (together)	Make agreements in advance with your children on chores, homework, etc.	Make agreements in advance with your employees
Schedule regular time for problem solving	Hold weekly family meetings	Hold regular staff meetings
Give compliments and show appreciation regularly	Start family meetings with compliments and appreciate your children often	Start staff meetings with appreciations and make a habit of pointing out the positive in your employees
Create routines or procedures together	Make routines with your children	Create policies and procedures with your employees
Ask for input, respect input, act on input	Children feel respected when asked for input; doing so minimizes power struggles and invites cooperation	Employees feel respected when asked for input; doing so minimizes power struggles and invites cooperation
Put warring factions in the same boat	Put fighting siblings in the same boat by not taking sides; and have them work it out	Never take sides with employees or teams in conflict; stay neutral and let them work it out

Positive Discipline Management Tools in Action

MELANIE MANAGES THE customer service department for a large manufacturing company. A group of internal and external auditors told her that she was required to produce a "how to" manual documenting every policy and procedure in the customer service department step-by-step. This was a daunting task for Melanie and her employees who were responsible for answering nonstop customer service requests and complaints.

Melanie immediately called a meeting with all of her direct reports. She explained the difficult assignment being asked of the department, shared her concerns, and expressed her need for help and support. She asked everyone to share their ideas for how they could meet the requirements and still keep up with their daily responsibilities.

After brainstorming, Melanie's group decided that each person would volunteer to write one of the step-by-step procedures. Every person then committed to meet a non-negotiable deadline. Melanie expressed gratitude for their willingness to take on this extra challenge and acknowledged the difficulty they would face in juggling this new task along with nonstop customer service orders. She assured them that she would be with them each step of the way to help them through any obstacles that could prevent them from meeting the agreed-upon deadline. She also promised them that if the whole group met the deadline, she would personally make each of them hot fudge sundaes and throw a big party.

Melanie held a brief training on using a template she designed for the group to use for each policy and procedure. This ensured that they would understand the audit requirements and create a uniform manual. She also gave them freedom to use their knowledge and creativity in filling in the templates as they saw fit.

Realizing that her team was going the extra mile, Melanie met with them frequently to offer support and encouragement. She gave public appreciation to those who completed the assignment. She asked those who were struggling what support they needed from her to be successful. Some of them expressed frustration because they were not good at getting their ideas down on paper. Melanie would then ask for a volunteer to help them put their ideas in written form. She would compliment each of them on their progress and give practical pointers and tips for getting the job completed. Sometimes it required moving the workload around so those who were behind would have uninterrupted time to write their procedure. Those who were struggling were offered help and support rather than criticism or blame.

In the end, every single person in Melanie's department met the deadline. As a group they created an outstanding product in which everyone in the department could take pride and ownership. True to her word, Melanie made each one of her employees a made-to-order hot fudge sundae. They felt cared about, appreciated, valued, and capable. Melanie felt thankful and proud that together they had suc-

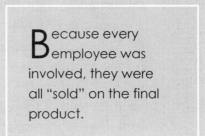

Because every employee was involved, they were all "sold" on the final product.

ceeded. Everyone in the department used the manual and followed the protocols. Because every employee was involved, they were all "sold" on the final product.

Managing Without Positive Discipline Management Tools

BARBARA WAS THE accounts receivable department manager at the same company where Melanie works. She was also asked by the auditors to create a step-by-step "how to" manual for all of the policies and procedures in the accounts receivable department. In her rush to please the auditors with outstanding work, Barbara holed up in her office and worked long, grueling hours detailing the procedures in her department. She didn't explain the project to her employees or seek any formal input. She came out of her office once in a while to seek clarification on certain aspects of their work, but she never told them what was happening. The employees suspected something was going on because Barbara seemed so stressed and overwhelmed. When they finally caught wind of her attempt to write a procedures manual without them, they rolled their eyes and said, "How would she know? We're the ones who do the work every day. She ought to be asking us!"

After weeks of hard work, Barbara contacted the auditors to tell them she had single-handedly completed the manual. She then called a meeting with her staff to deliver the finished product. She was exhausted but proud of her success in meeting the audit deadline. She handed each of them a procedures manual and told them they would need to be diligent in following all of the steps and guidelines it contained. Now that the auditors had received it they were all committed. Their future reviews would be based on how well they performed according to the stated policies and procedures.

As her staff members thumbed through the document, hands were raised in frustration as they objected to policies they felt were unrealistic, unfair, or just plain incorrect. One employee objected to the new policy on handling credit memos. "I thought the first priority was to meet our customers' needs. According to this manual, we now only get twenty-four hours to do credit memos instead of the forty-eight hours we agreed on previously. I disagree with the way you have prioritized our time. Twenty-four hours is unrealistic and will hurt our first priority: the customers!"

All of the employees resented being told how they had to do things when they had never been asked to give input. They felt angry that they were committed to doing things that were unrealistic given the sheer volume of their daily responsibilities. In the end, the employees felt so overwhelmed by the requirements and so disrespected by Barbara that they ignored the manual and carried on doing business as usual. Barbara was furious that her employees had so little regard for her hard work and frustrated that they refused to comply with the guidelines.

> When a manager does not seek input from her employees and is unwilling to delegate to them, they feel incapable and disrespected.

When the credit department complained that credit memos were not being done in the stated twenty-four-hour period, Barbara would attack the offending employee for not meeting the regulations. The employees commiserated behind Barbara's back. They felt misunderstood, discouraged, unappreciated, unvalued, and unimportant. They were not motivated to help Barbara succeed. They quietly sabotaged her behind her back. When a manager does not seek input from her employees and is unwilling to delegate to them, they feel incapable and disrespected. This invites resentment, not cooperation.

Encouragement Brings Out the Best in Everyone

MELANIE IS A REAL person and a truly gifted manager. Melanie is still (many years later) adored by her employees. When she got married, her staff threw her a huge party. When her baby was sick, they did Melanie's work as well as their own. When Melanie had to leave temporarily to do a company-wide project, she pleaded with her replacement, "Please walk around and talk to them every day. Don't let a day go by that you don't check in with them personally and professionally."

Melanie used the positive discipline attitude tools in her management style. First, Melanie clearly communicated respect and caring for her employees. She was empathetic to the difficulties they would possibly face and cared enough to help them meet those challenges. She was a constant source of encouragement to her employees—she built them up and was careful not to tear them down when they were struggling. This invited them to want to extend themselves to help and support her. Melanie showed a good balance of kindness and firmness. She showed firmness in giving her employees parameters and deadlines for the project but kindness and respect for their individual needs. She kept the long-range result in mind as a manager and avoided autocratic methods that may have given her short-term results but sabotaged long-term good will and cooperation. She sought input from her employees and did regular problem solving. She empowered her employees by giving them the template for a tool, but allowed them to get to the final product in their own way. She focused on solving problems when they were behind schedule or having difficulties rather than finding fault and blaming. When mistakes were made, she gave pointers to help employees be more successful. She understood that her success as a manager was contingent on building her employees up and that encouragement would make them more capable and valuable employees.

We also see that Melanie used all of the positive discipline action tools. She spent special time with her employees. We know that the term "special time" is not an appropriate business term, but it is a very important principle that good managers follow. She knew each of her employees personally and professionally. She knew what was going on at home and gave support and showed caring when children or family members were sick or when there were personal challenges. She supported them in finding success on the job and in their lives. It is impossible to encourage people you don't know.

In Melanie's staff and one-on-one meetings with her employees, she asked many what, why, and how questions in order to fully understand their point of view. She asked questions such as, "How can we accomplish this goal?" "What will be the easiest and fairest way to everyone?" and "How can I give you the support you need?"

Melanie also took time for training. She taught them how to use the template and did ongoing training to ensure they could meet the goal. She demonstrated the skill of making agreements in advance with her employees and then respectfully followed through. Melanie held regular staff meetings and gave constant compliments and appreciations. She created every policy and procedure *with* her employees rather than coming up with policies on her own and then *telling* them, like Barbara. She asked for her employees' input and then acted on it. This helped her staff feel that their contributions were important and meaningful.

The next few pages will offer additional ideas and tips on applying the positive discipline attitude and action tools.

Cool Off Before Communicating or Problem Solving

BE SURE TO correct your employees with compassion. Whether you need to give feedback on something minor like a missed day of work or major like consistently not doing his or her share of the work, you must build the person up rather than tear him or her down. It is important to take some time to cool down if you are really irritated. The following scenario points out two ways of handling the same stressful situation—one without the positive discipline tools and one with them.

> Be sure to correct your employees with compassion. . . . You must build the person up rather than tear him or her down.

John was furious that he didn't have the report in his in-box that he desperately needed for his 4:00 presentation to the Board. He saw Jill, his office manager, and confronted her immediately, "Do you know how stupid I'm going to look in front of the Board today because you and Nancy failed to get me the report! I told you three days ago I needed it!" Jill felt unprepared for such an attack and responded with anger and defensiveness. She curtly tried to explain that the computers were down yesterday, but John was so angry he couldn't hear her. Shaking with anger, Jill yelled at Keri, her secretary, who had been busy working on the report all morning. All of them felt angry, disrespected, and unappreciated.

Contrast this with scene two, in which positive discipline tools are used. John felt his anger and took ten minutes to calm down. He then asked Jill if he could speak with her for five minutes. He calmly shared his concern about doing well in the Board meeting and asked her for the status on the report and what she could do to help him avoid a potential problem. He listened attentively as Jill explained that the computers were down the day before, but that she and her secretary, Keri, came in early to get it done and they would have it to him before 2:00 P.M. so he would have two hours to review it. John's anxiety evaporated and he thanked Jill for her help. Jill was able to tell Keri how much she appreciated her extra work in getting the report out. All of them felt respected, valuable, and supported.

Under which of these scenarios do you think Jill and Keri could do their best work? If you take the time to calm down when you are angry, you will avoid the "reptilian brain" approach that destroys morale and people's sense of belonging and capability. When you are calm you can keep rapport and respect and everyone can do their best work. Nobody likes to have his or her worth trampled on. It is humiliating and disrespectful and encourages people to get revenge.

Take Plenty of Time for Training

MANY MANAGERS HAVE such a heavy individual workload that they mistakenly view time with their employees as an interruption of their own productivity. In the name of individual productivity, many managers spend too little time training their employees. Bob, the manager of a golf course, often felt irritated when his employees interrupted him from his personal "to do" list. (In reality, Bob needs to learn to delegate more of his responsibilities to his employees so he can spend more time on his primary job—to manage.) Eventually Bob was written up and put on formal probation because his employees were so poorly trained that they lacked the knowledge to do their jobs properly. Bob had to learn (the hard way) the importance of taking time for training. He learned from his mistakes and found that regularly scheduled trainings saved him countless hours of aggravation and interruption. Training helped his employees perform with more confidence and competence and minimized their need to ask routine questions about aspects of their jobs. Bob now holds monthly trainings with each of his groups. Productivity, revenue, and job satisfaction have gone up for Bob and his employees. (He also gets to keep his job!)

> In the name of individual productivity, many managers spend too little time training their employees.

Hold Regular Staff Meetings

STAFF MEETINGS (LIKE family meetings) are important and serve multiple purposes: to communicate new ideas and information, set goals, inspire and motivate employees, solve problems, build consensus on policies, team-build, and boost morale. When staff meetings are well run and kept short, they are an enjoyable and effective way to meet these purposes. One group dubbed their weekly staff meeting the weekly "huddle." During extremely challenging or busy periods they would call daily "huddles" to help everyone succeed by moving the workload around so the whole group could meet their goals.

The following is a list of don'ts and do's for staff meetings.

Don't:

1. Don't make meetings too long by allowing people to ramble, dominate, or go off on tangents. These meetings are boring, ineffective, and people feel angry that they have wasted time that could have been productive.

2. Don't allow the tone in meetings to become argumentative and nega-
    tive. Your employees will leave feeling resentful and uncooperative.
    In effectively run meetings, people freely share ideas. They tend to
    leapfrog, not in a competitive way, but in a synergistic way, which al-
    lows each idea to improve with input from the entire group.

Do:

1. Have a regularly scheduled staff meeting each week with a publicized
    time limit (thirty to forty-five minutes, for example).

2. Post an agenda to which all participants can contribute.

3. Start with appreciations and compliments (see compliment section on
    the next page).

4. Brainstorm solutions for each item on the agenda. (Wait until the fol-
    lowing week if time will not allow you to brainstorm all items on the
    agenda. End on time!)

    a. State the problem to be solved.

    b. Rapidly brainstorm ideas for solving the stated problem, even if
        they are unrealistic or ridiculous. Write down every suggestion and
        don't censor at this point.

    c. Vote on each of the ideas without criticizing or judging the ideas
        with which you disagree. Draw people out with numerous what,
        why, and how questions. When you have a complete list of ideas,
        choose the solution everyone (or almost everyone) can support,
        and agree to try it for a specific period of time. Pick a date to eval-
        uate if the solution is working or if another round of brainstorm-
        ing is needed.

5. Review important projects and deadlines and make assignments. Seek
    input on these items.

Other fun ideas for staff meetings are as follows:

•   Plan fun events.

•   Celebrate birthdays.

•   Do skills training.

- Give surprise awards or recognition (public encouragement).
- Share your wins.
- Share your losses (and have the group give suggestions for how to handle the situation the next time).

Give Compliments and Appreciations Constantly

ONE MANAGER HAD a little plastic horse he would give to the "Greatest Workhorse" at the first staff meeting every month. Everyone in the room gave the recipient a sincere compliment and appreciation for their contributions. Employees would proudly display the tacky, plastic horse throughout the month.

Another creative manager blew up pictures of employees with extraordinary performances and glued them on a Wheaties box. She held well-publicized "Breakfast of Champions" meetings that honored employees who had gone the extra mile. Everyone in the department attended to watch the honoree eat his or her Wheaties cereal and give appreciation for the hard work. The "Breakfast of Champions" became a coveted award within her department.

The weekly staff meeting is a good place to regularly appreciate your employees. Some supervisors throw a Koosh ball to each person in the room and give a compliment to whoever has the ball. Fellow employees also can throw the Koosh ball to their colleagues followed by an appreciation. Appreciations are extremely encouraging. They elevate each person's sense of belonging and create an energetic, positive, cooperative, and creative atmosphere for work to take place. This provides a wonderful foundation for miracles to happen.

Never Take Sides with Employees in Conflict

STAY NEUTRAL AND let those who have a conflict work it out. If you take sides, you will leave someone with the sense that he or she does not belong or is not valued. This will invite the conflict to escalate and exacerbate both parties' efforts to prove they are "right." They will use you as their proving ground. If they get you to side with them, they will feel justified and "right." Taking sides is damaging to both parties and will invite more rivalry in the future. Your best bet is to have them brainstorm solutions together after a cooling-off period. Admonish them to "focus on solutions rather than assign blame" and ask them to come up with a creative way to honor both sides.

> Appreciations are extremely encouraging. They elevate each person's sense of belonging and create an energetic, positive, cooperative, and creative atmosphere.

Positive Discipline Can Transform Your Workplace and Home

POSITIVE DISCIPLINE OFFERS a wonderful opportunity for you to become the best parent and the best supervisor you can be. Success in both arenas depends on being highly skilled in the art of encouragement. As you apply the positive discipline attitude and action tools you will find that you become expert in encouraging the best from your children, employees, and everyone who is important to you in your life. This will give all of you the opportunity to live and love at your highest level of capability and personal fulfillment.

We can promise you this: If you consistently persevere in utilizing the positive discipline tools and principles outlined in this book, your relationships will absolutely be transformed. How can we promise you this? We can because we have learned the tools, used them most of the time (with plenty of lapses and mistakes), and have kept practicing the principles imperfectly one day at a time. The results have been nothing short of spiritual—deep, satisfying connections with our children and our mates and contentment and harmony at work. It is our hope that you will have the same transforming experience.

INDEX

ABOUT THE AUTHORS

Jane Nelsen is a popular lecturer and coauthor of the entire POSITIVE DISCIPLINE series. She also wrote *From Here to Serenity: Four Principles for Understanding Who You Really Are.* She has appeared on *Oprah* and *Sally Jesse Raphael* and was the featured parent expert on the "National Parent Quiz," hosted by Ben Vereen. Jane is the mother of seven children and the grandmother of eighteen.

Lisa Larson is a popular keynote speaker, parent educator, and corporate trainer whose workshops are dynamic and entertaining. She has appeared on numerous radio and television shows sharing practical tools, creative solutions, and humor with parents, teachers, and corporations. Lisa has an M.A. from the University of San Francisco and is a marriage and family therapist. She lives with her husband and three children near Sacramento, California.

FOR MORE INFORMATION

THE AUTHORS ARE available for keynotes, workshops, and seminars for corporations, associations, and parent and teacher groups. Their topics include titles such as:

Positive Discipline in the Classroom (a two-day workshop or a one-day inservice)

Balancing Family and Work

Leadership Skills: Better Parents Make Better Supervisors and Better Supervisors Make Better Parents

21 Tools for Avoid Power Struggles at Home and at Work

Team Building

Managing to Have Fun: Those Who Play Together, Stay Together

"The Color Code": How Your Core Personality Affects Your Interpersonal Relationships (At Home or in the Workplace)

Discover your Core Mission and Values

The Overload Syndrome: Finding Balance & Peace in a Crazy World

Managing Transitions (Reorganizations or Life Transitions)

Two-Day training for Positive Discipline Lunch and Learn programs

Jane Nelsen, Ed.D.
969 W. Harmony Rose Circle
South Jordan, UT 84095
JaneNelsen@aol.com
(800) 456-7770
www.positivediscipline.com

Lisa Larson, MFT
Positive Paradigms
507 Natoma Street
Folsom, CA 95762
(916) 608-4569
laf@pacbell.net

ORDER FORM

To: Empowering People, P.O. Box 1926, Orem, UT 84059-1926
Phone: 1-800-456-7770 (credit card orders only)
Fax: 801-762-0022
Web Site: www.positivediscipline.com for discount prices

BOOKS

	Price	Quantity	Amount
Positive Discipline for Working Parents, by Nelsen & Larson	$16.95	_____	_____
Positive Discipline for Childcare Providers, by Nelsen & Erwin	$16.95	_____	_____
Positive Discipline for Single Parents, by Nelsen, Erwin, & Delzer	$16.95	_____	_____
Positive Discipline in the Classroom, by Nelsen, Lott, & Glenn	$16.00	_____	_____
Positive Discipline: A Teacher's A–Z Guide, by Nelsen, Duffy, Escobar, Ortolano, & Owen-Sohocki	$16.95	_____	_____
Positive Discipline for Preschoolers, by Nelsen, Erwin, & Duffy	$16.95	_____	_____
Positive Discipline: The First Three Years, by Nelsen, Erwin, & Duffy	$16.95	_____	_____
Positive Discipline, by Nelsen	$12.00	_____	_____
Positive Discipline A–Z, by Nelsen, Lott, & Glenn	$16.95	_____	_____
Positive Discipline for Teenagers, by Nelsen & Lott	$16.95	_____	_____
Positive Discipline for Parenting in Recovery, by Nelsen, Intner, & Lott	$12.95	_____	_____
Raising Self-Reliant Children in a Self-Indulgent World, by Glenn & Nelsen	$15.95	_____	_____
Positive Time-Out: And 50 Other Ways to Avoid Power Struggles, Nelsen	$12.95	_____	_____
From Here to Serenity, by Nelsen	$14.00	_____	_____
Positive Discipline in the Christian Home, Nelsen, Erwin, Brock, & Hughes	$16.95	_____	_____

MANUALS

	Price	Quantity	Amount
Teaching Parenting the Positive Discipline Way, by Lott & Nelsen	$49.95	_____	_____
Positive Discipline in the Classroom, by Nelsen & Lott	$49.95	_____	_____

TAPES AND VIDEOS

	Price	Quantity	Amount
Positive Discipline audiotape	$10.00	_____	_____
Positive Discipline videotape	$49.95	_____	_____
Building Healthy Self-Esteem Through Positive Discipline audiotape	$10.00	_____	_____

SUBTOTAL _____

Sales tax: UT add 6.25%; CA add 7.25% _____

Shipping & handling: $3.00 plus $0.50 each item _____

(Prices subject to change without notice.) **TOTAL** _____

METHOD OF PAYMENT (check one):
_____ Check made payable to Empowering People Books, Tapes, & Videos
_____ MasterCard, Visa, Discover Card, American Express

Card # _____ Expiration _____ /_____

Ship to _____

Address _____

City/State/Zip _____

Daytime phone (_____)_____